The Process of Highly Effective Coaching

The Process of Highly Effective Coaching offers a unique blend of theory and practical methods for conducting effective coaching conversations. It provides an umbrella under which all of the major conceptual models for helping people change can not only coexist but work together. In addition to using this integrative approach, *The Process of Highly Effective Coaching* presents a framework for conducting coaching conversations and for relating the coaching process to the coaching competencies defined by the International Coach Federation, the largest coach-credentialing organization in the world.

Robert F. Hicks, PhD, is a clinical professor of organizational behavior at The University of Texas at Dallas and founding director of the Organizational Development, Coaching and Consulting program in the Naveen Jindal School of Management. He is a licensed psychologist and holds an appointment as faculty associate in the Department of Psychiatry at UT Southwestern Medical Center. He has more than 30 years of experience coaching executives of Fortune 500 companies and teaching coaching methodology to both leaders and practitioners.

The Process of Highly Effective Coaching

An Evidence-Based Framework

Robert F. Hicks

Routledge
Taylor & Francis Group

NEW YORK AND LONDON

First published 2017
by Routledge
711 Third Avenue, New York, NY 10017

and by Routledge
2 Park Square, Milton Park, Abingdon, Oxon, OX14 4RN

Routledge is an imprint of the Taylor & Francis Group, an informa business

Library of Congress Cataloging in Publication Data
Name: Hicks, Robert F., author.
Title: The process of highly effective coaching: an evidence-based
    framework / by Robert F. Hicks, Ph.D.
Description: New York, NY: Routledge, 2017. | Includes bibliographical
    references and index.
Identifiers: LCCN 2016022949 | ISBN 9781138906006 (hardback : alk. paper) |
    ISBN 9781138906013 (pbk. : alk. paper) | ISBN 9781315692418 (ebook)
Subjects: LCSH: Personal coaching.
Classification: LCC BF637.P36 H53 2017 | DDC 158.3—dc23
LC record available at https://lccn.loc.gov/2016022949

ISBN: 978-1-138-90600-6 (hbk)
ISBN: 978-1-138-90601-3 (pbk)
ISBN: 978-1-315-69241-8 (ebk)

Typeset in Minion Pro
by Apex CoVantage, LLC

To my family, both near and far.
And to my faithful companions, both here and there.
Thank you for your love.

Contents

Acknowledgments

Although this book has but one author, it was not written alone. I have had the support of many people. My staff at The University of Texas at Dallas have, through their competence and care, made it possible for me to devote the requisite time and attention to this book. For that, I am truly grateful. To those colleagues who graced me with their feedback along the way, thank you for your insights. I especially want to thank Lorrie Groll and Diane Whiting whose eagle eyes and sharp minds helped refine the finished product. Finally, I owe a special debt of gratitude to my family. Writing, at least for me, is an arduous process and consumes my attention for long periods. I was asked, more than once, by my children and grandchildren when I would be finished so I could do things with them again. Not to mention that my wife had to put up with me, daily. God bless all of you.

Introduction

In my first book for Routledge, *Coaching as a Leadership Style: The Art and Science of Coaching Conversations for Healthcare Professionals* (2014), I had four goals: 1) to introduce the Foursquare Coaching Framework to practitioners and leaders as a process for conducting coaching conversations that help others resolve problem situations and develop professionally; 2) to connect the competencies utilized within the Framework to the practice of transformational leadership; 3) to illustrate how a coach-like interpersonal style can contribute to effective interactions with professional colleagues and direct reports, whether or not actual coaching is occurring; and 4) to speak specifically to healthcare leaders and professionals about coaching because of the emerging need for coaching in this field. Since I was writing for two audiences, i.e., practitioners and leaders, I had to walk a narrow path so as to provide a practical, how-to approach to coaching that non-practitioners could relate to, and at the same time explain the science behind the framework as well as how to use it so that those who were already skilled coaches would have enough new information to find it professionally worthwhile.

Although coach practitioners will find *Coaching as a Leadership Style* very useful, in the end, I made compromises because of the dual audience. For example, I omitted an important facet of the Framework (the cognitive-behavioral component) and simplified some of the techniques. Moreover, I abridged my explanation of the relevant psychological theories that are integrated with the Framework. This book is written to remedy those shortcomings.

This book draws from many wells. Its content contains methods and techniques from an array of evidence-based psychological theories and models that are proven to assist people in their developmental or change efforts. Even though these theories and models are reframed so that they are congruent with the aims and philosophy of coaching, that, in and of itself, is not what distinguishes this book from others that have been written to apply psychological theory and practices to coaching. In this book, I present a unifying framework—the Foursquare Coaching Framework—that *integrates* the multiplicity of these psychological constructs in a way that organizes and simplifies their use.

Perhaps more importantly, however, is that this book shows readers how to use the Framework as a schema for managing the *process* of a coaching conversation. It is not enough to have a working knowledge of the psychological constructs that inform the coaching process, or to be adept at using the evidence-based practices and techniques that are derived from those constructs. Coaches must be able to use their knowledge and skills in an intuitive and spontaneous manner as guided by their professional judgment. To do so requires a precise understanding of the landscape of a coaching conversation so that the coach knows, moment by moment, where the conversation is within that landscape and what process options are available to him or her. For that, coaches need a cognitive structure that serves as a map for the conversation. The Foursquare Coaching Framework is such a map.

The goals of this book are:

1. To introduce, or increase your understanding of, the Foursquare Coaching Framework as a cognitive structure to guide the coaching process.
2. To link prominent psychological theories and evidence-based methods to the practice of coaching, and to integrate these divergent approaches within a single, easy to follow Framework.
3. To teach the competencies necessary to use the Foursquare Coaching Framework during a coaching conversation.

Chapter Descriptions

1. Becoming a Master-Level Practitioner

Chapter 1 explores the road to becoming a master-level practitioner by explaining how master-level practitioners think differently from novice or journeyman practitioners. Based on current research, the behavioral distinctions that differentiate Level I (novice), Level II (journeyman), and Level III (master) practitioners are explained. Two models—the Scientist-Practitioner and the Reflective Practitioner—both influential in the development of professionals in the behavioral sciences, are described as to their advantages and drawbacks for use in the development of coaches on their path to mastery. A third model, the Informed Practitioner, is introduced as a way of combining the strengths of both models and incorporating the use of evidence-based practices as a hallmark of the master-level coach. A short history of psychology's influence on coaching illustrates how the evidence-based practices derived from both clinical and educational psychology inform the coaching process. Finally, an argument is made that evidence-based practices are necessary but not sufficient for becoming a master coach. Master-level coaching requires non-linear thinking and the ability to demonstrate reflection in action. A case is made for the use of a schema that facilitates a coach's ability to do both.

2. The Foursquare Coaching Framework: A Schema for Coaching

Chapter 2 explains the structure of the Foursquare Coaching Framework. This chapter describes the similarities between coaching and the Socratic Method. Two processes elemental to the Socratic Method—support and challenge—are discussed and then applied to two types of content that serve as the basis for all coaching conversations: thoughts and actions. The interaction between these two processes and two types of content create a two-by-two matrix that provides a schema for coaching named the Foursquare Coaching Framework (FsCF). The purpose of each quadrant in this structure is defined and illustrated with examples. The non-linear nature of the Framework is stressed with the idea being that the FsCF is used as a process map for the coaching conversation as opposed to a linear structure that prescribes a set of sequential steps. The chapter closes with a deeper explanation of how the Framework functions as a structure for focusing client awareness. Each square of the Framework steers the client's attention in different ways and produces changes in the energy and information flow of the coaching conversation.

3. Support-for-Thought: Connecting with and Engaging the Client

The efficacy of the coaching conversation rests, first and foremost, on the coach's ability to connect with and engage the client. The concept of empathy is addressed as it applies to creating the relational conditions for productive thinking and problem solving between the coach and client. Specifically, this chapter spotlights the Empathy Cycle—a specific type of interactional process that facilitates all types of helping conversations. The Empathy Cycle consists of four steps. Each step is explained in detail with instructions on its use and implementation while in the Support-for-Thought quadrant. Among the instructional points included in this chapter are guidelines for maintaining focused attention while coaching, how to use the messages coaches send themselves during a coaching session to enhance the coaching effectiveness, listening from the correct ego state, understanding the four levels of affective empathy, self-assessing one's aptitude for empathic resonance, and the use of reflection and summary to establish rapport. Additionally, the neuroscience of empathy is examined as it relates to the Empathy Cycle.

4. Support-for-Thought: Setting the Agenda and Clarifying the Narrative

This chapter teaches the specific linguistic techniques for identifying and recovering missing information in the stories, anecdotes, problem statements, and chronologies of clients as a means of building a platform of understanding about the client's current situation. Three types of deleted information are defined, and guidelines for constructing inquiries specific to each type are provided. A special point of instruction in this chapter is the use of inquiry to clarify the client's agenda for the coaching session. Since clients can be incredibly vague about what they want, typical client requests are examined and the reader is provided with a systematic method for converting ambiguous responses to a well-defined agenda. A distinction is made between conversations that start from scratch and those that are a continuation of previous discussions. Finally, the concept of using springboards to smoothly transition from Support-for-Thought to other quadrants in the FsCF is explained. Specific kinds of springboards are named, defined, and exemplified.

5.   Challenge-for-Thought: Constructing a Well-Formed Outcome

The Foursquare Coaching Framework draws heavily on the solution-focused approach to facilitating individual change and problem solving. This chapter sets out the organizing principles for using this approach as a means of constructing positive outcomes in a way that increases the probability of goal attainment. The topic of goal hierarchies is discussed as it relates to the process of constructing a well-formed outcome. This chapter defines the components of a well-formed outcome and how to develop such an outcome to impart a clear and vivid picture of the client's desired future state. Developing discrepancy is introduced as a core competency used throughout the FsCF for different purposes. In Challenge-for-Thought, developing discrepancy is devoted to assisting clients in shifting their attention from their current state to their desired future state. The reader is instructed in a variety of solution-focused techniques for converting the client's wished-for future into actionable, goal-specific outcomes.

6.   Challenge-for-Thought: Eliciting Self-Talk and Beliefs

This chapter focuses on the cognitive methods and practices used to challenge erroneous conclusions, limiting assumptions, maladaptive self-talk, and impoverished beliefs. The cognitive-behavioral approach to analyzing and reality-testing existing patterns of thinking is explained. A distinction is made between cognitive therapy and cognitive coaching, and only those parts of the cognitive-behavioral model that fit the purpose of coaching are highlighted. The reader is taught how the feeling states of clients are produced by their thinking patterns and, therefore, can be altered by changing the way clients talk to themselves. Parent, Child, and Adult ego states are reintroduced as coherent systems of thought, with each ego state having a cognitive structure of self-talk unique to that ego state. This chapter describes how the self-talk associated with the Parent and Child ego states can become debilitating to goal achievement. Techniques for eliciting the client's self-talk are spelled out so that it can be examined as to functionality. Finally, the reader is informed as to how to teach clients to use Thought Records as a means of increasing client awareness of thinking patterns interfering with goal achievement.

7.   Challenge-for-Thought: Changing Contaminated Self-Talk and Counterproductive Beliefs

This chapter introduces methods and tools to be used in Challenge-for-Thought when refuting and replacing contaminated self-talk and counterproductive beliefs interfering with goal attainment, or when the regulation of emotions and behavior is, in and of itself, the client's goal. Specifically, common patterns of cognitive distortions are defined so that, when detected, they can be exposed and challenged as to their validity. Readers are provided with several methods for testing the accuracy of distorted thinking and uncovering the faulty reasoning underlying counterproductive beliefs. Special attention is given to irrational "should" statements that indicate the presence of internal beliefs about oneself or the world in general that are likely to be extreme, rigid, and blindly followed. Readers are instructed in cognitive-behavioral techniques for using Socratic questioning to induce more objective and balanced thinking on the part of the client.

8.   Support-for-Action: Strengthening Motivation for Change

The purpose of this chapter is to delineate the motivational determinates of committed action and to provide the reader with proven methods for strengthening clients' readiness, willingness, and ability to act in quest of their well-formed outcomes. The reader is taught Motivational Interviewing techniques that spotlight client speech favoring movement in the direction of their desired change. To this end, precise methods for recognizing, magnifying, and reinforcing speech that increases goal attainment value and self-confidence are explained and illustrated. Particular attention is given to the the challenge of helping clients resolve mixed thoughts and feelings about moving forward so that they are ready to take action. As with each chapter, the fluidity of the Foursquare Coaching Framework is illustrated with a demonstration of how to seamlessly navigate from Support-for-Action to other quadrants within the Framework.

9.   Challenge-for-Action: Generating Movement

This chapter explains the principles and practices that generate movement toward the client's change goal and desired future state. The heuristic approach to action planning is discussed, and guidelines for creating successful action experiments are presented, along with tactics for helping the client overcome inertia. Three types of action experiments are examined—informational, cognitive, and behavioral—and guidelines for their use prescribed. The reader is provided with a step-by-step formula for using the scaling technique within the Challenge-for-Action quadrant to identify and reinforce practical steps toward goal achievement. Several additional methods are described and illustrated for assisting clients in the development of action strategies that will help them achieve their goals. Finally, a rationale is given for the use of small steps as a stratagem when using the heuristic approach to goal attainment.

10.   The Coaching Alliance: Putting the Framework in Context

The purpose of this chapter is to provide a larger context for understanding the use of the Foursquare Coaching Framework. The focal point of this chapter is the Coaching Alliance: coaching's version of the helping or working alliance between the person who seeks change and the change agent. The Coaching

Alliance has both cognitive and relational aspects, and evidence is presented as to why it is one of the keys, if not *the* key, to the change that occurs during the coaching engagement. The relational aspect of the Coaching Alliance is the primary topic of emphasis in this chapter. With that in mind, this chapter discusses, in depth, the personal qualities and competencies that nourish the coach-client relationship. A case is made for the proposition that the Coaching Alliance, and particularly the relational aspect, is the foundation upon which the Foursquare Coaching Framework rests. Lastly, a summary is given as to why the Framework succeeds in its purpose and the value it brings to any coaching conversation.

CHAPTER 1

Becoming a Master-Level Practitioner

In the Disney movie *Fantasia*, Mickey Mouse is the sorcerer's apprentice. As an apprentice, he is consigned to perform menial tasks while watching and learning from the master. But Mickey aspires to be a great sorcerer himself, so one night when the master sorcerer leaves he puts on the sorcerer's hat and copies one of the sorcerer's techniques to perform a laborious task: getting water from the well for the household. Mickey proceeds to cast a spell to animate a broom to fetch the water for him and, to his surprise and satisfaction, he is successful. The broom does his work for him and fetches the water repeatedly. Mickey starts to imagine himself as a master sorcerer having command over all of the elements. However, a problem arises: he cannot make the broom stop fetching water, and it begins to flood the house. In an attempt to stop the water Mickey chops up the broom, but that only makes the problem worse as pieces of the broom multiply into new brooms that also fetch water. Finally, Mickey frantically turns to the sorcerer's book of magic to look for another technique that will counter the first. Just when it seems that there is no hope of stopping the water, the master sorcerer appears, takes his hat back from Mickey, and magically dries up the flood and restores order.

What was Mickey's error? Mistaking technique for mastery. This is the very same mistake made by coaches who assume that the use of coaching tools and techniques equates to mastery. It is the reason that so many coaches and coach training programs emphasize the "coaching toolbox." But what actually distinguishes a master-level practitioner from those less competent? This subject has not been well researched in the field of coaching, but it has been a topic of research in psychology, specifically counseling psychology, and the results of that research can inform the coaching community. Mozdzierz et al. (2014) argue that master-level practitioners *think differently* than other practitioners. Specifically, they employ a non-linear thinking strategy that gives them the ability to evaluate the client's situation in real time and know just what to say or ask, when to say or ask it, and how to do so in ways that those who are less advanced do not—or seemingly cannot—do!

As in all professions, the path to master-level coaching competence can be described on a continuum from novice to journeyman to the master-level practitioner. Stoltenberg (1993, 1997) has described an integrated developmental model for psychotherapists that describes points of reference for three levels of counselor development culminating in "Level III" mastery—the integrated level. While not all elements of his model apply to coaching, his descriptions of each level do serve as a guide for distinguishing among novice, journeyman, and master-level coach practitioners.

According to Stoltenberg, Level I Practitioners are characterized by a strong internal focus, feelings of anxiousness, and the use of structure and specific techniques with clients, often in a formulaic manner. Coach practitioners at this level are very self-conscious and apprehensive about their abilities. Their anxiety tends to cause the Level I coach to focus "on his or her own fears and lack of knowledge and leaves little remaining attentional capacity to effectively attend to the [client]" (Stoltenberg, 1993, p. 133). Their strong internal focus interferes with insightfulness, causing them to emphasize the use of specific techniques to the detriment of seeing the big picture. The thinking of Level I coaches is primarily linear as opposed to the non-linear thinking of more advanced practitioners. They want to know what steps to follow. Due to their heightened anxiety, they have a great concern about not making mistakes. They have a strong desire to learn the "correct" way to coach so that their anxiety is reduced and self-efficacy is increased. This desire is typically demonstrated by "How to" questions, e.g., "What do you say when the client says (or does) . . . ?" or "What does it mean when . . . ?" The motivation for perfection is driven by a genuine aspiration to do good work, help clients, and develop expertise. When asked to go beyond technique or learn an approach that is not immediately within their skill set, they often become bewildered and frustrated.

With time and practice Level I coaches move to Level II. Level II coaches have developed more confidence in their skills and are comfortable in the role of coach. This comfort level allows them to be less mentally distracted and better able to attend to the client's needs and goals. Overall, their attention is less on themselves and their internal processes and more on the client and the client's narrative. Such a shift in orientation takes place only when the coach has an increased sense of calm, comfort, interest, and fundamental understanding of the nature of the coaching process. This *other-awareness* allows for a more careful and accurate assessment of the client's view of the world as well as his or her thinking and emotional state. At the same time, the other-awareness that is symbolic of the Level II practitioner may cause the coach to attend too closely to the client's narrative and become lost in irrelevant details or inaccurate perceptions. Also, at times, the coach may over-identify with the client. Over-identification can cloud the coach's objectivity, rendering her less able to assist the client in developing appropriate goals and pathways to those goals because of an unwillingness to challenge the client when needed.

Level II practitioners are on the way to learning how to think differently. A more complex view of the coaching process is beginning to develop, and they are more comfortable with not knowing because they understand and appreciate the power of the coaching process itself. They can begin to relinquish their struggle to make something happen in coaching and instead let it happen. Level II practitioners are less enamored with "the coaching toolbox" as they begin the shift from linear to non-linear thinking. In other words, micro-level skills, which have been the focus of their operational model, are starting to be replaced by a more sophisticated cognitive map of the coaching process. They are better able to put what they do within the context of a larger conceptual (and theoretical) framework. The Level II practitioner begins to understand that there is value in knowing the evidence-based models and methods that can be applied to the practice of coaching.

Level III (master-level) practitioners are much more balanced than Level I or Level II practitioners. They can engage in an empathic understanding of the client while simultaneously pulling back into a more objective, third-person view of the situation. In other words, they can be a part of, and apart from, the conversation simultaneously (this is called a dual level of consciousness and is discussed in Chapter 10). This ability allows the master-level coach to relate what is happening in the coaching session to previously learned theory and to make reasoned decisions about how best to manage the coaching conversation for the client's benefit. Level III practitioners comfortably engage in non-linear thinking by taking in and integrating information from the client while adapting to the needs of the situation and flow of the coaching conversation. Chi (2006) attributes this ability to being able to detect and recognize features of a given situation that Level I and Level II practitioners cannot. To do this, master-level practitioners have a schema, a mental framework that allows them to assimilate and accommodate information intuitively so that they can demonstrate coaching agility by "dancing in the moment" (a popular phrase in the coaching community).

Coaches at this level experience a sense of comfort with their ability while simultaneously remaining realistically aware of their limitations. Miscues are taken in stride without an undue sense of guilt or failure. Instead, frustrations, reversals, or adversities become a source of learning. The master-level coach understands that his or her approach to coaching is continually evolving as a product of personal maturation and professional growth. However, perhaps the most interesting characteristic of the master-level practitioner is that practicing at this level becomes less of a goal and more of an expression of self-actualization. Mozdzierz and his colleagues make this clear in their book, *Advanced Principles of Counseling and Psychotherapy*:

> The irony is that once someone achieves true mastery of his or her province, the person seems to care less about being a master and more about bringing out the best in himself or herself. Paradoxically, master practitioners understand that although earlier aspirations (i.e., those described in our introductory volume as being at Levels 1 and 2) may have been driven by a desire to be a master, they now have little concern or preoccupation with such matters. They are more concerned with being themselves, relating in an authentic way, and being fully available to clients.
>
> (2014, p. 10)

The path to mastery is not a straight one. It is fraught with frustration and stumbling blocks. In fact, Michelangelo reportedly said, "If people knew how hard I worked to get my mastery, it wouldn't seem so wonderful at all." Although the process of mastery does take time and hard work, it does not have to be painful—nor mysterious. Two models, in particular, the Scientist-Practitioner model and the Reflective Practitioner model, have been very influential in developing professionals in the behavioral sciences. Each model has something to offer the coaching community and both outline a path to mastery.

The Scientist-Practitioner

Kurt Lewin, the renowned German-American psychologist and pioneer in the field of social psychology, declared, "There is nothing more practical than a good theory" (Lewin, 1952, p. 169). The simplicity of this phrase understates the power and complexity of the ideas that led to its creation. Its principal message is that evidence-based theories and models not only can, but also should, provide ideas for understanding and conceptualizing how a practitioner approaches the task of helping individuals. Lewin's statement draws attention to the linkage between the theoretical and the practical: a linkage that he believed must not be ignored by everyday practitioners. His message spawned interest in understanding how practitioners learn and improve professionally and gave rise to the development of the Scientist-Practitioner model.

A major tenet of the Scientist-Practitioner model is the notion that clinical practitioners should be trained in research and those theoretical models that will enable them to apply informed critical thought to the practice of helping others. It is based on the belief that psychology incorporates science and practice, and, therefore, each must continually inform the other. Currently, however, the Scientist-Practitioner model is not accepted by everyone. David Shapiro (2002) points out the fact that clinicians, as a rule, do not see themselves as theorists and researchers. In their minds, there is often a divide between research, theory, and practice. This observation holds true for coaches as well—perhaps even more so. It is not a stretch to say that doing research is not in their DNA; they would rather be coaching.

Coaching as an Expression of Personality

For most people who choose to coach as a vocation, their innate interest is in helping others. Coaching is their passion and helping others is a natural extension of who they are as people. John L. Holland—the creator of the well-known career development model, Holland Occupational Themes—argued as far back as 1959 that an individual's vocational choice was very much a product of personality. He explained that one's personality interacts with his or her environment and produces, what he termed, an adjustive orientation. Holland stated, "The person making a vocational choice in a sense 'searches' for situations which satisfy his hierarchy of adjustive orientations" (Holland, 1959, p. 35). Holland developed a typology of six personality types and corresponding occupational environments that ultimately produced the Holland Codes (Occupational Themes).

Briefly, each Holland Code represents a vocational environment that people with a matching personality would find to their liking. Each code or theme is symbolized by a letter and the corresponding word that represents the essence of that occupational environment: R-Theme (Realistic), I-Theme (Investigative), A-Theme (Artistic), S-Theme (Social), E-Theme (Enterprising), and C-Theme

(Conventional). Those who would embrace the Scientist-Practitioner model gravitate toward the Investigative theme. The Investigative occupational environment is a fit for people who are scholarly, scientific, and technical by nature. Their personalities are described as analytical, introspective, reserved, and logical. They enjoy conducting research, developing theory, and solving problems.

By contrast, literature reviews of the personality characteristics of coaches and counselors conclude that traits such as warmth, friendliness, acceptance, patience, sensitivity, sociability, empathy, and cooperativeness typify those who are attracted to, and most active in, helping others (Pope & Kline, 1999). These characteristics fit the Social occupational theme precisely. The work represented by this theme attracts people who are concerned about the welfare of others. They are helpers who like tasks involving social interaction and relationship building. This theme embodies an interest in working to enlighten, inform, help, train, or counsel. It is difficult to imagine practitioners who are typified by the Social occupational theme gravitating to the Scientist-Practitioner model since it does not fit their personality or perceived self-image. Perhaps that is one reason it has not resonated with the coaching community. Coach education programs (primarily in the United States) have largely ignored the tenets of the Scientist-Practitioner model. However, by doing so, they may have stunted the ability of coaches to apply scientific theory to practice and, in the process, slowed the acceptance of coaching as a discipline.

The Reflective Practitioner

The challenge of professionalizing a vocation is certainly not limited to coaching. Most established occupations have had to deal with the issue of how best to increase the professional competence of their members. During the 1980s, educators reexamined the process of training teachers and administrators with the goal of producing more capable practitioners within the field of education. This effort led to the adoption of the Reflective Practitioner model as a means of developing fresh insights and ideas that advance the practitioner's work. Reflective practice is different from merely reflecting. Reflecting is the act of thinking carefully about something, while reflective practice is "the mindful consideration of one's actions, specifically, one's professional actions" (Osterman, 1990, p. 134) to develop one's skill as a professional.

The process of reflection as a means of enlightenment stretches as far back as Socrates. His use of inquiry to induce reflection, self-discovery, and learning became known as the Socratic Method. This method is very much a part of coaching as it exists today (Hicks, 2014). The modern roots of reflection as a learning process are attributed to John Dewey. In his book *Experience and Education* (1938), he argued that learning is foremost an activity that arises from a person grappling with, and thinking about, a problem or one's experiences. However, this approach did not become fully operational until Chris Argyris and Donald Schön began researching professional effectiveness in the early 1970s. Their research investigated how professionals become skilled. They concluded that accomplished practitioners are Reflective Practitioners. They use their experience as a basis for assessing and revising their existing "theories of action" to develop more effective intervention strategies.

According to Schön (1987), learning and growth take place by purposely reflecting on what occurred as a result of one's professional actions as compared to what was expected or desired. From reflective practice, alternate action strategies (i.e., theories of action) are then developed, which, when constantly refined, enable the practitioner to become more skillful and ultimately professionally effective. However, Schön believed that reflective learning is not always possible because of the intuitive nature of our actions:

> When we go about the spontaneous, intuitive performance of the actions of everyday life, we show ourselves to be knowledgeable in a special way. Often we cannot say what it is that we know. When we try to describe it, we find ourselves at a loss, or we produce descriptions that are obviously inappropriate. Our knowing is ordinarily tacit, implicit in our patterns of action and in our feel for the stuff with which we are dealing.
>
> (Schön, 1983, p. 49)

A Case in Point

When I began coaching, it didn't exist. In the late 1970s, I was a newly minted Ph.D. and had just finished my internship as a clinical psychologist in the state hospital system of California. After passing my state psychology exams, I was faced with a decision: Do I start a clinical practice or do something different? After due consideration, I decided to apply my psychological training to the "people problems" found in organizations as a consulting psychologist.

During my consulting activities, I would often be pulled aside by managers and executives for personal consulting. They would be struggling with some issue and wanted advice. However, there was a problem: I didn't have any advice to give as I did not have the professional experience from which to draw upon to offer advice. When asked to answer a question such as "How do I lead people with whom I was previously a peer?" or "How do I handle this politically charged situation?" I had no clue.

Since I could not offer solutions, I could do but one thing: help them find their own answers. I used a variety of approaches that were extracted from different therapeutic models; e.g., person-centered therapy, solution-focused counseling (brief therapy), cognitive-behavioral therapy, and behavioral modification—to name a few. Over time, I was able to facilitate a discussion that helped clients think through their situation, overcome limiting assumptions and counterproductive thinking patterns, develop paths to action, and experience the positive effect of their actions.

After twenty-five years of coaching executives and professionals, as well as consulting to a myriad of organizations across a range of industries, I entered academia. The University of Texas at Dallas provided me an opportunity to create a Graduate Certificate in Executive and Professional Coaching and I was privileged to teach in it. I quickly realized that my coaching was very intuitive at this point in my life. As Schön would say, my knowing was in my action. I was now challenged to make my coaching process explicit so that I could teach others what had served me so well over the years. I became more conscious of what I was doing and how I was doing it. Again, in the words of Schön, I was turning "thought back on action and on the knowing which is implicit in action" (1983, p. 50). The Foursquare Coaching Framework is the result of that reflective process.

The Reflective Practitioner model is considered to be an antidote to the problems associated with the technical rationality inherent in the Scientist-Practitioner model. Schön argued that "technical rationality depends on agreement about ends. When ends are fixed and clear, then the decision to act can present itself as an instrumental problem, but when ends are confused and conflicting, there is as yet no 'problem' to solve" (Schön, 1983, p. 41). To paraphrase, the problems and situations faced by those in the behavioral sciences (i.e., coaches) do not lend themselves to a purely "scientific" approach because human problems are characterized by uncertainty, uniqueness, instability, and confusing and conflicting ends. Schön goes on to say,

> In the varied topography of professional practice, there is a high, hard ground where practitioners can make effective use of research-based theory and technique, and there is a swampy lowland where situations are confusing "messes" incapable of technical solution. The difficulty is that the problems of the high ground, however great their technical interest, are often relatively unimportant to clients . . . while in the swamp are the problems of greatest human concern.
>
> (1983, p. 42)

While reflective practice may help in the professional development of coaches who deal with the swampy problems of clients, reflective practice is not for everyone. According to Finlay (2008), there is a dark side to reflective practice. She points out that the critics of reflective practice contend that over-stretched professionals do not have the time to engage in quality reflection, which results in it being an inconsistent practice or a perfunctory, superficial process. When the process of reflective practice is poorly executed, the practitioner does not benefit from additional insight or knowledge and may, in fact, reinforce existing prejudices and habits. Finlay suggests that the inappropriate use of reflective practice leads to self-absorbed navel gazing, which may diminish a practitioner's professional work instead of promoting it. Furthermore, one wonders if an emphasis on self-discovery as a basis for developing action strategies does so at the expense of ignoring models for helping others derived from sound research. It may be, as Rolfe suggests, that "the highest price paid by Reflective Practitioners is undoubtedly the devaluing of the kinds of knowledge traditionally associated with expertise" (2002, p. 25).

The Informed Practitioner

Clearly, there are strengths and weaknesses in both the Scientist-Practitioner and the Reflective Practitioner models. The Scientist-Practitioner model has paved the way for the application of theory to practice in the behavioral sciences but possibly at the expense of benefiting from experiential learning. The Reflective Practitioner model has opened the door for the development of professional insight through the mindful consideration of, and learning from, one's experiences but perhaps to the detriment of utilizing the results of applied research to increase professional effectiveness. There is a third path: the Informed Practitioner. This model combines the strong points of both the Scientist-Practitioner and the Reflective Practitioner models:

> The strength of the informed-practitioner model lies not in developing scientifically tenacious prescriptive intervention models to be applied with unquestioning confidence. Rather, its strength is that it provides theoretical frameworks, information, critical thinking, and methodological rigor that the practitioner can use to navigate the ever-changing waters of the coaching intervention.
>
> (Grant & Stober, 2006, p. 6)

As Parker and Detterman (1988) mention, informed practitioners are not presumed to be significant producers of research. Instead, informed practitioners draw on the evidence-based knowledge *produced* by research, apply it in their practice, and then act as a reflective practitioner to further refine the use of those frameworks in their work.

Evidence-Based Practice: Theory Is for the Coach; Coaching Is for the Client!

Evidence-based practice defines the informed practitioner. Evidence-based practice means that the coach's work is explicitly grounded in up-to-date information drawn from relevant and valid research, theory, and practice so as to optimize outcomes. Rolfe (2002) refers to this type of information as propositional knowledge. He argues that expert practitioners can draw on such existing knowledge, adapt it, and use it to apply informed critical thought to what they do. Many coaches, by contrast, are often keen to use skills, tools, and techniques before building a repertoire of propositional knowledge. Gray (2006) points out that, "far from utilising specific theoretical models to underpin their practice, some coaches, at least, may only do this at a subconscious or, at least, tacit level" (p. 4). It follows, therefore, that if this is their custom, the work that is done with clients may remain superficial, lack nuance, and be reduced to a rote application of coaching tools and techniques because there is no conceptual depth from which to operate.

The over-reliance on skill, ability, and behaviorally based competencies as a measure of coaching expertise is exacerbated by the fact that many coach training programs focus exclusively on these types of competencies as a structured guide for developing proficiency as a coach. That is not to imply that the mastery of these competencies is not required for effective coaching—they are. The International Coach Federation (ICF), arguably the most well-known coaching organization in the world, has defined eleven such competencies (ICF Core Competencies—International Coach Federation, n.d.) as the foundation for its credentialing process.

These competencies serve the coaching conversation well and even assist in building the Coaching Alliance (Chapter 10). However, while necessary, Bluckert (2005) argues that skill, ability, and behaviorally based competencies are not sufficient for master-level coaching without being combined with what he terms higher-level competencies. Higher-level competencies include the comprehension of psychologically based theoretical frameworks (domains of knowledge) that provide the underpinning for evidence-based practice, and out of which these skill and ability-based competencies have emerged. Mozdzierz and his colleagues buttress the idea that skills and techniques, by themselves, are but a shallow substitute for domains of knowledge. They point out that for a set of skills to be more than a rote application of techniques they must be applied *within the context* of a domain:

> [S]kills are applied within the context of a domain of knowledge (or field). As such, they represent a *refinement of one's thinking within a certain area* rather than an application of mechanical skills. The refinement of one's thinking within particular domains includes the thought processes behind skills, explanations, and theories regarding the topic, and research about the subject area. It represents an *understanding and discernment.*
>
> (2014, p. 4)

This line of reasoning makes it apparent that the ability to coach at the highest professional level requires both skills-based competencies *and* the propositional knowledge that supports the use of those competencies. This point is easily illustrated with the ICF competency *Powerful Questioning*. Powerful Questioning as defined by the ICF is the "ability to ask questions that reveal the information needed for maximum benefit to the coaching relationship and the client" (ICF Core Competencies—International Coach Federation, n.d.). By itself, this competency includes such skills as reflective listening and open-ended questioning to create greater clarity, possibility, or new learning that moves the client toward what he or she desires. However, when the skills associated with this competency are utilized in conjunction with an understanding of different psychologically based frameworks, the result is even more potent. For example, powerful questions asked from a solution-focused domain of knowledge have a different intent and structure than powerful questions posed from a motivational interviewing domain of knowledge. Both are essential to the coaching process, but without an understanding of these domains of knowledge the coach practitioner will be unable to make a conscious distinction. Clearly then, coaches—as Informed Practitioners—should have a thorough grasp of the psychological domains of knowledge from which their methods and practices stem. To this end, the coaching profession would be well-served to understand and appreciate the influence that different branches of psychology have had on how coaching is practiced today.

Psychology's Influence on Coaching

Coaching, in its present form, is a relatively young discipline. With the need to establish its unique identity and to set ethical boundaries, there has been a concerted effort to distinguish it from counseling and psychotherapy, and rightly so. As Kemp (2005) correctly asserts, making this distinction has some practical, professional, and commercial benefits. However, he also warns that by attempting to construct such an impermeable barrier, "it fails to acknowledge the widespread applicability and utilization of therapeutic models of understanding and intervention within the positivist, developmental coaching context" (p. 37). One only has to witness the emphasis that coaching places on learning, development, personal growth, and transformation to see the influence of its psychological roots. In fact, it has long been a mission of psychology to develop people's strengths for optimal functioning so that their lives are more productive and fulfilling. This mission, however, has been overshadowed by the public's perception that psychology only focuses on mental illness—a perception drawn from psychology's origins.

Psychology has a long past but a short history. Its roots extend as far back as Aristotle and Plato, but it did not emerge as a separate discipline until the late 1800s. With the publication of his classic textbook, *The Principles of Psychology* in 1890, William James established himself as the father of American psychology. While a descendant of the philosophical tradition, James was also a medical doctor, and it was during this period that other physicians such as Sigmund Freud began using the medical model to treat mental illness and other psychological disorders. This trend continued during the early part of the twentieth century with the development of psychoanalysis and the introduction of behaviorism—led by Pavlov in Europe and Skinner in America (Brock, 2014). After World War II, there was additional emphasis placed on pathology and mental illness due to the need for psychologists to help post-war veterans with their problems.

The tide shifted, however, during the 1950s with the emergence of humanistic psychology, as the discipline reconnected with its "positive side." The work and writings of people such as Abraham Maslow, Erich Fromm, and Carl Rogers focused on those influences that allowed people to be at their very best. More recently, the study of positive subjective experience and how to improve one's quality of life has been reenergized with the rise of Positive Psychology—the intent of which mirrors the goals and outcomes of coaching. The link between coaching and psychology, however, is not as simple as a one-to-one correlation with Positive Psychology. Many facets of psychology impact the practice of coaching.

Although it is difficult for many coaches to accept, coaching and psychotherapy are based on similar theoretical constructs (Hart et al., 2001). The content and issues addressed in therapeutic and coaching conversations may differ, but there are similarities in what must happen for both the therapist and coach to provide the help to the client that is their intention. In both cases, the practitioner must induce the client to discuss items of a private nature—whether they are personal or professional issues. To assist the client in gaining new perspectives and insights, blind spots and shortcomings are explored and become targets for action. The client is also encouraged to "look inside" and reflect on the desires, needs, concerns, and fears that impact motivation for change and resolve any conflicting internal forces (a practice fundamental to the Freudian approach to psychotherapy). Moreover, establishing a dialogue with the client and observing the processes that take place during that dialogue is an essential component of the Gestalt approach to psychotherapy, as it is to coaching. Therapists and clients work together in a collaborative relationship to raise clients' "awareness of the constructive solutions already in their lives and to help them to find ways to expand upon them" (O'Connell, 2003, p. 5). Coaches do the same. Furthermore, just as psychotherapists administer tests to assess the client's effectiveness and personality dynamics, coaches often use assessments to identify personality traits, strengths, and cognitive predispositions and to understand their clients better. The point here is that, although coaches must be vigilant about not straying into therapeutic issues, they share common methods and practices with psychotherapists.

Clinical psychology is not the only branch of psychology with which coaching shares similarities. Educational psychology—the scientific study of human learning—has produced theories, models, and methods that offer useful underpinnings to coaching. Adult learning theory, for example, emphasizes many of the same goals for learners that coaching does for clients, i.e., self-determination, self-actualization, and self-transformation (Jarvis et al., 1998). Learners are viewed as autonomous and self-directed and as responsible for their personal growth and development. Similarly, coached clients are considered in control of and accountable for their desired outcomes. Additionally, the conversational climate for the self-directed learner, as for the coached client, must be one of feeling valued and supported.

Previously in this chapter, the Reflective Practitioner model was discussed as it applies to coaching. This model is grounded in experiential learning theory, another topic researched and developed by educational psychologists. Research in experiential learning has become critical to understanding how adults learn. It explains how experience is turned into knowledge, skills, attitudes, values, and even emotions through the process of conscious reflection (Jarvis, 1987). Coaches rely on experiential learning when they ask clients to recall, and reflect on, past success experiences to help clients discover and reinforce strengths that enhance confidence and increase capacity to achieve valued goals. Coached clients are also encouraged to use past experiences to discover previously fruitful paths of action as a means of achieving current objectives. Even failure is reframed as a learning experience and used to promote growth and development.

The next evolutionary step in experiential learning is transformative learning. The originator of transformative learning, Mezirow (1994), defines it as "[t]he social process of construing and appropriating a new or revised interpretation of the meaning of one's experiences as a guide to action" (pp. 222–223). Thus, while transformative learning, as with previous models of adult learning, is a co-created experience that promotes critical reflection, it adds a new element to the transformative process: reconstructing the meaning derived from one's experiences. Gray (2006) explains it this way: "Rather than knowing the learner's experiences and using them as a resource for discussion, the educator comes to encourage a critical examination of these experiences and the assumptions that underlie them—a process aimed at transforming the learner's meaning perspectives" (p. 486). Transformative learning's emphasis on encouraging reflection as a prerequisite for promoting action, examining underlying assumptions and beliefs, reframing one's interpretation of experiences to develop new meaning, and co-creating the learning experience are all premises and practices of coaching. Coaching, then, is a form of transformative learning.

Evidence-Based Practices Are Not Enough

It is apparent from this brief overview that coaching has benefited from psychologically based theory, models, and methods—both clinical and educational. To become an Informed Practitioner, a coach must have a working knowledge of the psychological constructs (theories) that inform the coaching process and utilize the evidence-based practices (EBPs) derived from those constructs. Being an Informed Practitioner, however, is not sufficient to become a Level III coach. Master-level practitioners have the ability to use EBPs in an intuitive and spontaneous manner while simultaneously navigating the ever-changing landscape of a coaching conversation. This ability is also recognized as important by the ICF because behavioral descriptors for the competency *Coaching Presence* include being flexible during the coaching process ("dancing in the moment") and accessing one's intuiton and gut feel when guiding the coaching process (ICF Core Competencies—International Coach Federation, n.d.). Pure intuition is not sufficient, however, to demonstrate this competency. Coaches must have an *educated* "feel" for what to do and when that allows them to be artful in the performance of their craft. Schön (1983, 1987) describes this activity as *reflection-in-action*.

Reflection-in-action involves processes that allow people to reshape what they are doing while doing it. "In such processes, reflection tends to focus interactively on the outcomes of action, the action itself, and the intuitive knowing implicit in the action" (Schön, 1983, p. 56). Schön illustrates how this improvisational process works within the context of a jazz performance:

> When good jazz musicians improvise together, they also manifest a "feel for" their material and they make on-the-spot adjustments to the sounds they hear. Listening to one another and to themselves, they feel where the music is going and adjust their playing accordingly. They can do this, first of all, because their collective effort and musical invention makes use of a schema—a metric, melodic, and harmonic structure familiar to all the participants—which gives a predictable order to the piece. In addition, each of the musicians has at the ready a repertoire of musical figures that he can deliver at appropriate moments. Improvisation consists in varying, combining, and recombining a set of figures within the schema which bounds and gives coherence to the performance. As the musicians feel the direction of the music that is developing out of their interwoven contributions, they make new sense of it and adjust their performance to the new sense they have made.
>
> (1983, p. 55)

This description is not unlike what takes place during a coaching conversation. Just as the jazz musician has a repertoire of musical riffs and scales that can be spontaneously retrieved and delivered at suitable points to create a coherent performance, a coach has a set of evidence-based methods and techniques that can be accessed *in the moment* to facilitate a coaching conversation. For the master jazz musician, it is a feel for what musical figures should be played in response to where the music is going that allows him to demonstrate his art. For the Level III coach, it is also a feel—in the form of intuitive judgment—about what to do and when in response to where the coaching conversation is going that allows for a masterful coaching session. In both cases, reflection-in-action is at work. Jazz musicians can do this because they make use of a schema—a musical blueprint familiar to all players—that gives a predictable order to the piece of music. To do the same, master-level coaches must also have a schema that gives a predictable order to the coaching conversation.

A Schema for Coaching

A schema is "a knowledge structure that guides information processing" (Kendzierski, 1980, p. 23). To put it another way, it is a cognitive framework that helps us organize and use information. For jazz musicians, it is the metric, melodic, and harmonic structure of music that serves as a cognitive "map" allowing them to use their knowledge, skills, and abilities to play what feels right at the moment by informing them of their artistic choices. Similarly, a coach must have a cognitive map for coaching. Without such a map, it is easy to get lost in the fluidity of the conversation and lose your "feel" for what to do and when, even if you have a storehouse of evidence-based knowledge, methods, and techniques. Such a map facilitates non-linear thinking and fosters reflection-in-action. The remainder of this book will describe a cognitive map of the coaching process—the *Foursquare Coaching Framework*—its evidence-based practices and related domains of knowledge.

Chapter Summary

The conduct of coaching exists on a continuum from novice to master level. There are recognizable indicators that provide clues as to where a practitioner is on that continuum. Anchoring one end of the continuum is the novice or Level I practitioner. Coaches at this level are self-conscious about their efforts and have great concern about not making mistakes. Apprehensiveness about their competence leads to an over-reliance on structure and technique. Their thinking process is quite linear, as they want to use a formulaic approach that ensures success. By contrast, master-level (Level III) practitioners process information differently. Their thinking can be described as non-linear since they integrate a variety of information simultaneously while coaching. Their ability to process information in this way combined with their professional confidence enables them to focus more on the client and less on themselves. To put it another way, they integrate an array of information while simultaneously adapting to the needs and flow of the coaching conversation in an intuitive way that facilitates the helping process.

Over the years, two models have emerged that have been helpful in assisting practitioners in their efforts to achieve mastery: the Scientist-Practitioner model and the Reflective Practitioner model. The Scientist-Practitioner model is based on the premise that science and practice must continually inform each other. In this model, professionals engage in research, develop evidence-based practices, and apply those methods to their work. The Reflective Practitioner model encourages practitioners to use the process of critical thinking to examine their work experiences so as to develop theories of action that lead to increasingly successful intervention strategies. For coaches, the best approach seems to be to combine the strengths of both models. In other words, to draw upon relevant evidence-based research, apply it to the process of coaching, and then act as a reflective practitioner to refine their coaching methods and techniques. This paradigm is called the Informed Practitioner model.

In this chapter, it was argued that master-level coaching does not result from evidence-based practices or reflective observation alone. Master-level coaching can only occur if a cognitive structure exists that makes it possible to engage in reflection-in-action, i.e., to reshape what one is doing and how it is being done, in real time, during the flow of a coaching conversation while simultaneously focusing on the outcomes of those actions. To accomplish this, coaches must have a knowledge structure—a schema—that guides information processing for this purpose. Simply put, coaches need a cognitive map that allows them to navigate the coaching landscape in a non-linear, masterful way. That map is the Foursquare Coaching Framework.

CHAPTER 2

The Foursquare Coaching Framework
A Schema for Coaching

Imagine leading a safari through the jungle. Your journey begins on a tall hill overlooking a lush, green jungle, on the far side of which is a long winding river. Standing with you is the group of people you are guiding who want to reach the river and who are depending on you to take them through the jungle to their goal. From the hill, the journey looks easy, but once you have entered the jungle things change. The destination is no longer as clear; the path forward is obscured by vines that must be cleared away a little at a time to see what is ahead. Even then, your route is constantly changing due to unexpected challenges, e.g., a damaged bridge, a fallen tree, a washed-out trail. Occasionally, a wild animal is encountered and must be avoided.

The way through a jungle is never straight and narrow. It is like finding your way through a labyrinth. To fulfill your role as a safari guide, you must have many competencies. You must know first aid, you must know where and how to set up camp each night, you must have the survival skills necessary to deal with every threat the jungle offers. This knowledge and these skills notwithstanding, nothing is more important than being able to navigate the jungle. You must know at all times where you are and what options are available to get where you want to go. Knowing how to navigate the jungle is particularly important when the terrain changes unexpectedly and the path forward becomes ambiguous, or when the unforeseen happens. Coaching is similar to leading a safari, except that you are in a different kind of jungle. It is a jungle of thoughts and actions through which you must lead clients to the destination of their choosing, but instead of using a physical map you must rely on a cognitive map of the process of the coaching conversation.

Coaching and the Socratic Method

Socrates (470–399 BC) was a Greek philosopher who used a dialectic method of inquiry to develop the critical thinking skills of his students. This approach became known as the Socratic Method. Coaching and the Socratic Method are similar in three ways. First, they are both inquiry-based methodologies that involve the systematic use of questions to facilitate learning, problem solving, and self-discovery. Second, both require a collaborative and egalitarian relationship between parties. Finally, and most importantly for this book, they rely on two cardinal methods of helping: support and challenge.

Support and Challenge

To support means to encourage, comfort, strengthen, validate, reinforce, serve as a foundation for something, or maintain the existence of something. To challenge means to confront, question, test, dare, or insist on an explanation or clarification. Coaching has traditionally emphasized support over challenge. This practice is undoubtedly due to the influence of its humanistic roots; specifically, the person-centered approach of Carl Rogers (1951). The person-centered approach stresses the importance of a warm, positive relationship between the practitioner and client as a prerequisite for helping. The Rogerian approach is a non-directive methodology in which practitioners operate on the premise that clients have, within themselves, immense resources for personal development and problem solving. Establishing a supportive climate of empathy, positive regard, and genuineness creates the conditions whereby the client's capacity for self-growth is unleashed.

The idea of affirming the value of the client and building a productive helping relationship is well-known to coaches and is accentuated in the coaching literature. However, coaches would do well to follow in the footsteps of Socrates and, more recently, Laurent Daloz (2012) by using inquiry to challenge clients when needed. Daloz's model of mentoring adult learners is widely used in education. He argues that support without challenge can be detrimental to the adult learning process. In fact, John Blakey and Ian Day claim that support without challenge is a form of collusion:

> *Collusion* arises when the coach is only asking questions in a very supportive fashion, being nonjudgmental, and listening. Here, there is a risk that the coach colludes with the coachee; that is, aligns 100 percent with their worldview and fails to challenge or give feedback from a different perspective.
> (Blakey & Day, 2012, p. 16)

So, what is the intent of challenge? Simply put, it is to create *productive discomfort* so that critical self-reflection occurs. An important part of the coach's role is to be an "empathetic provocateur" (Cranton, 1992). Master-level coaches challenge their clients by highlighting incorrect assumptions, bringing to light contradictions in the client's thinking, and pointing out inconsistencies between what the client says and what the client does. In addition, clients are challenged to specify what they want and then challenged again to *do* something to achieve it. The point is, challenge is an essential element of the coaching process. It is the *push* that complements the *pull* provided by support.

Support and challenge work hand in hand. Support closes the distance between the practitioner and the client. It creates a safe space where clients can satisfy their need for intimacy and trust. Challenge, by way of contrast, adds distance to the relationship, drawing clients outward to fill the gap, causing them to move in some way in response to the distancing (Daloz, 1999). Support and challenge are the yin and yang of coaching because they are interdependent halves of a whole. They must work together in a balanced way if they are to be effective. Daloz's concept of the relationship between support and challenge is illustrated in the graphic below.

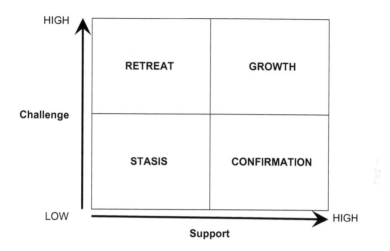

When support and challenge are low, there is inertia and apathy. Little is likely to happen (stasis), and things stay pretty much as they are. If there is high support and low challenge, clients will feel validated (confirmation), but they will not be pushed to act or see things differently. The coach becomes a cheerleader rather than a facilitator of change. Conversely, if there is too much challenge in the absence of support, clients will experience undue stress and be driven into a defensive posture (retreat), leading to intellectual sparring and arguments. The coach is a driver rather than a facilitator. Balancing support and challenge, on the other hand, can lead to sustainable growth and change on the part of the client. The coach can utilize the natural tension that results from support equipoised with challenge to propel the client toward his or her preferred future.

Thought and Action

No matter the purpose for which clients come to coaching, the common denominator among all clients is that they want to experience a change in some way, shape, or form. Change does not happen without engaging thought and action; clients have to think about what they want and then take action to achieve it. In fact, it is the congruence between thought and action that makes change possible. Thoughts and actions are to a coach what clay is to a potter. They are the material a coach works with to help clients achieve their goals.

Dr. Francis is an excellent emergency room physician with years of experience. In many ways, her peers and certainly the younger professionals she works with, both nurses and physicians, see her as a role model. The chair of the department is aware of her reputation and has encouraged her to take on more formal leadership responsibilities. While flattered, Dr. Francis is uncertain. On the surface, it seems like a pretty good idea. She feels that she has the necessary experience and skills to be a good leader, but she doesn't know if this is what she really wants. She is concerned that taking on more of a leadership role would reduce the time she is able to devote to her clinical work; therefore, she feels stuck and can't seem to find the motivation to move forward. She wonders if she has not thought it through enough while at the same time worrying that she is over-thinking the decision. Sometimes she thinks that maybe she should just start taking on more leadership responsibilities and see what happens. However, even if she decides to act on that idea, she is not sure what to do first.

Dr. Francis is doing a lot of thinking but lacks clarity about her priorities. She wants to act but is not sure what to do. In order for her to find a resolution, she must decide what is important to her and what actions she will take based on those priorities. Dr. Francis is not unlike any other client, in that the content of the coaching conversation will revolve around her thoughts and actions. Coaching, then, can be thought of as applying the practices of support and challenge to the elements of thought and action (Pemberton, 2006). The relationship of support and challenge to thought and action creates a foursquare matrix—or framework— that serves as a cognitive map (a mental schema) that allows you to navigate the ever-changing landscape of the coaching conversation in an artful manner using the non-linear thinking approach that typifies master-level coaches.

Foursquare Coaching Framework

The Foursquare Coaching Framework (FsCF)

Each quadrant in the Foursquare Coaching Framework contributes to the overall coaching process and directs the coaching conversation in a way consistent with its purpose. For example, Support-for-Action focuses the conversation on the client's motivation to act in pursuit of his or her goals and objectives, and the methods and practices used in Support-for-Action support this purpose. It is analogous to going to Disneyland. Each "land" has a theme, and the rides in each land reinforce that theme. For instance, the theme of *Tomorrowland* is different than that of *Adventureland*. Consistent with its theme, *Tomorrowland* has rides similar to Hyperspace Mountain while *Frontierland* has rides like the Indiana Jones Adventure. To fully experience Disneyland, you will want to explore all of the theme parks: *Tomorrowland, Adventureland, Frontierland,* and *Fantasyland.* Similarly, to fully manage the process of an effective coaching conversation, you will want to spend time, at some point, in each quadrant of the Foursquare Coaching Framework: *Support-for-Thought, Challenge-for-Thought, Support-for-Action,* and *Challenge-for-Action.* The purpose and goals of each quadrant are briefly explained and illustrated below so that you will have an overview of the Framework as a precursor to the in-depth discussion that occupies the remainder of this book.

Support-for-Thought

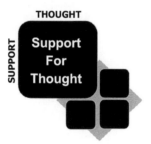

Support is the underpinning for challenge and thought paves the way for action. Therefore, Support-for-Thought is a foundational piece of the FsCF. The purpose of Support-for-Thought is to create the requisite conditions that *support* the client's willingness and ability to think constructively. To accomplish this, Support-for-Thought has three objectives: 1) connect with and engage the client; 2) set the coaching agenda; and 3) build a platform of understanding about the client's current situation. These objectives, when met, provide a launching pad for the exploration of additional thoughts about what clients want, their motivational readiness to take action, and the specific actions they will take to accomplish their goals. The example below illustrates a coaching conversation that begins in the Support-for-Thought quadrant of the FsCF.

Support-for-Thought: Building a Platform of Understanding

Coach: How are things going since the last time we talked?

Client: Okay (with a so-so expression).

Coach: I hear some frustration in your voice.

Client: Honestly? Yes. That's what I wanted to talk about today.

Coach: What specifically do you want to talk about?

Client: My frustration at work.

Coach: And what about your frustration do you want to talk about?

Client: Well, I've tried to be a team player, but I don't seem to be fitting in with my team. Everybody seems so distant and unfriendly—at least with me. I've been there for a good six months now, and it seems as if I started yesterday as far as my relationships go. I mean, my colleagues work with me in the sense that they give me the information I need and cooperate with me on tasks, but that's about it. The rest of the time, everyone is so distant and business-like.

Coach: Let me see if I understand what you're saying. Your frustration is not with the way they work with you on tasks, but more about how you seem to be treated as a person and that's not what you want from your work relationships.

Client: Yes! That's it exactly! (With a smile and head nodding). They don't show any interest in me as a person.

Coach: How do you know that they don't show any interest in you as a person?

Client: Well, for one thing, they never ask me about how my weekend was or what's going on outside of work. They don't invite me to lunch—even though they go to lunch together.

Coach: Okay, so what would you like from today's conversation?

Client: That is a good question. I think I would like to find a way for them to be more sensitive to me as a person and accept me as one of the team.

Coach: How will you know if we accomplished what you wanted from today's discussion?

Client: (pause . . . eyes go up and to the right, and after a moment refocuses on the coach) I want to have some actions that I can take that might get them to relate to me as a person, not just as a co-worker.

During this segment of the conversation, the coach is connecting with and engaging the client and building a platform of understanding about the client's current situation. Along the way, he sets the agenda for the coaching conversation. Support-for-Thought requires the coach to demonstrate empathy, display positive regard, engage in Adult-to-Adult interactions, and recover deletions in the client's narrative. These elements and their associated techniques are discussed in detail in Chapters 3 and 4.

Challenge-for-Thought

In the classic book, *Alice's Adventures in Wonderland* by Lewis Carroll, there is an exchange between Alice and the Cheshire Cat during which Alice asks the Cat, "Would you tell me, please, which way I ought to go from here?" The Cat answers by saying, "That depends a good deal on where you want to get to." This short exchange illustrates an important point: You can't get "there" when you don't know where "there" is. The first purpose of Challenge-for-Thought is to use the rigorous discipline of inquiry to *challenge* clients to think about, and then describe, their preferred future. In other words, to tell you where they "want to get to."

The example below continues the coaching conversation from above, which has now shifted to the Challenge-for-Thought quadrant. During this segment of the conversation, the coach is facilitating the client's thinking about her preferred future by engaging in two quadrant-related activities: developing discrepancy and constructing a well-formed outcome.

Challenge-for-Thought: Describing Their Preferred Future

Client: (pause . . . eyes go up and to the right, and after a moment refocus on the coach) I want to have some actions that I can take that might get them to relate to me as a person, not just as a co-worker.

Coach: How do you want them to relate to you as a person that is different from what you are experiencing now?

Client: I wouldn't be excluded from some of the things they do outside of work.

Coach: What would be happening instead?

Client: They would say things like, "Hey, we're going to lunch, want to come along?"

Coach: What stops you from asking them to go to lunch?

Client: If I have to ask them, then they're only going because I asked and not because they really want to.

Coach: Interesting . . . let's come back to that later. What else would let you know that they are relating to you as a person?

Client: We'd talk about what was happening outside of work, our kids, that sort of thing.

Coach: Anything else?

Client: I would feel more comfortable asking them about what's going on in their world. I would feel more of a connection with them. Right now, I would feel like I'm intruding if I did that.

Coach: How would you know if you had more of a connection with them?

Client: I would know them better as people, and they would know me better.

Coach: Let me pull together what I hear to this point. You want a more personal relationship with the people that you work with. And you'll know when that's happening because you'll be included in their social activities outside of work, like going to lunch and things like that. Also, you'll be having conversations about things other than work-related matters. In fact, you'll feel more comfortable asking them about what's going on in their lives because you'll feel a connection with them personally. You'll know them better, and they'll know you better. Is that about right?

Client: Yes, it is. I think if that were to happen I'd be much happier at work—and more productive.

In addition to challenging clients to think about, and ultimately describe, what they want, coaches need to be able to help clients spot and overcome cognitive roadblocks in the form of counterproductive self-talk and limiting beliefs. This aspect of coaching is one of the purposes of Challenge-for-Thought. To illustrate, we pick up the previous coaching conversation.

Challenge-for-Thought: Overcoming Cognitive Roadblocks

Client: Yes, it is. I think if that were to happen I'd be much happier at work—and more productive.

Coach: I'd like to go back to something interesting that you said earlier. You said that if you had to ask your co-workers to go to lunch that they'd only be going because you asked. Is that correct?

Client: That's right.

Coach: How do you know that?

Client: Because if people really want to do something with you, they will ask you to join them. If they don't, it means that they're not interested.

Coach: Would you be offended if they asked you to go to lunch?

Client: No, I wouldn't, I'd like it.

Coach: So, what if your co-workers held that same belief?

Client: What do you mean?

Coach: Suppose they believed that if you really wanted to go to lunch with them that you would initiate it by asking them, and because you don't it means that you're not interested in joining them.

Client: Well, they'd be wrong.

Coach: So is it at all possible, even slightly, that you might be wrong too? That perhaps they are waiting for you to ask them to do something to show that you are interested in spending time with them? After all, you're fairly new, and they don't know you that well.

Client: (pause) . . . I hadn't thought about it like that.

Coach: If you were to think of it like that, how would it help you?

Client: For one thing, it would free me up to take the initiative in asking them to do things with me. But, I must admit, that's not easy.

During this segment of the conversation, the coach is challenging a limiting *if-then* belief, i.e., "If people really want to do something with you, they will ask you to join them. If they don't, it means that they're not interested." Counterproductive automatic thoughts in the form of contaminated self-talk and limiting beliefs can interfere with the goal setting as well as the action choices available to clients. When these types of cognitive roadblocks surface during the conversation, the coach has the option to move to Challenge-for-Thought so that they can be explored and replaced with more productive thinking.

To summarize, conversations in the Challenge-for-Thought quadrant are intended to help clients think about what they want and remove mental barriers that can impede progress toward reaching their goals. The quadrant-related activities in Challenge-for-Thought are developing discrepancy between the client's current state and desired future state, constructing well-formed outcomes, and changing contaminated self-talk and counterproductive beliefs. These activities and their related techniques are discussed in detail in Chapters 5, 6, and 7.

Support-for-Action

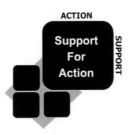

Coaches typically proceed from the assumption that clients are inherently motivated to take action in pursuit of goals. This assumption is reasonable because coming to coaching is a voluntary activity and clients drive the agenda, which is presumed to be about issues and goals important to them. Unfortunately, clients are not as uniform in their motivation to act as one would think. Therefore, goal-related actions must be *supported* by sufficient levels of motivation for those actions to be initiated and sustained. Support is more than encouraging, comforting, validating, and reinforcing. In this case, it means creating the *motivational foundation* to ensure a strong impetus for action. In Support-for-Action, the coach tests and strengthens that motivational foundation. This is illustrated below as the coaching conversation continues.

Support-for-Action: Strengthening Motivation for Change

Client: For one thing, it would free me up to take the initiative in developing a more personal relationship with some of the people I work with. But, I must admit, that's not easy.

Coach: What is not easy for you?

Client: Taking the initiative in reaching out to people. This is an area that I've struggled with for a long time. For example, I don't even like to ask people for help at work, and it creates problems for me at times. It even affects my personal life.

Coach: So, if you were to become more comfortable reaching out to people for help or to get what you want or need, that would be beneficial.

Client: Very! In fact, the more I think about it, my real challenge is not that my teammates don't accept me, but that I need to learn to ask people for what I want and take the initiative in getting it.

Coach: It sounds like learning to take the initiative with other people is something that would help you in all areas of your life—not just at work.

Client: Exactly, I think my situation at work is just a symptom of a larger issue. If I can make progress on it, that would help me in many ways.

Coach: In what other ways might it help you?

Client: It would help me at home. Sometimes I expect my husband to recognize what I want or need without me having to ask, and when he doesn't, I get resentful. It's kind of like feeling resentful when my teammates didn't invite me to lunch even though I never asked.

Coach: What would happen if you did not become more proactive about getting what you want from others?

Client: It puts me at the mercy of others because I have to wait for them to make the first move. It's like I'm expecting them to read my mind. I want to feel like I am in control of getting what I want from others—both at work and at home. I'm tired of feeling anxious about asking people for help or feeling resentful when people don't automatically include me in their activities—even though I haven't made it clear that I would enjoy being included.

Coach: Okay. So, let me see if I can summarize what you're saying. Becoming more proactive about getting what you want from others is very important to you at this point because it will help you in both your professional and personal life. (Client is nodding her head.) When you are successful in doing this, you will feel more in control and experience fewer negative feelings like anxiousness or resentment. Plus, you'll get more of what you want from others, like help with work and so forth. Is that about right?

Client: Yes, it is, and now that I hear it again, it definitely makes this an important goal.

Coach: Initially, you said that you wanted to focus on being accepted by your team so that you have a more personal relationship with the people you work with. Now it seems as if you have a new goal, which is to be more proactive about getting what you want from others, in general. And that you're strongly motivated to do this, correct?

Client: (head nodding) That's correct.

Coach: On a scale from zero to ten, with ten being very motivated and zero being the opposite, where are you on that scale?

Client: I'd say I'm at least an eight.

During this segment of the conversation, the emphasis is on strengthening motivation by enhancing the *goal attainment value* of the client's desire to be more proactive about getting what she wants from others. Specifically, the coach did this by having the client talk about the advantages of goal accomplishment and the disadvantages of maintaining the status quo. Finally, the coach used the technique of scaling to quantify the client's subjective measure of her level of motivation. These are methods and techniques used in Support-for-Action to strengthen motivation. They are discussed in detail in Chapter 8.

Now the coach is at a decision point in the conversation. The client began with the goal of wanting her co-workers to relate to her as a person, not just as a co-worker. However, during Support-for-Action, the client's goal has changed. She wants to become more proactive about getting what she wants from others in general. Since the purpose of Support-for-Action is to strengthen motivation, the coach pursued this objective given the enhanced motivational value of the new goal. Once the discussion in Support-for-Action is complete, the coach has options: move to Challenge-for-Thought to develop a well-formed outcome or, alternatively, proceed to Challenge-for-Action to develop action experiments. The coach can even stay in Support-for-Action to strengthen the client's *confidence* with regard to being more proactive about getting what she wants from others. Which option is best? That is a judgment call on the part of the coach. Staying within Support-for-Action will continue to build motivation by focusing on capability and readiness to act, while moving to Challenge-for-Thought adds depth to the conversation by fleshing out details regarding indicators of success. Challenge-for-Action, on the other hand, promotes movement by having the client talk about what she is going to do, specifically, to be more proactive in getting what she wants.

The critical point here is that this schema (the FsCF) guides information processing and informs the coach as to his or her options available at the moment. This process is not a zero sum game. All of the options can be pursued at some point. Furthermore, this example demonstrates the fluidity that is inherent in the use of the Framework. Moving from quadrant to quadrant is not a linear progression, but a process dictated by the intentions of the coach as he or she moves to the part of the Framework that best serves the client at that point in the coaching conversation. Without this *cognitive map*, it is easy to get lost in the jungle of thoughts and actions.

Challenge-for-Action

Action makes things happen. In the Challenge-for-Action phase of the coaching conversation, the client defines steps to be taken in pursuing something that he or she deems important. *Challenging* people to act, even in some small way, to get what they want begins the overt manifestation of the change process and initiates the most active and obvious stage of change: *doing something differently* to get what one wants. Now, the coaching conversation example shifts to the Challenge-for-Action quadrant.

Challenge-for-Action: Creating Movement toward the Desired Objective

Coach: On a scale from zero to ten, with ten being very motivated and zero being the opposite, where are you on that scale?

Client: I'd say I'm at least an eight.

Coach: What would you like to start experimenting with to become better about asking for what you want from others?

Client: I want to go back to my original situation. I would like to start making the first move toward building more personal relationships with my co-workers.

Coach: Great! I think that is a good place to start. So, what are you going to start doing differently going forward to accomplish this?

Client: I am going to start showing an interest in their personal lives.

Coach: How are you going to do that?

Client: I'm intentionally going to ask how their weekend was, or what's going on with their kids. In fact, now that I think about it, June—one of my co-workers—has kids the same age as mine. She might be someone who I can begin to connect with.

Coach: What else might you start doing differently?

Client: I don't think I want to start by asking the entire group out to lunch.

Coach: What can you do instead?

Client: I can start joining them over coffee and things like that. I've pretty much stayed away from the informal get-togethers because I've just focused on my work. I can start taking some time to join the group when they are in casual conversations.

Coach: By doing that, what will it get you?

Client: I think it will show that I am not standoffish and that I'm interested in them.

Coach: Are there any other ways you want to start being proactive about getting what you want from others?

Client: Actually, yes. My father is getting along in years, and I spend a lot of time checking on him and taking care of his needs. I have a sister who lives here in town that could help, but she has not offered to do much. I think it's because she sees me doing everything and feels that everything is being taken care of, therefore, she doesn't have to do anything. I am going to sit down with her and ask for her help with Dad.

Coach: What do you think her response will be?

Client: My guess is she will be open to it if I ask. I just haven't asked.

Coach: You've talked about doing three things going forward. First, you are going to connect with one of your co-workers—June—with whom you have things in common, like your kids. And second, you are going to begin to join the group at work when they are having coffee for some informal conversations. Finally, you said that you are going to reach out to your sister for help with your dad. Is this accurate?

Client: It is.

Coach: Do you feel comfortable doing these things?

Client: I don't know if "comfortable" is the right word because I will be outside my comfort zone, but I think these are good first steps.

Coach: When are you going to start?

Client: I am going to start doing them next week.

Coach: We are scheduled to meet again in a couple of weeks. When we meet at that time, is it safe to say that you will have had conversations with June, joined the rest of the group at work for some informal interactions, and had the conversation with your sister so that we can talk about how they went?

Client: Absolutely.

Coach: Great, then we can see what you have learned from doing this.

The biggest roadblock to action is inertia. The important thing is to *challenge* the client to do something (no matter how small) toward their goal. These small experimental steps are designed to get the client to behave differently from what she would otherwise and to experience some early success from her efforts. These aims reflect the activities in the Challenge-for-Action quadrant: identifying what clients can do to move forward, specifying how they are going to go about it, pinpointing when and where they will start, and using the results from their actions to promote learning and identify additional actions. Challenge-for-Action is discussed in detail in Chapter 9.

Using the FsCF is a Non-Linear Process

In the sci-fi thriller *Prometheus*, the crew of the spaceship (*Prometheus*) follows a star map discovered among some ancient earth artifacts to find the origins of humanity. As the spaceship is about to land on a distant world, the archeologist on board, Charlie Holloway (played by Logan Marshall-Green), spots a series of straight lines on the surface and declares, "God does not build in straight lines." He believes it is a sure sign of intelligent life because straight lines are a rarity in nature. And so it is with coaching; it is rare that a coaching conversation follows a straight path. As I indicated in my analogy of the coach as a safari guide, the path through the jungle is winding and unpredictable, and the process of coaching reflects this reality.

The Foursquare Coaching Framework is a conceptual structure that helps you plot a route through the ever-changing terrain of the coaching conversation. It is not a rigid set of sequential steps. Instead, it is a non-linear framework that facilitates the type of thinking practiced by Level III coaches. The conversation can begin in any square and move through the other squares as dictated by the flow of the conversation. The conversation may switch squares because of statements made by the client or inquiry by the coach. For example, if clients begin talking about what they want in the future, the conversation has moved to the Challenge-for-Thought square. If during the same conversation, clients mention what actions they might want to take, they have dipped their toe into the Challenge-for-Action quadrant. The coach may also intentionally move the conversation to a specific quadrant with an inquiry, e.g., "What makes this important to you at this point in time?" (Support-for-Action). By picturing all four squares and knowing where you are at any point in the conversation, you can recognize what has been discussed and what conversational territory remains to be explored.

The following simple coaching conversation demonstrates how the coach can use the FsCF to navigate smoothly through the coaching conversation. Specifically, it shows a coaching conversation that begins in Support-for-Thought because of the client's comments, moves to Support-for-Action due to an inquiry by the coach where it stays until the coach transitions to Challenge-for-Action. Throughout this example, graphic symbols represent each of the squares and allow you to track the conversation as it progresses through the Framework.

Support-for-Thought

Support-for-Action

Challenge-for-Thought

Challenge-for-Action

A Process Map

Coach: You mentioned that you wanted to talk about a couple of things. What would you like to talk about today?

Client: I'd like to bounce some ideas off of you. I'm not very good at setting boundaries for myself. I need to improve that.

Coach: What specifically do you need to improve?

Client: I am too willing to take on additional work. I don't speak up enough in my meetings; in my team meetings and my departmental meetings. I don't resist enough when decisions are being made that will create a lot of additional work for my team and me.

Coach: I can understand why you might find that frustrating.

Client: Yes, exactly. It is just my inability to say no when I have too much work on my desk, and I'm being asked to take on more.

[Commentary: The conversation begins with some clarification of the narrative (i.e., "What kind of boundaries specifically do you need to improve?") and a display of empathy (i.e. "I can understand why you might find that frustrating") to connect with and engage the client (Support-for-Thought). However, very little time is spent building a platform of understanding here because the client began the discussion by stating his problem and what he wants to improve upon (i.e., setting boundaries). Additionally with the client's statement "I need to improve on that" the client has indicated a sense of importance for what he wants to do; thereby providing the coach with an opportunity to move to Support-for-Action to enhance goal attainment value and client confidence. The coach also has the option of moving to the Challenge-for-Thought square to develop a well-formed outcome.]

Coach: You just said that you need to improve on setting boundaries. What is different now that makes it important for you to make a change?

Client: Well, you know that I am working with different people now, and there are some very strong personalities in my department. Frankly, I feel like I'm just not assertive enough with some of the people that work with me on the committees.

Coach: And that creates problems because . . . ?

Client: I usually leave a meeting having not resisted enough on ideas that I know were not in the best interest of my department. Also, I leave with a bunch of additional tasks that leave me feeling quite overwhelmed.

Coach: Are there other times when you do not feel that you're assertive enough?

Client: I think that I'm not assertive enough even within my own team. I look at myself and think that my personality is such that I do not delegate enough. I am simply too willing to say, "Yes, I'll be the one to do that"; and that is everywhere in my life generally, and with my family for sure. Now it's just looking at that for what it is and realizing that this is my fault. I've gotten to this place where I feel overwhelmed, stressed out, and not working at the level I would like because I do not draw boundaries well.

Coach: So, this is not just something that you want to do for professional reasons. You're saying that this is important for personal reasons as well.

Client: Definitely, very much so.

Coach: Have there been situations in the past where you have been assertive in the way that you want to be, going forward?

Client: Well, yes, there have been times—as I think about it—that I did not say "Yes" immediately. I was more aware that when people said: "Will you do this?"; "Will you take that on?"; or "Will you participate on this committee?" I simply responded, "I'll get back to you on that." I think that helped me limit my tasks a little bit better.

Coach: How did that help you limit your tasks a little bit better?

Client: I was not impulsive with my decision by reacting to the pressure of the moment. I went away and thought about it. This allowed me to make a more considered decision, and many times I would be able to be assertive and say no.

Coach: So going forward, this is not something that you've never done before, so that means that you are perfectly capable.

Client: Yes, I just think I've fallen into some bad patterns.

Coach: Okay, that makes sense. I mean, we all fall into some bad patterns from time to time.

Let me see if I can summarize what I've heard you say. First, you said that being assertive by setting boundaries is important to you, for both personal and professional reasons. Second, you know that you are capable of this because you've been able to be assertive and set boundaries in the past. Is this correct?

Client: Yes, I think that's accurate.

[Commentary: The coach has chosen to use the client's statement, "I need to improve on that" to move to Support-for-Action by asking the client to talk about "Why this, why now?" In so doing, the client is induced into thinking more deeply about the reasons for wanting to make this change, thereby increasing motivation in the process. The coach then reinforced the importance of the change by reflecting back to the client that he has indicated both personal and professional reasons for making the change. Finally, the coach elicited a previous success experience that proves the person is capable of doing what he wants to do (confidence building). This past success will also be available for use in the Challenge-for-Action quadrant as a basis for identifying actions that have worked in the past that may be reapplied or expanded to help him achieve his current goal. Finally, the coach shifted briefly to Support-for-Thought through a show of empathy (i.e., ". . . that makes sense . . . we all fall into some bad patterns from time to time") and then went back to Support-for-Action by, again, summarizing the importance of the goal and reemphasizing the client's capability.]

Coach: OK, the question I have for you now is, "Based on what you have said, what do you want to do differently going forward to start setting boundaries for yourself?"

[Commentary: The coach's question shifts the conversation to the Challenge-for-Action quadrant to begin devising action experiments that will move the client toward his goal of learning to set boundaries.]

As you might expect, there are other paths this conversation could have followed. For example, Challenge-for-Thought has not yet been explored (i.e., a well-formed outcome has not been developed). So, the coach could have ignored the client's statement of need *("I need to improve on that")* and gone directly to Challenge-for-Thought, returning to Support-for-Action at a later point. It is also possible that the coach could have moved to Challenge-for-Action sooner by asking the client to describe what he will start doing differently in the future to begin setting boundaries in the way that he wants to—even without creating a well-formed outcome. The salient point is that, just as a jazz musician has musical choices to make that are informed by his or her knowledge of the structure of music, you have coaching choices to make that are informed by your knowledge of the structure of coaching as defined by the Foursquare Coaching Framework. Your choices depend on your professional judgment in the same way that a jazz musician relies on his or her musical judgment.

A Deeper Explanation

What does the Foursquare Coaching Framework actually do? To answer, let's start with a different question: Is the mind different from our brain? Dr. Daniel Siegel, a professor of psychiatry at UCLA School of Medicine and author of the book *Pocket Guide to Interpersonal Neurobiology* (2012) states that the answer is "Yes." He makes it clear that the brain is a neural mechanism, an organ in the human body that coordinates the flow of energy and information, whereas the mind is our consciousness or awareness of our inner, subjective experience produced by the flow of energy and information in our brain. The mind is the home for our mental lives—thoughts, feelings, memories, and other mental activities (i.e., beliefs, hopes, dreams, perceptions, intuition, and images). The mind is the seat of consciousness, our experience of being aware.

Awareness and Attention

Awareness has always been a subject of psychology. Awareness is the spontaneous sensing of what arises in you (Perls et al., 1951). It is our "subjective sense of knowing or being conscious of something" (Siegel, 2012, p. 5–1). For example, you may notice the scissors on your desk, feel a sense of hunger, have a specific thought, memory, or daydream. In doing so, you have become conscious or *aware* of something internal or external. However, awareness is not the same thing as attention.

Although attention and awareness are intimately connected, we can be aware, or conscious, of something without attending to it. How often have you been aware of other cars around you when you are driving but not focusing your attention on them? Attention throws a spotlight on particular aspects of our awareness. It is, according to James, "the taking possession by the mind, in clear and vivid form, of one out of what seems several simultaneously possible objects or trains of thought. Focalization, concentration of consciousness are of its essence" (as cited in Ahmadi et al., 2011, p. 1366). In fact, attention is so different from awareness that recent research seems to indicate that they are distinct neuronal processes, with distinct functions (Koch & Tsuchiya, 2007). What does all of this mean for coaches? Coaches are in the business of directing attention. In truth, powerful questions manipulate attention in ways that will assist clients in goal attainment, change, and growth.

Questions are like a spotlight in a dark room; they focus the person's attention (mental processes) toward whatever is "lit up" by the nature and purpose of the question. Have you ever had a client say, "Wow, good question" or "I haven't thought about that before" in response to something you've asked them? Such a reaction usually indicates that your question focused the client's attention upon something new, something that has not been considered before in the mind of that person. Through inquiry, coaches focus people's attention on thoughts and ideas that are useful while avoiding thoughts and ideas that are unproductive.

How does the Foursquare Coaching Framework fit into this? We can envision the Framework as being a metaphoric map, a visual image that signifies the reality of the coaching process with four interdependent facets. The Framework represents different focal areas for a client's attention that, when considered as a whole, will assist a client in achieving his or her goals and objectives. Each facet or quadrant focuses the client's attention in different ways and produces changes in the energy and information flow of the coaching conversation. The coach manages this process to the benefit of the client.

Chapter Summary

Coaching is an extension of the Socratic Method because it relies on inquiry to achieve its purpose within the context of an egalitarian relationship. Additionally, both the Socratic Method and coaching employ the complementary processes of support and challenge as the means for accomplishing their purposes. During coaching, support strengthens the relationship and serves as a foundation for much of the work that is done to buttress goal achievement. Challenge is a balancing activity that induces the client to answer the tough questions that must be addressed to overcome obstacles and stimulate movement toward desired outcomes. The push-pull of both processes are required, as each without the other creates a vacuum that diminishes the coaching process.

Just as the members of a safari depend on their guide to navigate the jungle, clients rely on the coach to manage the process of coaching for their benefit.

However, the content of a coaching session will always be client driven and will consist of a conversation about the client's thoughts and actions about some desired goal state. Therefore, the activity of coaching is the application of the practices of support and challenge to the elements of thought and action. The relationship of these processes to the content of coaching produces a foursquare framework that serves as a cognitive map of the coaching landscape.

The Foursquare Coaching Framework consists of four quadrants, each with a different purpose and accompanying methods and techniques. Support-for-Thought establishes rapport and builds a platform of understanding about the client's current situation. When the conversation moves to Challenge-for-Thought, clients are prompted to think about what they want in specific terms, how it is different from what they have now, and then receive help in removing any mental barriers that impede progress. Support-for-Action ensures that clients are sufficiently motivated to take action in pursuit of goals. Finally, in Challenge-for-Action clients define their first (or next) steps on their path toward goal attainment and the resources available to maximize their success.

Each quadrant is a waypoint on a conversational journey that has many twists and turns. They are not sequential steps but markers that inform the coach as to his or her location in the "coaching jungle" so that he or she can guide clients to the destination of their choice. At a deeper level, the Framework represents different focal areas for the client's attention and serves as a metaphoric map of the conversational landscape. Using the Framework as a guide, the coach directs attention, energy, and information flow in ways that serve the client's agenda.

CHAPTER 3

Support-for-Thought
Connecting with and Engaging the Client

The efficacy of your coaching conversation rests, first and foremost, upon your ability to connect with and engage the client. Doing so promotes an open and honest dialogue between coach and client that creates the conditions for productive thinking and problem solving. The use of empathy is one means of connecting with and engaging the client. In fact, it is so important that it is one of five pillars that support the relational aspect of the Coaching Alliance generally (self-awareness, positive regard, genuineness, and presence being the others). These pillars are defined and discussed in Chapter 10. This chapter describes the use of the Empathy Cycle to connect with and engage the client during Support-for-Thought.

Empathy

Facilitating a client's learning, change efforts, and problem solving is accomplished primarily through inquiry. Each quadrant in the Foursquare Coaching Framework uses distinctive inquiries to achieve its purpose and objectives, but *inquiry without empathy is an interrogation*. The word itself was invented by Edward Titchener, a British psychologist, as a translation of the German word "Einfuhlung," which means "to project yourself into what you observe" (as cited in Baron-Cohen & Wheelwright, 2004, p. 163). When you are able to do this with clients, there is a felt understanding as to what they are thinking and feeling. Your understanding of their internal world builds rapport and mutual respect that, in turn, engenders trust, which leads to a deeper connection and more understanding.

It is important to note, however, that empathy is not a one-way process. It is a dialogical in the sense that it utilizes the empathic faculties of *both* the coach and the client. These faculties are "activated automatically through verbal and nonverbal exchanges, and enhanced by conscious efforts by each to understand the other" (Dekeyser et al., 2009, p.114). This dialogical process is illustrated by the "tuning fork" experiment:

> If a tuning fork is struck, it vibrates. If the vibrating tuning fork is then moved close to a nonvibrating fork of the same (or similar) frequency, the nonvibrating fork will begin to resonate with the frequency of the vibrating fork (without ever directly contacting the vibrating fork). In other words, the vibrations in the air are picked up by the second tuning fork, causing it to vibrate in sync. Consider also the opposite situation, as when a vibrating fork is brought near another tuning fork that does not a have a similar frequency—the second fork will barely vibrate or not vibrate at all.
>
> (Mozdzierz et al., 2014, p. 137)

The coach and the client are like the two tuning forks of similar frequencies; they are empathic partners in the coaching process, and one affects the other. When coaches and their clients are in sync, there is an empathic exchange such that the coach is freer to challenge the client in ways that stimulate reflection, resourcefulness, and self-efficacy. The client in return is more open and receptive to hearing and understanding the coach, willing to discuss deficits and limitations, and more likely to imagine and pursue new possibilities. Although empathy ensues from the interactions of both the coach and client, one person is the initiator, just as one tuning fork must be struck before the other can resonate with it. Because of the dynamics of the coach-client relationship, that person is the coach.

The Empathy Cycle

Barrett-Lennard (1981) in his pioneering article "The Empathy Cycle: Refinement of a Nuclear Concept" construed empathy as a cycle of attentional, experiential, and communicational processes that he termed the "Empathy Cycle." Using the Empathy Cycle is a matter of following a series of steps that, while distinct, overlap or interlock with each other.

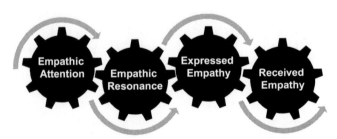

Step 1 is *Empathic Attention* (EA). The coach actively attends to the client and what the client is expressing about his experience through his narrative.

Meg, an executive coach to a large professional services firm, is listening to her client, Claude, a senior manager. Claude is describing how he is having problems staying focused on work. He talks about how complicated his life is given the demands some of the partners are placing on him. He also brings up the fact that he is dealing with pressures at home. He and his wife have a new baby, and one of her parents is having health issues with which they have been trying to assist. Throughout the client's narrative, Meg's attention is solely on the client. She is processing what Claude is saying and is absorbed in his story—even while a part of her is mapping the conversation to the Foursquare Coaching Framework and deciding on where to take the conversation next.

Step 2 is *Empathic Resonance* (ER): the inner process of empathic listening and observing to achieve a personal understanding of another person's current state or reality. In this step, the coach reads and "resonates" to the client in such a way that expressed aspects of the client's experience become alive, vivid, and known to the coach.

While listening, Meg is aware of Claude's increasing pace of speaking and a slight change in his physical demeanor. She judges the match between his words and his behavior. She can hear the stress in his voice and notices that his level of energy is much less than in previous sessions. She visualizes the details of his story, and in so doing "feels" his sense of helplessness. Her internal reactions become the basis for her empathic response to Claude.

Step 3 is *Expressed Empathy* (EE): the communication or expression of empathic understanding. The coach demonstrates to the client her felt awareness of what she is experiencing from the client.

Claude: I have been trying to push things out of my mind, but every time I sit down, I forget what I'm doing. I just sit there trying to regain focus. I'm so tired I feel like I am going around in circles. Everything is just a big mess.
Meg: Yeah, it must be really hard being pulled in a million different directions. There hasn't been time for you, and with all of the demands on you no wonder it feels like everything is a big mess. I imagine it's like being caught up in a whirlpool, and it's hard to swim your way out of it.

Step 4 is *Received Empathy* (RE): the client assesses the coach's responses sufficiently to measure the extent and accuracy of the coach's personal understanding of his experience. The client then self-expresses in a way that provides feedback to the coach that either confirms or corrects the coach's empathic response. This step is sometimes referred to as *perceived empathy*.

> Claude listens to Meg's verbal statements of empathy. As he does, he engages in an appraisal process (usually non-conscious) that evaluates the congruency of Meg's statements with his internal state and situation. He wants to know that he is being heard and understood.
>
> **Meg**: Yeah, it must be really hard being pulled in a million different directions. There hasn't been time for you, and with all of the demands on you no wonder it feels like everything is a big mess. I imagine it's like being caught up in a whirlpool, and it's hard to swim your way out of it.
>
> **Claude**: That's exactly how I feel! I mean, it's so frustrating feeling stuck. I know I have to do something to get back on track.

Finally, assuming a continuation of the coach's empathic attention and a resumption of the client's narrative, the Empathy Cycle is completed and returns to step 2, with added or fresh content. The remainder of the chapter explains, in more detail, each step in the Empathy Cycle.

Empathic Attention (EA)

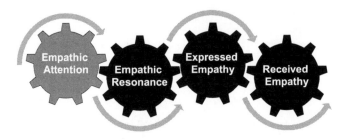

"Pay attention!" This familiar directive tells us something about attention: there is a cost associated with it. We have to "pay" for our attention with something; but what? To answer this question, first consider the fact that our attention has two masters: the experiential world and the person doing the attending (Schmeichel & Baumeister, 2014). The experiential world stimulates our senses and provides stimuli that have the power to attract our attention quickly and effortlessly—especially when the stimulus is novel. Imagine driving around town in your car when, all of a sudden, you hear a honking horn. Without even trying, your attention shifts toward the sound regardless of where your attention was previously focused. The same is true if it is an internal stimulus, such as an emotion. Although it is a product of our inner world, it still has an experiential quality that can attract our attention without us consciously having to direct it there. When our attention is drawn to the external or internal experiential world, there is no cost because our attention effortlessly flows to whatever attracts it naturally. The cost occurs when we must do the opposite of what is natural: resist attention-grabbing stimuli and focus it toward other tasks or events. "We suggest that moving attention away from attention-grabbing events exacts a psychological cost because this entails the self-control of attention" (Schmeichel & Baumeister, 2014, p. 30).

The second master of attention, therefore, is you. With self-control, you can intentionally shift or refocus your attention, even though the experiential world may try to capture it. Imposing self-control on your attention extracts a cost because there are often powerful experiential stimuli you are compelled to counteract or resist, e.g., pressing personal or professional matters tugging at your consciousness, something the client says that prompts an unexpected shift in your thoughts, or the fatigue of seeing your final client after a long day when you are mentally worn out. Whatever the reason, as soon as your attention shifts from the client to somewhere else the Empathy Cycle is interrupted.

Arguably, then, the most valuable thing you can offer clients is your focused attention because that is what initiates the Empathy Cycle. Barrett-Lennard (1981) emphasized this point when he said that the person doing the empathizing must *attend* to the person being empathized with as another "self." This practice ensures that the client is at the heart of what the practitioner does. He termed this an "empathic attentional set" (Barrett-Lennard, 1981, p. 93). An empathic attentional set means that you are giving clients your full and undivided attention in the present moment. Wilson and DuFrene (2008) speak to the importance of staying in the moment when they write:

> By increasing our own ability to focus on what's happening in the present moment, we can sharpen our [coaching] skills. Our interaction with clients is a sort of dance. . . . We need to determine when it's time to intervene and when we'll accomplish more by sitting back and listening. Sometimes we need to speed things up; at other times, slowing down is what the situation demands. In all of these cases, studied and practiced attention to the present moment is one of our greatest [coaching] resources.
>
> (p. 127)

As mentioned above, one of the five pillars of the coaching relationship is presence; the state of being completely in the moment when you are with a client. Presence makes Empathic Attention possible. Although similar, presence is an overriding way of being that affects the larger coach-client relationship, while Empathic Attention is a more directed means of focusing awareness for the purpose of initiating the Empathy Cycle.

Curiosity Is Key!

The curious mind is a focused and receptive mind. Mozdzierz (2014) and his colleagues believe curiosity may be the greatest asset a practitioner can bring to the helping conversation. It certainly is a characteristic of master-level practitioners. When master-level practitioners meet with clients, they connect with them through curiosity (also known as receptive awareness). Being intensely curious automatically focuses attention because it restricts awareness to our current experience—the client.

Curiosity requires an open and accepting (non-judgmental) attitude. The idea of withholding judgment is certainly not a new one. Carl Rogers considered it essential that a helper withholds all judgments about the client. Stober (2006) echoed Rogers's belief that to achieve accurate empathy, "practitioners must set aside their own feelings, reactions, and thoughts in order to sense the client's world as if it were their own" (p. 23). This aspect of empathy is often captured by the image of hands *letting go*, a metaphor for surrendering preconceptions about the other person and taking judgments out of the relational equation. This process is also referred to as bracketing. Bracketing is the first step in the phenomenological method of investigation. This method requires the practitioner to "bracket" all presuppositions regarding the client as much as possible by setting aside any initial biases and prejudices. Instead, practitioners are asked to focus on "what presents itself as it presents itself so that the client's currently lived worldview can be more adequately disclosed" (Spinelli, 2014, p. 98). The point here is that attention, when focused on the client, opens the door to a wealth of information.

Active Listening Focuses Attention

Curiosity focuses our attention, but so does active listening. Active listening puts our attention squarely on the client because we must listen with all of our senses and then send signals assuring the person that we are listening and interested. To show interest, we use verbal and behavioral cues that *invite* clients to tell us more or elaborate on what they are saying. Inviting is accomplished verbally with small verbal comments like "yes" and "uh-huh" and behaviorally by conveying an appropriate amount of eye contact and providing signals such as a nod of the head, smiling, or other facial expressions that reinforce the message "I am paying attention to you." Sincere active listening requires that you pay attention to the client.

Second Channel Communication

> Of course, I talk to myself. Sometimes I need expert advice.
>
> —Anonymous

The fact is, however, that our attention is rarely unidirectional. There are always two conversations going on within any coaching session: the one we have with the client and the one we have with ourselves—our self-talk. While some would say that self-talk is distracting and counterproductive, in truth, it is the type of self-talk that determines whether it is an impediment. Egan (2010) believes that it is important to listen to ourselves—if we do it correctly. Egan calls this type of listening "second channel communication." To clarify, if listening to your internal dialogue overrides your ability to listen to the client because you are the object of your attention, it will naturally be a barrier to empathic resonance. On the other hand, second-channel communication can "help you identify both what you might do to be of further help to the client and what might be standing in the way of your being with and listening to the client" (Egan, 2010, p. 154).

Second Channel Communication

Coach: What would you like to talk about today?

Allison: What's on my mind now is being able to leverage and capitalize on all the things I've gone through in my coaching sessions—and actually my whole life. At the same time, I need to be okay with the fact that it doesn't have to happen all today. I always tend to feel I'm slow in getting things done and accomplishing things, and that weighs on me at times. And I always feel, well, I should be moving along faster with this or that or whatever.

[Second Channel Communication: "There is a lot of ambiguity in what she is saying."]

Allison (continuing): I really want to get better at that and try my own way of getting things accomplished. I want to feel that is okay. I know that maybe it sounds simple, but it causes me a great deal of anxiety at times because I will fret about it, right? And yet, I do get things done and I do make things happen, and I am successful in all of those things.

[Second Channel Communication: "She is contradicting herself. It's not clear what she wants. I think I need to ask her to clarify what she wants from this conversation since she seems to be happy with some of what she is already doing."]

Allison (continuing): . . . but for some reason, I still torture myself a little bit about some of this. So I want to move into this fully. I want to move into this phase of my life and not stress about it anymore.

This example illustrates the idea behind second channel communication. The client is presenting a very confusing narrative. Meanwhile, the coach is assessing what he is currently experiencing during the session, what he is thinking about what the client is saying and what he might want to do next. Fauth and Williams (2005), in a study of therapists in training, found that internal conversations during sessions were more helpful than hindering—up to a point. A low-to-moderate amount of second channel communication allows the helper to become more interpersonally engaged and productive in the session. Although, when the level of self-talk reaches a certain threshold or is of a self-critical nature, it ceases to be helpful—such as that experienced by Level I (novice) practitioners. Master-level practitioners, by contrast, have learned to listen to their second channel communication to manage themselves and the coaching process, while simultaneously being fully present for the client.

Empathic Resonance (ER)

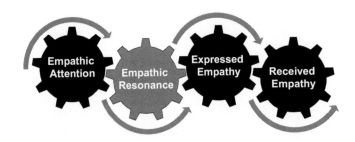

Carl Rogers (1961) defined empathy as "an accurate, empathic understanding of the client's world as seen from the inside" (p. 284). For Rogers, empathy is both a cognitive and emotional process, and he defined it as such:

> [the] . . . sensitive ability and willingness to understand the client's thoughts, feelings, and struggles from the client's point of view. [It is] this ability to see completely through the client's eyes, to adopt his frame of reference. . . . It means entering the private perceptual world of the other . . . being sensitive, moment by moment, to the changing felt meanings which flow in this other person. . . . It means sensing meanings of which he or she is scarcely aware.
> (1980, p. 142)

This description captures the essence of Empathic Resonance. The goal of ER is to be in tune with your client's experience so that you are prepared to express your understanding as a means of creating a supportive conversational climate. Empathic Resonance gives you access to a different type of information about the client. Without this type of information, the coach's formulations about what the client is experiencing are educated guesses at best.

The Cognitive Component

That empathy includes both a cognitive and feeling component is confirmed by recent research in the field of neuroscience that sheds light on how the brain correlates these two subprocesses of empathy. Elliott et al. (2011) cite studies showing that the cognitive component of empathy is localized in the medial and ventromedial areas of the prefrontal cortex as well as the temporal cortex. The cognitive aspect of empathy emphasizes *understanding* the mindset of others by switching your attention to mentally simulate their point of view. This process is sometimes referred to as *perspective-taking*: a cognitive, intellectual understanding of the perspective of another (Davis, 1983). A simple illustration of perspective-taking can be found in a delightful story related by Alfred Benjamin in his book *The Helping Interview* (1981); it is paraphrased below.

In a small village in Israel, there was a donkey. It had long and silky ears, large and shiny eyes, and all of the children loved it very much. Every day the parents would bring their children to pet it or ride it, or just give it treats. Indeed, it was the most popular animal in the village, but one day the donkey went missing. The people looked everywhere, but it was nowhere to be found. Needless to say, all of the children and their parents were very upset. The people in the village were so distressed that they gathered together to decide what to do next.

In that same village lived an old man, the father of one of the earliest settlers. He was so old that he had become somewhat senile, and, sometimes, people even made fun of the old man behind his back. While the people were gathered together wondering what to do, in walked the old man leading the donkey. The jubilation was great, and their astonishment was even greater. "How is it," they asked him, "that you of all people have found the donkey? What did you do?" "It was simple," he said. "I just looked at it from the donkey's point of view and asked myself 'Where would I go off to?'" I went there, found him, and brought him back.

Attempting to understand the world through another's eyes shows an interest in and sensitivity to their world-view. The challenge for most of us is suspending our perspectives, opinions, and judgments long enough to understand the thoughts, feelings, and struggles of another person from their point of view.

Listen from Your Adult Ego State

It is natural for people to listen judgmentally; that is, to pronounce what is said as good or bad, right or wrong, relevant or irrelevant, acceptable or unacceptable. However, judging while listening interferes with Emotional Resonance. The real culprit in this process is our Parent ego state. During the late 1950s and early 1960s, psychiatrist Eric Berne developed a theory of interpersonal interaction that he named Transactional Analysis (TA). Central to TA is the concept of *ego states* (Berne, 1964). An ego state is a cognitive structure that stores information, filters our present experience, and determines our attitude and response to people and situations. Berne identified three ego states that are a part of our personality: Parent, Adult, and Child. Empathic listening is inhibited when we listen from our Parent ego state and is facilitated when we listen from our Adult ego state.

The Parent ego state contains values and opinions copied from emotionally significant parental figures. While the Parent ego state can act as a conscience and provide a moral compass to guide our behavior, the value-based judgments that flow from this ego state are potentially lethal to Empathic Resonance. Only when you suspend Parent judgment are you free to take on the perspective of your client. The Adult ego state, on the other hand, does not draw from the value-based relics from our past to evaluate the present. Instead, it observes, reality-tests, analyzes, and acts accordingly. It enables us to listen to our client's conversation with neutral ears and without the distraction of judgment and criticism. "The Adult structural ego state is the major asset of a coach; the capacity for most of their energy to be focused on the current experience with the client" (Napper & Newton, 2014, p. 172).

The Affective Component

In the 1997 film *The Lost World: Jurassic Park*, Sarah (played by Julianne Moore) has fallen onto the windshield of an RV, now dangling over a cliff, and if she shifts her weight at the wrong angle, the windshield's glass will break. As the glass slowly splinters under her, viewers live the fear experienced by Sarah until she finally makes it to safety. For a long time, filmmakers have known and capitalized on our innate capacity to resonate emotionally with the experiences of others. Recently, findings from the field of neuroscience have opened the door for understanding how this process of empathic resonance truly works. Brain mapping has led to the discovery of mirror neurons—a type of brain cell present in the frontal lobes, the back of the parietal lobes, the top of the temporal lobes, and the insula which allows us to mirror another person, or to feel what another person is experiencing without even thinking about it (Arden, 2010).

Research in mirror neurons shows that the same brain regions are activated in an observer as those activated in a person experiencing a particular sensation or performing a certain action (Rankin et al., 2006). Moreover, the same phenomenon occurs in emotional processing. That is to say, regions of the brain associated with feeling or emotion are activated by observing that emotion in another person. Sometimes—as the scene in the movie illustrates—even seeing a person in a situation that would normally elicit a particular emotion may very well cause us to experience that same emotion, even though we are not in that situation. Jeanne Watson and Leslie Greenberg (2009) draw attention to the fact that these and other findings in neuroscience have particular significance for understanding empathy in ways that are relevant for practitioners in the helping professions. They assert that the physiological correlates of affective empathy support what practitioners have known intuitively through their subjective experience of empathizing with clients.

Affective empathy has two aspects to it: 1) the recognition of what your client feels as expressed by his or her words or non-verbal behavior and 2) understanding the reasons for those feelings in terms of your client's experience. This kind of Empathic Resonance is sometimes confused with sympathy, but sympathy is feeling pity or sorrow for someone's plight, whereas emotional empathy is the ability to enter your clients' private worlds and understand their feelings and struggles. In their book, *Coaching with Empathy*, Brockbank and McGill (2013) refer to four levels of affective empathy: 1) zero empathy, 2) partial empathy, 3) primary empathy, and 4) advanced empathy.

1) Zero affective empathy is when—instead of engaging in empathic listening and personal understanding—you give your client advice or ask him or her questions rather than providing an appropriate empathic response when the situation calls for it. You may even recognize a feeling state in your client but remain silent assuming that you are empathic because of the recognition alone. Zero empathy is a missed opportunity to connect with your client.

> **Zero Affective Empathy**
>
> **Client**: I'm really in a panic (anxious, looking plaintively at the coach). I feel anxious all the time in my new job because I worry that I'm not measuring up. I'm actually afraid of completely failing (looks down and away with a sad expression). Nothing like this has happened to me before (wobbly voice). I always felt in control, but now I don't know what's happening.
> **Coach**: What makes you think that you are failing now?

2) Partial affective empathy is when you only attend to part of your client's emotional world. Your client is expressing his or her feelings verbally and non-verbally, but your response only refers to the verbal expression of feelings and does not include a reference to what the client's non-verbal language suggests. In the example below, there is no response to the tone of voice, which may indicate a lack of self-confidence—the reason for the emotions and the key to change.

> **Partial Affective Empathy**
>
> **Client**: I'm really in a panic (anxious, looking plaintively at the coach). I feel anxious all the time in my new job because I worry that I'm not measuring up. I'm actually afraid of completely failing (looks down and away with a sad expression). Nothing like this has happened to me before (wobbly voice). I always felt in control, but now I don't know what's happening.
> **Coach**: So, you feel a real sense of vulnerability like your future is something you have no say in.

3) Primary affective empathy is a response that includes recognition of all the feelings expressed by the client—both verbally and non-verbally. The response also includes the reasons underlying the coach's response.

Primary Affective Empathy

Client: I'm really in a panic (anxious, looking plaintively at the coach). I feel anxious all the time in my new job because I worry that I'm not measuring up. I'm actually afraid of completely failing (looks down and away with a sad expression). Nothing like this has happened to me before (wobbly voice). I always felt in control, but now I don't know what's happening.

Coach: So, you feel a real sense of vulnerability which makes you anxious. I also hear in your voice what sounds like a lack of confidence.

4) Advanced affective empathy is a response for which there may not be sufficient evidence and is the result of a "hunch" or reading between the lines. In effect, it is a hypothesis being offered by the coach based on what is known about the client or the client's situation from previous discussions. It may be incorrect and, therefore, must always be validated by the client as to its accuracy.

Advanced Affective Empathy

Client: I'm really in a panic (anxious, looking plaintively at the coach). I feel anxious all the time in my new job because I worry that I'm not measuring up. I'm actually afraid of completely failing (looks down and away with a sad expression). Nothing like this has happened to me before (wobbly voice). I always felt in control, but now I don't know what's happening.

Coach: So, you feel a real sense of vulnerability which is making you anxious. I also hear in your voice what sounds like a lack of confidence. I know that you've said that your new manager's style is much more controlling than you're used to. Could it be that you are having trouble adjusting to this new style, and that is what's causing you to feel out of balance and confused? If so, that would certainly be understandable.

Developing Affective Empathy

Based on their research, Watson and Greenberg (2009) believe that there are at least two evidence-based means for practitioners to enhance their empathic capacity: 1) using visualization to actively imagine the experiences and events in their client's lives; and 2) paying close attention to visceral responses as you watch and listen to client narratives.

Visualize Your Clients' Experiences

Mirror neurons allow us to mimic the intentions, sensations, and emotions of people around us—in other words, to experience what they are experiencing. Add to this the fact that deliberate acts of imagination produce stronger responses in the neuronal empathy circuit than observation alone (Jackson & Decety, 2004). Thus, Watson and Greenberg suggest that empathizing with another person's emotional state can be enhanced by actively visualizing the details of the client's experience. The more intensity you add to your visualizations, the more it will amplify your neural response such that you will have a better sense of what is happening for your client.

This type of interaction is a different experience than if you are passively listening to narratives about your clients' experiences. Think of it this way: If you are watching a movie that captures your attention and interest such that you feel part of the action, neuroscience indicates that you will have a richer emotional experience in response to what you see because of the intensity of your visualization. Contrast that to passively attending to what you are seeing and hearing in the movie. The empathic resonance produced by the neuronal circuitry will be much less.

Monitor Your Visceral Responses

As mentioned, mirror neurons imitate the subjective experience in another through the observational process and produce an analogous state in the observer similar to what the other person is experiencing. Therefore, it is through the activation of these mirror neurons that we can use the visceral reaction our body produces to "track" another person. To paraphrase Watson and Greenberg (2009), this will help coaches "feel" themselves into their clients' world. This form of empathic resonance begins with the observations we make by watching and listening to our clients, and then paying attention to the "gut" reactions we have to those observations.

Observing

According to Carkhuff (2009), observational skills are fundamental to any helping conversation. Because a significant amount of client communication is non-verbal, Carkhuff asserts that we learn much of what we need to know about what is going on with clients by watching for and intuiting the meaning of their non-verbal behavior. Non-verbal behavior refers to body movements, facial expressions, posture, and tone of voice. As an example, when a client looks as though he is carrying the weight of the world on his shoulders, it is not something the client tells us; it is something that we *see* in the person's body language. Our motor mirror neurons help us to resonate empathically to the fact that they are "down" emotionally, and we may decide to use that information to respond empathically, e.g., "It seems like something's really weighing you down right now."

In a song, the music and lyrics complement each other to create a musical message. If the music does not fit the lyrics, there is dissonance. Similarly, the non-verbal communication (the music) of people must match or be congruent with what they are saying (the lyrics), or it sends a mixed message. The ability to notice mixed messages in your client's communication is a critical observational skill. Suppose a client is talking about an emerging opportunity for career advancement, but for her to take advantage of the opportunity, it would require a relocation of her family to another state and her husband would be forced to find new employment. As she talks about this career opportunity her body language is subdued, there is a hesitancy in her voice, and her eyes are focused down and away, even as she is telling you how great it would be for her career. She is saying one thing, but her body language communicates something different altogether.

Your ability to notice the mixed message in the client's communication helps in three ways. First, it allows you to resonate empathically to the ambiguity the client is obviously experiencing. Second, were you to reflect back to the client what you are sensing, it brings the mixed thoughts and feelings she has about the career opportunity to the forefront of the conversation, even though she may not be totally aware of her internal conflict. Finally, once the issue of her ambiguity is on the table, it gives you the opening to shift the conversation to Support-for-Action where her ambiguity can be explored and, ultimately, resolved.

Empathic Resonance: How Easy Is It for You?

Empathic Resonance requires the ability to step inside another's frame of reference both cognitively and emotionally. How easy is it for you to engage in empathic resonance? In his book, *Zero Degrees of Empathy*, Simon Baron-Cohen (2012) published an Empathy Quotient Questionnaire. Here are some statements from his questionnaire that describe behavior associated with Empathic Resonance. How do you measure up?

1. I find it easy to put myself in somebody else's shoes.
2. I can usually appreciate the other person's viewpoint even if I don't agree with it.
3. I am quick to spot when someone is feeling awkward or uncomfortable.
4. I am good at understanding how others are feeling.
5. Friends usually talk to me about their problems because I am very understanding.
6. I can easily tell if someone is interested in what I am saying.
7. I can rapidly and intuitively tune in to how someone feels.
8. I can easily work out what another person might want to talk about.
9. I can pick up quickly if someone says one thing but means another.
10. I can tell if someone is masking his or her true emotion.

If you are interested, the entire questionnaire can be found in Baron-Cohen's book. Even if you responded with "No" or "Not exactly" to these statements, take heart because Empathic Resonance can be developed with practice.

Warning: Stay Empathically Connected but Professionally Detached

If you have coached for any length of time, it would be rare that you have not had a client cry or express strong emotions during a coaching session. While it may sound contradictory to the idea of Empathic Resonance, professional detachment is necessary to do your job as coach. There is plenty of evidence that suggests that people do indeed "catch" the emotions of others (Hatfield et al., 1993). In fact, there is a term for it, *Emotional Contagion*: the tendency for people to emotionally converge and to feel and express emotions similar to and influenced by those of others. This idea aligns with the most recent research on mirror neurons as discussed above. At any rate, if you over-identify with the experiences of your clients to the point where you are *emotionally* engrossed by the client's problems, it will interfere with the empathic process and your ability to lead the client in a solution-focused direction. To fully comprehend the client's experience, it is important that the coach remains differentiated. Master-level coaches know this and have learned to resonate with what the client feels, while at the same time not succumbing to the emotional reactions being triggered within. Getting a sense of how clients are feeling or what they are experiencing is very different from feeling distress or overwhelming concern over their pain. It is for this reason that *self-regulation* is an underlying competency needed for the healthy expression of empathy.

Expressed Empathy (EE) and Received Empathy (RE)

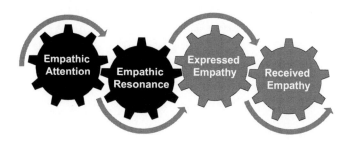

Our brain's neurological capabilities allow us to put ourselves in the shoes of our clients emotionally and cognitively, either on a moment-by-moment basis or by developing an overall sense of what it is like to be in their situation. However, merely responding inwardly with empathic understanding is not enough. The coach may have a felt awareness of what the client is experiencing (Empathic Resonance), but if the coach does not provide an empathetic response, the client will never know it. It reminds one of the philosophical thought experiment that asks the question, "If a tree falls in a forest and no one is around to hear it, does it make a sound?" Therefore, the Empathy Cycle requires that the coach not only has an understanding of the world from the client's point of view (his or her feelings, experience, and behavior) but communicate that understanding in full. Therefore, step 3 of the Empathy Cycle is called Expressed Empathy: the *reflection*

and *summary* of core meanings, sentiments, and feelings communicated by the client during the session.

The power of Expressed Empathy is that it engages people such that when clients hear an accurate interpretation of their message or their experience, it produces a *recognition reflex* (Dreikurs et al., 1982). A recognition reflex is an automatic response that people exhibit when their point of view or feeling is reflected back to them in an insightful way. It may take the form of a smile, head nodding, or even a verbal response such as "Yes! That's it!" Whatever the response, it is a confirmation that Expressed Empathy has hit the mark and has been *received* by the other person. Received Empathy (step 4) completes the Empathy Cycle.

Reflection

Reflection and Summary are discussed in detail in Chapter 8, but an initial explanation will be provided in this chapter. Briefly, reflection is the process of restating the client's explicit or implicit message in order to demonstrate and test your understanding of what the client is communicating.

Reflection

Client: I don't know why I feel this way. I feel like everyone depends on me, but none of my attempts to provide direction come off correctly. And then, everyone looks at me like I've failed. I always end up thinking to myself, "I can't do this."

Coach: So, you feel like you're letting people down.

[The coach conveys an understanding of the client's experience through a simple and concise paraphrase of the client's core message.]

Client: Exactly! It makes me feel pathetic—like I can't just do what I need to do without worrying about what other people think. I feel as if I have to watch everything I do, every word I say. Therefore, I end up not doing or saying anything.

[The client's empathic response ("Exactly!") is a recognition reflex indicating Received Empathy. The phrase "It makes me feel pathetic" is disowned language because the client is not acknowledging how he is bringing this on himself. It presents an opportunity to transition into Challenge-for-Thought to change contaminated self-talk and counterproductive beliefs.]

Coach: Kind of like paralysis by analysis, but, in this case, paralysis by other people's analysis.

[The coach brings to life the client's experience by using a metaphor to paint a word picture of what she is hearing from the client.]

Client: That's right (smiles and nods). I'm so concerned about the opinions of others that it's like a giant roadblock to my decision making and actions.

[A recognition reflex.]

Coach: So, the leadership role may not fit with who you are or what you really like to do.

[The coach restates what seems to be implicit in the client's message, but which is not openly expressed.]

Client: Yes, that's right. I am beginning to question whether or not I'm cut out for this. It's something that I need to think through a little more. I mean, the question for me is whether this is a normal part of the transition when assuming a leadership role or a reflection of my lack of self-confidence and what I feel most comfortable doing.

This example is illustrative of the Empathy Cycle. The coach is actively attending to the client and what the client is expressing through his narrative (*Empathic Attention*). The coach then begins to achieve a personal understanding of the client's current state such that the client's experience becomes alive, vivid, and known to the coach (*Empathic Resonance*). Through the technique of reflection, the coach *responds* to the client in an empathic way (*Expressed Empathy*). The client evaluates the congruency of the coach's reflections with his internal state and situation and provides feedback that confirms or corrects the coach's empathic response (*Received Empathy*). The client's narrative resumes with added content that may spark another Empathy Cycle at some point in the conversation.

A common fear among coaches (especially level I and even some level II coaches) is the fear of articulating an inaccurate reflection (e.g., a reflection is given, and the client says, "No, that's not what I was saying"). It is true that sometimes you will be off the mark, but if your intentions are authentic, clients will not be put off by an occasional inaccurate reflection. In fact, it gives them an opportunity to provide a correct interpretation of what they have said or meant to say. When clients correct you, it forces them to rethink their message and restate it in a way that provides more clarity for both parties.

Brammer provides a helpful summary of guidelines for reflecting. They are as follows:

1. Read the *total message*—stated feelings, non-verbal body feelings, and content.
2. Select the best *mix* of content and feelings to fulfill the goals for understanding at this stage of the helping process.
3. *Reflect* the experience just perceived.
4. *Wait* for helpee's confirming or disconfirming response to your reflection as a cue about what to do next (Brammer, 1973, p. 93).

Summary

Summary is assembling the themes and ideas that you have heard from clients into a succinct outline of their main points and then providing that summary at strategic points in the conversation.

Summary

Coach: Let's see if I can pull together what you've been saying. First, you said that you feel like everyone depends on you, but none of your attempts to provide direction seem to be working for them. Second, you're worrying a lot about what people think. As a result, you feel like you have to watch everything you do and say, which is kind of like a giant roadblock to making decisions and taking actions. Finally, now you're starting to wonder whether you're cut out for this type of leadership role. Is that about right?

Notice that summary is somewhat similar to reflection in that it helps clients know that you are listening to what they are saying, but it is different in that the coach is giving a more literal translation of the highlights of the conversation, rather than an interpretation of selected messages. As with reflection, summary gives the client the opportunity to add to or modify what was said.

Summary can also be used for transitional purposes. Transitional summaries (Miller & Rollnick, 2002) mark and announce a shift from one focus to another, or in the case of the FsCF, from one quadrant to another. For instance, in the example above, the coach provides a summary of the client's narrative, and once the summary has been confirmed, corrected, or expanded on by the client, the coach has choices. He can help the client define what he wants to be different going forward (Challenge-for-Thought), develop action steps for helping the client think through the situation (Challenge-for-Action), or strengthen his motivation and resolve ambiguity about whether this is the role for him (Support-for-Action). Here is an example.

Summary with Transition to Support-for-Action

Coach: Let's see if I can pull together what you've been saying. First, you said that you feel like everyone depends on you, but none of your attempts to provide direction seem to be working for them. Second, you're worrying a lot about what people think. As a result, you feel like you have to watch everything you do and say, which is kind of like a giant roadblock to making decisions and taking actions. Finally, now you're starting to wonder whether you're cut out for this type of leadership role. Is that about right?

> **Client**: That pretty much covers it. I mean, I like where I am and what I'm doing, but now, because of the stress, I'm wondering whether I'm cut out for this. Maybe I should think about another role.
>
> **Coach**: Well, let's spend some time thinking about this. What would be the disadvantages of leaving what you're doing now? [The coach has transitioned into Support-for-Action.]

In Support-for-Action, the coach will continue exploring the drawbacks to changing roles and then eventually flip the discussion so that the client deliberates over the advantages of staying where he is and working on his leadership abilities. During this process, the coach will not be an advocate for any particular position but will merely help the client think through the situation from different perspectives to resolve his ambivalence. Once again, the fluidity of the Foursquare Coaching Framework is on display as the coach quickly and seamlessly moves from Support-for-Thought into Support-for-Action.

Chapter Summary

Support-for-Thought is about connecting with and engaging the client. Connecting with the client occurs through an empathic exchange called the Empathy Cycle—in which both parties participate. The Empathy Cycle is composed of four interlocking steps: Empathic Attention, Empathic Resonance, Expressed Empathy, and Received Empathy. Empathic Attention (EA) means giving the client your full and undivided attention in the present moment. A mindset of curiosity and the use of active listening techniques are methods for focusing your attention and displaying EA. Empathic Resonance means that you are tuned in to your client's thoughts and feelings so that you can *express* empathy in service of building a conversational climate that supports thinking and dialogue. Expressed Empathy is demonstrated by using reflection and summary. When clients hear an accurate interpretation or summary of their situation, they respond with a *recognition reflex* that signals Received Empathy. Assuming a continuation of the coach's Empathic Attention and a resumption of the client's narrative, the door remains open for another Empathy Cycle with fresh content.

Concerning the use of the Empathy Cycle in Support-for-Thought, remember:

- Empathy is not just a means for creating a supportive conversational climate but is part of the overall coaching relationship and, as such, permeates all interactions with your clients.
- Employing the Empathy Cycle is an influence technique, but it should always flow naturally from your genuine interest in the person you are helping.
- Do not let your attempt at being skillful in the use of empathic techniques interfere with your ability to see the big picture and navigate the Foursquare Coaching Framework.

- Do not get in a rut or stereotype your responses. Be creative and flexible in your use of techniques, particularly reflection. A "style rut" gives the impression of insincerity.
- Expressed Empathy may not always be accurate. Use your client's confirming or disconfirming response as a clue about what to do next.
- When using reflection, respond selectively to core client messages; it is impossible to respond to everything a client communicates through words or behavior.

The ICF competencies (ICF Core Competencies—International Coach Federation, n.d.) addressed by the content of this chapter are:

- **Establishing Trust and Intimacy with the Client**
  - Shows genuine concern for the client's welfare and future.
  - Demonstrates respect for client's perceptions, learning style, personal being.
- **Coaching Presence**
  - Is present and flexible during the coaching process, dancing in the moment.
  - Accesses own intuition and trusts one's inner knowing—"goes with the gut."
  - Demonstrates confidence in working with strong emotions and can self-manage and not be over-powered or enmeshed by client's emotions.
- **Active Listening**
  - Attends to the client and the client's agenda and not to the coach's agenda for the client.
  - Distinguishes between the words, the tone of voice, and the body language.
  - Summarizes, paraphrases, reiterates, and mirrors back what client has said to ensure clarity and understanding.
  - Encourages, accepts, explores, and reinforces the client's expression of feelings, perceptions, concerns, beliefs, suggestions, etc.
  - "Bottom-lines" or understands the essence of the client's communication and helps the client get there rather than engaging in long, descriptive stories.
  - Allows the client to vent or "clear" the situation without judgment or attachment in order to move on to next steps.
- **Powerful Questioning**
  - Asks questions that reflect active listening and an understanding of the client's perspective.
- **Direct Communication**
  - Uses metaphor and analogy to help to illustrate a point or paint a verbal picture.

- **Creating Awareness**
    - Goes beyond what is said in assessing client's concerns, not getting hooked by the client's description.
    - Invokes inquiry for greater understanding, awareness, and clarity.
    - Identifies for the client his or her underlying concerns; typical and fixed ways of perceiving himself/herself and the world; differences between the facts and the interpretation; and disparities between thoughts, feelings, and action.
    - Expresses insights to clients in ways that are useful and meaningful for the client.

CHAPTER 4

Support-for-Thought

Setting the Agenda and Clarifying the Narrative

To support people's thinking requires more than a show of empathy. It also necessitates that coaches clarify what is often a confused or incomplete depiction of what is going on in the life of their clients. Consistent with the ambiguity that regularly accompanies their narratives, clients are similarly opaque about their expectations for the coaching session itself. This chapter explores the practices of setting the coaching agenda and clarifying the client's narrative as part of connecting with and engaging the client.

Inquiry

> The art and science of asking questions is the source of all knowledge.
>
> —Thomas Berger (novelist)

Client narratives do not arrive in a nice, neat package. They are often a loosely knit web of incomplete information, vague issues, hidden concerns, and implicit goals which must be clarified through the skillful use of inquiry. Inquiry is the act of asking questions to gather missing information. It is virtually impossible not to respond to incisive questions as they stimulate the mind such that people are compelled to answer them.

In some ways, questions are almost magical. Imagine that you are asked this question: "If you could have anything in the world, what would it be?" Think about it. A question like this is irresistible. It forces you to think, and even if your answer is "I don't know," you must pause, reflect, and focus your attention on the intent of the question. Questions are like a spotlight in a dark room; they focus people's attention (and, therefore, their thinking) toward whatever is "lit up" by that particular question. Have you ever had someone say, "Wow, great question" or "I haven't thought about that before" in response to something you've asked them? Such a reaction indicates that your question focused the person's attention upon something new, something not previously considered. During Support-for-Thought, questions are used to clarify the narrative of clients: to make their communication less confused and more clearly comprehensible to you—and them. Since questions gather the missing information in a narrative, listening for what has been left out in their communication is a prerequisite to constructing inquiries to recover the deleted material.

A Map Is Not the Territory

Beginning in childhood, each of us experiences the world in different ways. From these experiences, we develop our unique picture of what the world is like. In Neuro-Linguistic Programming terminology, this picture is known as our model-of-the-world (M-O-W). By definition, the picture of our M-O-W is non-verbal, but language can be used to represent and communicate aspects of that picture. For instance, if I say to you, "Fred is difficult to work with," those words are a linguistic representation of a belief that exists within my M-O-W that has evolved from my personal experience with Fred. In this sense, language is analogous to a map because just as a map is a representation of a territory and not the territory itself, language is a representation of our M-O-W, but not the M-O-W itself. "A map is *not* the territory it represents, but, if correct, it has a *similar structure* to the territory, which accounts for its usefulness" (Korzybski, 1994, p. 58). Therefore, language, functioning as a map, is useful only to the degree that it accurately describes the territory it represents, namely one's M-O-W.

According to Richard Bandler and John Grinder (1975), the fullest, and most accurate, linguistic representations of the client's model-of-the-world is *Deep Structure* language. Deep Structure language is the best way for a client to communicate his or her M-O-W because it contains enough linguistic detail and richness that both the client and the coach understand the client's message. Unfortunately, people do not typically use Deep Structure language: they tend to think and speak in *Surface Structure* language. Surface Structure language is only "a representation of the full linguistic representation from which it is derived—the Deep Structure" (Bandler & Grinder, 1975, p. 41). In other words, Surface Structure language is a short-hand version of a person's Deep Structure language and is missing the requisite detail to communicate what is needed for effective coaching. To use an analogy, suppose you are accessing Google Maps to find a particular location in the United States. When the map first opens, it defaults to a high-level view. If left there, it is not very useful for finding the location you want. You must "zoom in" to see more detail. Clients' linguistic habits function the same way; when they talk about their current situation, issues, wants, or concerns they usually do so using Surface Structure language. If a client says, "Fred is difficult to work with," important details have been deleted (e.g., in what way he is difficult, what is the reasoning that leads me to believe he is difficult to work with, and what do I want from Fred that I am not experiencing now?). Recovering deleted information in clients' Surface Structure language illuminates their thinking.

Recovering Deletions

The purpose of recovering deletions is to assist clients in restoring a fuller linguistic representation of their model-of-the-world. There are three categories of deletions in particular that, when recovered, magnify a client's linguistic map in order to retrieve the detail needed to better understand their stated narrative: Unnamed References, Unspecified Actions, and Unstated Reasoning.

Unnamed References

The easiest way to understand unnamed references is to start with the most obvious. What is unnamed in this statement?

"They need to understand our situation."

The most prominent unnamed reference is when the client is referring to a person or a group of people, but not naming them. In all fairness, many times in the context of the conversation you will intuitively know to whom the client is referring. Nevertheless, it is not uncommon for clients to provide you a narrative that refers to people without specificity as to who they are. In some cases, it may not matter; however, in others clarity about who the players are is essential.

If clients deleted only unnamed persons from their linguistic map, recovering unnamed references would be simple, but that is not the case. Reexamine the statement "They need to understand our situation." What else is unnamed in this Surface Structure statement? What about the word *understand*? What is it *specifically* that they need to "understand" about our situation? This question helps to zoom in on their linguistic map so that more detail is added. There is also an unnamed reference with respect to the word "situation." To which specific situation is the client referring? In fact, contained within this simple Surface Structure statement are three unnamed references.

Who specifically needs to understand our situation?
"They need to understand our situation."
What specific situation?
What specifically do they need to understand about our situation?

How do you know which deletions to recover? The answer is simple: whichever ones help you clarify for yourself and the client what he or she is thinking about.

Martha—Unnamed References

Martha is a long-time client. During one of your coaching sessions, she says she has a concern that she would like to talk about, and you say, "Sure, what's going on?" Martha begins her narrative with these words:

"I'm feeling stuck right now. I have a sense that I should be more proactively involved in advancing my career. I'm happy with what I'm doing, but I feel as if I'm missing something. I'm at a point where I feel that if I don't make a concerted effort in order to advance my career in some way, opportunities will pass me by, and I'll have no choice but to stay where I am. I have to challenge myself. I need to decide what I should do."

Martha's short narrative contains several important unnamed references. The unnamed references are listed below along with suggested inquiries (questions) designed to recover the missing information. Please note that the questions are constructed using the client's language.

* *"I'm feeling stuck right now."*

    In what way are you *"feeling stuck right now"*?
* *"I should be more proactively involved in advancing my career."*

    What specific aspect of your career *"should you be involved in advancing"*?
    In what way, specifically, should you be more *"proactively involved"*?
* *"I feel as if I'm missing something."*

    What specifically are you *"missing"*?
* *". . . opportunities will pass me by."*

    What particular *"opportunities"* will pass you by?

While there may be other unnamed references worth exploring in Martha's narrative, recovering the aforementioned deletions will be very helpful from a coaching perspective. Each time you recover an unnamed reference, it adds clarity to the conversation and prompts the client to reflect on what he or she is saying. For example, suppose a client says that he or she wants to become more assertive. Recovering the unnamed reference associated with the word "assertive" (*More assertive in what way?*) induces the client to be more specific about what he or she wants.

Unspecified Actions

Another common deletion occurs when a client's Surface Structure language contains words or phrases that convey an action but do not specify the behavior associated with that action. The words to listen for are called *action verbs*. Action verbs express something that a person can do. For example, "cooperate" and "help" are action verbs. Consider the following Surface Structure statement and notice the questions used to define the *actions* that need to occur for each of the unspecified verbs.

What do we need to do to help our clinical staff cooperate with each other?

"We need to help our clinical staff cooperate with each other.

What does our clinical staff need to do to cooperate with each other?

Recognizing unspecified actions becomes paramount when you are helping people move toward a goal. When asked what will be done to reach their objective, clients often say things like, "I will influence my direct reports in a positive way." Challenging people to define specific behaviors associated with action verbs (e.g., *influence*) will initiate a thought process that yields a more likely path to success. Now, let's review Martha's narrative for unspecified actions.

Martha's Unspecified Actions

"I'm feeling stuck right now. I have a sense that I should be more *proactively* involved in advancing my career. I'm happy with what I'm doing, but I feel as if I'm missing something. I'm at a point where I feel if I don't make a concerted effort in order to advance my career in some way opportunities will pass me by, and I'll have no choice but to stay where I am. I have to *challenge* myself. I need to decide what I should do."

The following inquiries will recover unspecified actions found in the phrase "I have to challenge myself."

- What can you *do*, specifically, to "challenge" yourself?
- *How* are you going to "challenge" yourself?

Did you notice that there is another word that suggests action? The word *proactively* is, technically speaking, an adverb. An adverb answers questions that begin with "how," "when," "where," and "how much." The Surface Structure phrase, "more proactively involved," is describing *how* something should occur. As used in this example, "proactively involved" is how Martha thinks she should be in advancing her career and, given that it is a Surface Structure statement, the behavior associated with it needs to be identified. Asking the question, "How are you going to be more proactively involved in managing your career?" will help clarify her thinking so that she creates a more useful internal map of the required behaviors to guide her.

It is not imperative that you know about parts of speech such as verbs and adverbs. What is important is to recognize when someone is describing an action, but does not specify the behaviors that will make the action happen. In other words, use your intuition and listening skills to guide you when clients do not provide the requisite level of detail to help either you or themselves. If you listen with the intent of recovering deletions, your intuitive grasp of the language will be sufficient to help the client add the missing information.

Revisiting Unnamed References

Consider this statement: "We need to help our managerial staff cooperate with each other." The words "help" and "cooperate" contain unspecified actions, but they also contain unnamed references.

What type of help (specifically)?

"We need to help our clinical staff cooperate with each other.

What (specific) type of cooperation is needed?

By recovering the unnamed references associated with action verbs, you can add even more clarity to their narrative.

Martha's Unspecified Actions with Unnamed References

"I'm feeling stuck right now. I have a sense that I should be *more proactively involved* in advancing my career. I'm happy with what I'm doing, but I feel like I'm missing something. I'm at a point where I feel if I don't make a concerted effort to advance my career in some way opportunities will pass me by, and I'll have no choice but to stay where I am. I have to *challenge myself*. I need to decide what I should do."

The following inquiries will recover the unnamed references associated with the unspecified actions in Martha's narrative.

- In what way should you "*be more proactively involved*"?
- How, specifically, do you "*have to challenge*" yourself?

After recovering the unnamed references, the behavior that is represented by the action words can be identified with even more precision.

Unstated Reasoning

Finally, when clients tell you their story they include opinions and conclusions, but very seldom do they share their logic or reasoning behind those opinions and conclusions. Their logic is buried deep within their linguistic map. When a person makes a Surface Structure statement such as "We need to help our managerial staff cooperate with each other," an important part of the map is missing: the reasoning underlying that conclusion. While the answer to that question may be intuitively obvious in the context of the conversation, there are many times when clarifying a client's reasoning is helpful.

Martha's Unstated Reasoning

"I'm feeling stuck right now. I have a sense that *I should be more proactively involved in advancing my career.* I'm happy with what I'm doing, but I feel as if I'm missing something. I'm at a point where I feel if I don't make a concerted effort in order to advance my career in some way opportunities will pass me by, and I'll have no choice but to stay where I am. I have to challenge myself. I need to decide what I should do."

The following inquiries will recover the unstated reasoning in Martha's narrative.

- What leads you to believe that you *"should be more proactively involved in advancing"* your career?
- What causes you to feel that if you *"don't make a concerted effort to advance"* your career opportunities will pass you by?

Unstated reasoning is almost always present in a client's Surface Structure language; the challenge is to recover the reasoning that is most relevant to the discussion. Use your judgment; there is no such thing as a bad question when it comes to building a platform of understanding. Remember to construct your inquiries using your client's idiosyncratic words and phrases.

Why Not "Why"?

One type of question to avoid, especially when recovering unstated reasoning, is a question beginning with the word *why*. People's first exposure to "why" questions come from their parents or parental figures, e.g., *"Why* did you leave your toys all over the place?"; or *"Why* didn't you start studying for the test earlier?" These questions were not inquiries as much as they were implicit judgments. "Why" questions, especially when posed with an interrogatory voice, leave people feeling as if they have to defend or explain themselves; communication is diminished, and support for thought suffers. "Why" questions are only useful when they are completely stripped of their negative connotations. However, because questions beginning with "why" are easily misread, you may inadvertently bring about an adverse reaction in the client, even with good intentions. It is usually best to eliminate them from your stock of inquiries.

Making It Simple

Understanding and recovering deletions may seem complicated, but by following a few simple rules, you can accomplish the task of clarifying a person's narrative in a natural, relaxed, and spontaneous manner.

1. Listen for What's Not There

Whether you can name a deletion is less important than knowing it is there and using your intuitive understanding about what is missing to recover that information through the use of intelligent inquiries. Egan (2010) says it this way:

> People offer points of view but say nothing about what's behind them or their implications. They deliver decisions but don't give the reasons for them or spell out the implications. They propose courses of action but don't say why they want to head in a particular direction, what the implications are for themselves or others, what resources they might need, or how flexible they are. As you listen, it's important to note what they put in and what they leave out.
>
> (p. 153)

2. Ask "What" and "How" Questions

Throughout this chapter, several questions were suggested as a way of clarifying Martha's narrative:

- In what way are you "feeling stuck right now"?
- What aspect of your career "should you be involved in advancing"?
- What specifically are you "missing"?
- What "opportunities will pass" you by?
- What can you do, specifically, to "challenge" yourself?
- How are you going to "challenge" yourself?
- In what way, specifically, should you "be more proactively involved"?
- How do you "have to challenge" yourself?
- What would happen if you weren't "more proactively involved"?
- What would happen if you didn't "challenge" yourself?
- What leads you to believe that you "should be more proactively involved in advancing" your career?
- What causes you to feel that if you "don't make a concerted effort to advance" your career opportunities will pass you by?

These questions all began with the words "what" or "how." "What" questions predominate because they are the most powerful way to clarify what a client means, but there are also reasons to use "how" questions. "How" questions explore the *means by which* a person is going to do something. "When" and "Where" questions are also useful, but, generally, you need to know the "What" and "How" before "When" and "Where" become relevant.

3.   *Use the Client's Language*

The questions listed above all contain quoted material. These quotes are the exact words and phrases from Martha's narrative. Using the client's own language causes him or her to feel understood and demonstrates that you are listening. This is an impossible task if your mental attention is not focused on what the person is saying. Furthermore, using literal words and phrases as part of your question makes it simple for people to respond because you are working within their linguistic frame of reference, making it easier for them to add more detail.

4.   *Create Follow-Up Questions from Previous Answers*

The best questions are based on previous answers. Initial questions are but starting points; answers to those questions are the material from which further inquiries are developed. In other words, questions elicit answers, which lead to further questions, and a flow of dialogue is created. This is called the *rule of circularity*. "In a true conversation, each contribution builds on the last. This, ultimately, is how we know that we are being listened to: when the other person says something that connects with and develops what we have just said" (Iveson et al., 2012, p. 12). This circular process not only helps to recover the linguistic detail needed to understand the client's narrative; it also simultaneously builds and maintains rapport because it signals that you are truly listening.

5.   *Inquire, Don't Interrogate*

Clarifying clients' narratives does not mean subjecting them to an unending barrage of questions. Inquiry must be accompanied by empathy lest it become an interrogation. Empathy and inquiry are complementary elements of the coaching conversation, particularly during Support-for-Thought. If you include the Empathy Cycle periodically as you clarify the client's narrative, you will be able to ask incisive questions without fear of being too harsh. Questions can challenge their thinking, but rapport can still be maintained if you ask your questions from the Adult ego state. Remember, questions that challenge your client, if delivered out of a Parent ego state, can cause defensiveness and diminish rapport.

6. Use Verbal Softeners

Verbal softeners are often helpful in transforming what might be misconstrued as a Parent-like statement or inquiry into one that is being delivered in an Adult-to-Adult manner. Verbal softeners are additional words or phrases that tone down or soften the directness of a statement or inquiry, i.e., "perhaps"; "maybe"; "somewhat"; "I was wondering"; "You might want to"; "I'm curious"; "You may want to consider." For example, the question "Did you follow through with the actions we discussed in our last session?" can come across as judgmental when delivered with a Parent-like tone of voice, but this is avoided by adding verbal softeners, e.g., "I'm curious if you had a chance to follow through with some of the actions we discussed in our last session." Notice how the words and phrases "I am curious" "had a chance" and "some" soften the question, making it an Adult ego state request for information rather than a "gotcha" question stemming from the Parent ego state.

7. Avoid Multiple Questions within a Single Inquiry

This is also known as a double question. For example, "In what way do you need to be more assertive, and what's stopping you from doing that now?" A double question like this can confuse the listener because the client does not know to which question she should reply. Additionally, in picking one, the other question is left unanswered. When more than one question is contained within an inquiry, the listener can feel bombarded, making it difficult to keep up with what she is being asked. Rapport may suffer in the process.

Recovering Deletions Is a Core Competency

Recovering deletions, as with reflection and summary, is a competency that is used throughout the FsCF any time you want or need more detail about what the client is saying. Use this skill in each of the quadrants to help achieve the purpose of that quadrant. During Support-for-Thought, recover deletions to set the agenda and determine what the client wants from that particular coaching session. Recovering deletions during Support-for-Thought will also add richness and detail to clients' narratives as they discuss their present situations—as illustrated by the above example with Martha. Recovering deletions in Challenge-for-Thought will surface information needed to construct a well-formed outcome and assist in challenging contaminated self-talk and counterproductive beliefs.

Recovering Deletions to Build a Well-Formed Outcome

Coach: How would you know if you were successful in getting a handle on your emotions and controlling your stress?
Client: I would be responding differently to my directors.

> **Coach**: In what way would you be responding differently to your directors?
> **Client**: Well actually, I would keep in mind that it's not just about me. I wouldn't be focusing only on my concerns, but instead focusing on the other person—or, in this case, the leader that I am trying to support. My focus would be on their needs and concerns rather than mine.
> **Coach**: What would you be doing specifically to focus on their needs and concerns rather than yours?

Recovering deletions during Support-for-Action encourages clients to elaborate on their Change Talk (see Chapter 8). In this quadrant, probing for specificity is used to build confidence or enhance the perceived importance of the client's goal. When clients explicitly acknowledge that their goals are important to them and proclaim confidence in their abilities to attain those goals it strengthens motivation.

Recovering Deletions to Elaborate Change Talk

Client: This is something I can do.
Coach: And you know this is something you can do because . . . ?
Client: I've done it before.
Coach: Given that you've done it before, what did you take away from that experience that gives you confidence in this situation?
Client: That I'm a pretty determined person.
Coach: In what way, specifically, are you are a determined person?

Finally, recovering deletions—particularly unspecified actions—during Challenge-for-Action adds behavioral specificity to whatever action experiments have been identified. When clients are asked what they will do differently in the near future to pursue their desired outcomes, it makes a huge difference in their ability to succeed if statements like, "I will be sensitive to the concerns of my direct reports" are translated into specific thoughts and actions.

Recovering Deletions in Challenge-for-Action

Coach: What are you going to try over the next few weeks to reduce the stress you are experiencing now?

> **Client:** I am going to be more assertive with the directors when they are making unrealistic demands.
> **Coach:** How specifically are you going to be more assertive with the directors when they are making unrealistic demands?
> **Client:** I'm going to ask them to set priorities when they have multiple requests so that I limit myself to what's really important to them. Right now, everything is a top priority for them—which isn't actually the case.
> **Coach:** What else are you going to do, specifically, to be more assertive with the directors over the next few weeks?

Regardless of where and how you are recovering deletions, remember these guidelines:

1. Identify the missing information. Ask open-ended "what" and "how" questions to probe surface-level language.
2. Determine which deletion is the most important to recover at any point in time. People's surface-level language is rife with deletions. Choose to recover the missing information that will be most helpful given the purpose of the quadrant you are in, e.g., in Support-for-Action recover deletions that strengthen motivation.
3. Construct your inquiry by weaving the client's idiosyncratic language into the question used to recover the targeted deletion.

Setting the Agenda

In a coaching conversation, there is always a point of departure. That point of departure is the client's agenda. It is the client who determines the goals and direction of the coaching engagement generally, and the subject and outcomes of the coaching session specifically. The client-driven nature of the coaching process is one of the differentiators between coaching and other kinds of helping conversations. Clients are encouraged and expected to take charge of specifying what they want and assuming responsibility for the choices they make. Client responsibility begins with bringing an agenda to each coaching conversation.

Bridging

Coaching sessions rarely start from scratch. That is, there is usually "old business" to discuss before moving forward. Connecting the current session with what happened in the previous session or sessions is called *bridging* (Beck, 1995). The use of bridging is essential to demonstrate the ICF competency *Managing Progress and Accountability*. Bridging usually includes a review of what was discussed in the prior session or what the client has been thinking about since the last meeting. Sometimes homework is reviewed, if any was assigned. For instance, after a brief welcoming exchange, it is not uncommon to begin the coaching discussion in the Challenge-for-Action quadrant by reviewing what the client said he or she was going to do, ascertaining whether it was done, how it worked, what was learned from doing it, and what actions might stem from what was learned. Usually, however, the coaching session returns to Support-for-Thought to discuss the client's current situation and what he or she wants from the coaching session.

Moving Forward

Asking the client what he or she would like to talk about or wants from the coaching session seems like a simple matter. However, in practice, a clear answer is not always easy to ascertain. Clients regularly fail to clarify the topic of discussion, and they can be incredibly vague about what they want to take away from the coaching session. This may be because they are unclear themselves or assume it is evident from what they are saying. When asked what they would like to talk about, clients will respond one of three ways: with a subject statement, a set of information, or a story.

A Subject Statement

A subject statement is a very short answer that does nothing more than provide a topic without any explanation or context. A subject statement is the very tip of the iceberg when it comes to determining what clients want to talk about or work on during the session.

A Subject Statement

Coach: So, what would you like to talk about today?
Client: My relationship with my manager.

With such an ambiguous response, you must recover deletions to clarify the subject statement.

A Subject Statement with Probes

Coach: What would you like to talk about today?
Client: My relationship with my manager.
Coach: What is it specifically about your relationship with your manager you want to talk about today?

Client: I don't think we communicate in a productive way when we have disagreements. We end up arguing, and, even if we are not that far apart in our ideas, it sounds as if there is nothing we agree on—which isn't true.
Coach: So, what exactly would you like to focus on in our session today?
Client: I want to come up with some different ways I can handle a conversation with her so that she is more likely to hear my point of view and I hers. I want to learn to decrease some of the tension that seems to be there.

While there is still much work to do to flush out a viable outcome, the coach has a better idea of the issue as represented by the client's initial subject statement. Moreover, asking for more information about what the client wants encourages the client to explore what she means by what she has said. From here, the coach has several paths available:

1. Remain in Support-for-Thought and gather more information about this issue to create a better understanding of the client's current situation;
2. Move into Challenge-for-Thought by probing for what success would look like if she were handling the conversation in the way that she would like (constructing a well-formed outcome);
3. Move into Support-for-Action by establishing the motivational value of her objective so as to build readiness for change and motivational support for any actions the client might consider; or
4. Move directly into Challenge-for-Action by asking for a previous experience in which she was able to get the manager to hear her point of view, even though there was disagreement. Using a past success experience as a starting point will provide clues as to what she might want to do the next time she has a conversation with her manager.

A Set of Information

A set of information is a series of facts or observations provided by the client that implies that there is a problem or issue but contains no direct statement about what the issue is or what the client wants from the coaching session.

A Set of Information

Coach: So, what would you like to talk about or work on today?
Client: Well, actually this is a very timely call because just this week—well, the past couple of weeks—I've gotten some new responsibilities. But we are in

an unusual place in the organization where we haven't fully transitioned some people who are going to be on my team. So basically, I've gotten increased responsibility but not the people to accomplish what I need to. So I'm supporting two significantly large groups in the company from an HR perspective, and this includes doing coaching with the leaders and managers. I'm feeling stressed out because these leaders and managers are coming to me with all sorts of questions and issues, and frankly I'm not able to keep up with the activity. I'm even a little frustrated with my own management because they have announced my name as the person responsible, but they know I don't have the resources. I feel as if I'm in over my head.

In this case, asking for more information is counterproductive as it does little to move the conversation forward. The next step is asking the client what she wants from the coaching session given the information she has provided. To this point, the client's narrative contains nothing but information in the form of facts and opinions.

A Set of Information—Clarifying What Is Wanted

Client: I am even a little frustrated with my own management because they have announced my name as the person responsible, but they know I don't have the resources. I feel as if I'm in over my head.

Coach: Okay, so here's a question: Given the situation as you've described it, what would you like to take away from our conversation today?

Client: I need to get a handle on my own emotions, my own stress level. I would also like to establish a plan that, even for the short term, will get me on track to managing my workload.

Coach: You've mentioned two things: getting a handle on your emotions and stress, and developing a plan for managing your workload, correct?

Client: Yes.

Coach: Which one would you like to focus on first in case we can't get to both of them during this session?

Client: My emotions, handling my stress.

Clients may also be overly ambitious about what they want from any particular coaching session. It is up to the coach to keep their expectations realistic. In this case, the coach did that by listing both desired outcomes and asking the client to prioritize them (i.e., "Which one would you like to focus on first in case we can't get to both of them during this session?"). Once the client said that he wants to come away from the conversation with an idea of how to better handle his emotions and stress, the natural next step is to move into Challenge-for-Thought. The coach can then focus the client's attention on the difference between his existing way of dealing with his emotions and stress and how he wants it to be different going forward as part of constructing a well-formed outcome. As always, there are other options available. The client made this statement: "I need to get a handle on my own emotions, my own stress level." This is a "Need-to-Change" statement (Chapter 8). The use of the imperative "need" suggests considerable dissatisfaction with the status quo. The coach can use this statement as a springboard into Support-for-Action to reinforce the importance of changing. Keeping the map of the FsCF in your head as you listen to clients informs you of your options.

A Story

A story is a verbal replay of some event or interaction the client has experienced. It is as if the client is providing a "verbal video" of what occurred. Although a story may be interesting, there is always missing information and usually no clear indication of how the story relates to what the client wants to work on during the coaching session. In the example below the client relates a story, but there is a lack of clarity about what the client wants—if anything—based on the story alone.

A Story

Coach: So, what would you like to talk about today?

Client: Well, the other day I was in a team meeting, and my manager asked me to comment on one of the projects my team is working on. I was caught off guard because this wasn't on the agenda. I wasn't prepared and just stumbled through. I felt embarrassed. This isn't the first time this sort of thing has happened. I don't know whether he does it on purpose or what. I've meant to talk about it with him, but it's hard for me to bring it up because he has such a dominant personality. When I bring something like this to his attention, he always makes me feel like it's my problem.

Whether clients respond to your request for what they want to talk about or work on in the session with a subject statement, a set of information, or a story, there is more work to do—in the form of recovering deletions—to obtain a clear picture of exactly what they wish to take away from the coaching conversation.

Springboards

During Support-for-Thought, you are setting the agenda and building a platform of understanding about the client's presenting problem or situation. Clients talk about where they are now, and this discussion sets the stage for ascertaining what they want going forward. However, if the coaching conversation does not move beyond a discussion of their current situation to include what they want to be different in the future, why it is important to them, and what actions they are willing to take in the near future to realize the changes they desire, the coaching session stagnates. Simply put, the coaching conversation must move from Support-for-Thought into other quadrants if the coaching is to be considered a success.

Moving from Support-for-Thought to other areas of the FsCF can be accomplished in a straightforward manner by asking a question that commences a change of direction from Support-for-Thought to another quadrant, e.g., "Now that we've talked about your present situation, let's focus on what you want to be different going forward." Moving to another quadrant can also be accomplished subtly by taking advantage of *springboards*. Springboards are spontaneous words or phrases uttered by clients that afford the opportunity to jump seamlessly from one quadrant to another.

Imperatives

An imperative is something that demands attention or action; in the mind of the client, it is a necessity. When clients use words such as "must," "need to," and "have to" in reference to something they want to change or some behavior or action in which they wish to engage, they are signaling the importance of either what they want or what they want to do. Establishing the importance of an action or objective is a part of building motivation for change: a component of Support-for-Action. When an imperative occurs in the narrative of the client, it presents an opportunity to transition smoothly into Support-for-Action to explore the disadvantages of the status quo or the advantages of making the change with the client.

An Imperative as a Springboard

Coach: What would you like to talk about today?

Jim: Time management.

Coach: And what about time management would you like to talk about?

Jim: I have a time management problem. I don't seem to be able to get enough done in my normal work day. I create a "to do" list, but I never get to everything on it. I get a lot of things done, but it seems like the more I get done, the more I end up adding new items to the list—and instead of getting to the end of the list, the list just keeps growing. I never feel like I've accomplished anything because there is more to do. *I have to do something* about this, and I know I can, but I'm confused about where to start.

Coach: You mentioned that you "have to do something about this," and yet, you say that you do get a lot of things done. What would happen if you just continued the way you are?

In this example, the coach recognized a springboard opportunity when Jim stated, "I have to do something about this." The coach moved into Support-for-Action by asking the question "What would happen if you continued the way you are?" This question induces Jim to argue against the status quo and explain why change is needed—building motivation toward the change in the process.

Unspecified Actions

An unspecified action (using words or phrases that convey an action but do not specify the behavior associated with that action) is a common deletion in the Surface Structure language of clients. Unspecified actions occurring in a client's narrative during Support-for-Thought serve as springboards into either Challenge-for-Thought or Challenge-for-Action. Here is an example of each using Martha's narrative.

An Unspecified Action as a Springboard to Challenge-for-Thought

Martha: I'm feeling stuck right now. I have a sense that I should be more *proactively* involved in advancing my career. I'm happy with what I'm doing, but I feel as if I'm missing something. I'm at a point where I feel that if I don't make a concerted effort to advance my career in some way, opportunities will pass me by, and I'll have no choice but to stay where I am. I have to challenge myself. I need to decide what I should do.

Coach: Suppose you were "more proactively involved in advancing your career" in the way that you want to. What would that look like; what would you see, hear, or experience that would let you know you were more proactively involved?

[The coach moves into Challenge-for-Thought by asking Martha to define what success would look like (part of constructing a well-formed outcome) if she were to be more proactive in advancing her career.]

An Unspecified Action as a Springboard to Challenge-for-Action

Martha: I'm feeling stuck right now. I have a sense that I should be more *proactively* involved in advancing my career. I'm happy with what I'm doing, but I feel as if I'm missing something. I'm at a point where I feel that if I don't make a concerted effort to advance my career in some way, opportunities will pass me by, and I'll have no choice but to stay where I am. I have to challenge myself. I need to decide what I should do.

Coach: What might you start doing differently over the next two or three weeks to be more proactive in advancing your career?

[The coach moves into Challenge-for-Action by asking Martha to think about what she can start doing differently in the near future to be more proactive in advancing her career.]

Statements of Want or Improvement

Sometimes clients come right out and tell you what they want to focus on as a goal (e.g., Coach: "So, what would you like to talk about today?" Client: "I want to become more assertive in my interactions with my peers."). When this happens, solution-focused thinking suggests that you immediately transition into Challenge-for-Thought to explore the discrepancy between the client's future state (the want) and his or her present state (see developing discrepancy, Chapter 5). For instance, you might ask, "What is the difference between the assertiveness that you want to exhibit going forward and the way you behave now?" This begins the process of describing the desired outcome for the client's change goal. Of course, it is also possible to first recover the lack of reference associated with the unspecified action by asking "In what way do you want to become more assertive with your peers?" Either way, moving to Challenge-for-Thought prompts clients to think about their desired future as opposed to the status quo.

Statements of improvement are also embedded within the stories clients tell as they talk about their current situation. They are identified by comparatives such as "more" or "better" in conjunction with some behavior, skill, or attribute, e.g., "a better leader" or "feel more confident when I'm in front of C-suite clients." The use of comparatives indicates that there is a disparity between the client's current state or condition and his or her desired future state. Making the difference explicit moves the conversation to the Challenge-for-Thought quadrant.

Statements of Improvement

Coach: So, what would you like to talk about today?

Client: I've been thinking about how I act in meetings. I really feel strongly about some issues and have a lot of experience to support my opinions. So, I'm pretty outspoken in meetings, and I don't respond well to differing views. I can get pretty passionate. Unfortunately, others don't interpret it that way. I think I want to do a *better job of expressing my experience and knowledge in meetings* so that others are likely to hear what I'm saying. I just wish that I didn't get worked up so quickly.

Coach: If you were expressing your experience and knowledge in meetings so that others are likely to hear what you are saying, what would people see, hear, or experience differently from what you do now?

[Asking this question begins the process of identifying demonstrable indicators of success and moves the conversation from Support-for-Thought to Challenge-for-Thought.]

To recap, springboards are spontaneous words or phrases uttered by the client that provide you with the opportunity to transition smoothly from one quadrant in the Framework to another. However, just because an opportunity presents itself to change the direction of the conversation does not mean it should be acted upon immediately—or at all. Use judgment in determining whether it is best to stay where you are in the conversation or strategically move into a new quadrant. The question to ask and answer for yourself is "What will best serve the client's interests at this point in the conversation?"

Chapter Summary

People use language to represent and communicate their perceptions about the world. People speak in Surface Structure language and, in so doing, leave out important information. Inquiry is the act of asking questions to gather the missing information (i.e., to recover the deletions that are inherent in clients' surface-level language). Three kinds of deletions are defined and discussed in this chapter: Unnamed References, Unspecified Actions, and Unstated Reasoning. Recovering these deletions helps to create a platform of understanding about the client's current situation or condition. Recovering deletions is a core competency. It not only helps to clarify the client's narrative in Support-for-Thought but is used whenever linguistic precision is needed to serve the purposes of any quadrant in the Foursquare Coaching Framework.

This chapter also focused on setting the agenda and clarifying the client's narrative as a part of Support-for-Thought. Although bridging from one session to another is common practice, setting the agenda is usually the point of departure for most coaching conversations. It begins by asking what the client wants to discuss or work on during the session. The answer will most often be a subject statement, a set of information, or a story. These responses require further inquiry until it is clear what the client wants as an outcome.

Lastly, as clients talk about their current situation, their narratives will include words and phrases that provide the opportunity to transition efficiently to another quadrant in the Framework. These words and phrases are called springboards, and there are three types: Imperatives, Unspecified Actions, and Statements of Want or Improvement. Springboards may occur at any time, so be alert for the opportunity they provide to transition from one quadrant to another.

The ICF competencies (ICF Core Competencies—International Coach Federation, n.d.) addressed by the content of this chapter are:

- **Establishing Trust and Intimacy with the Client**
    - Demonstrates respect for client's perceptions, learning style, personal being.
- **Coaching Presence**
    - Sees many ways to work with the client and chooses in the moment what is most effective.
    - Confidently shifts perspectives and experiments with new possibilities for own action.
- **Active Listening**
    - Attends to the client and the client's agenda and not to the coach's agenda for the client.

- Integrates and builds on client's ideas and suggestions.
- **Powerful Questioning**
  - Asks questions that reflect active listening and an understanding of the client's perspective.
  - Asks questions that evoke discovery, insight, commitment or action (e.g., those that challenge the client's assumptions).
  - Asks open-ended questions that create greater clarity, possibility, or new learning.
  - Asks questions that move the client toward what he or she desires, not questions that ask for the client to justify or look backward.
- **Direct Communication**
  - Clearly states coaching objectives, meeting agenda, and purpose of techniques or exercises.
- **Creating Awareness**
  - Goes beyond what is said in assessing client's concerns, not getting hooked by the client's description.
  - Invokes inquiry for greater understanding, awareness, and clarity.
  - Identifies for the client his or her underlying concerns.
  - Identifies major strengths vs. major areas for learning and growth, and what is most important to address during coaching.
- **Managing Progress and Accountability**
  - Demonstrates follow-through by asking the client about those actions that the client committed to during the previous session(s).
  - Effectively prepares, organizes, and reviews with client information obtained during sessions.
  - Keeps the client on track between sessions by holding attention on the coaching plan and outcomes, agreed-upon courses of action, and topics for future session(s).

Moving from Support to Challenge

Music is an interplay between consonance and dissonance; similarly, coaching is an interplay between support and challenge. Support increases rapport and creates harmony while challenge adds a discordant—but necessary—note to the conversation. Trevino (1996) makes the point that while supportive interactions between a helper and another person enhance the relationship, a healthy amount of discord facilitates change. Egan (2010) agrees with this idea when he writes, "Because helping at its best is a constructive social-influence process, some form of challenge is central to helping" (p. 211). In other words, to help clients you sometimes have to make them uncomfortable. Master-level coaches understand this while novice coaches have a difficult time embracing the concept that failure to challenge is an impediment to the coaching process.

Challenge is the use of incisive inquiry to induce people to think about what they want, how they are going to get it, how they might be getting in their own way, and how to commit to the actions needed to reach their goals. However, to challenge does not mean to confront. While challenge provokes people to think differently or more deeply, confrontation is a clash of opinions or ideas. Confrontation produces a defensive response, while challenge changes the way a person construes problems and considers solutions. Challenge is used to help, while confrontation is used to dominate. Challenge must be done properly—and in the right spirit—or it may create resistance and reduce rapport. In fact, as Egan (2010) reminds us, "Empathy should permeate every kind of challenge" (p. 252).

Challenge-for-Thought

Constructing a Well-Formed Outcome

A Solution-Focused Approach

Challenge-for-Thought and Challenge-for-Action draw heavily on the solution-focused approach to therapy and coaching developed initially by Insoo Kim Berg, Steve de Shazer, and their colleagues at the Milwaukee Brief Family Therapy Center in the early 1980s. Although the solution-focused approach was initially described by de Shazer (1985) and de Shazer et al. (1986), both de Shazer and Berg are considered to be its founders and principle ambassadors. They observed hundreds of hours of therapy and painstakingly analyzed the questions and client responses that led to viable, real-life solutions to client problems. Through this inductive process, they developed the solution-focused approach for which they are famous and what would become a breakthrough in therapy and coaching. The solution-focused approach is as much a paradigm for a way of thinking as it is a set of methods and techniques. As such, following its practices means understanding its organizing principles.

Principle #1: You Do Not Have to Understand the Cause of a Problem to Solve It

For the task of helping clients work their way out of problem situations or pursue their change goals, the processes of diagnosing problems and finding solutions are not necessarily related. As De Jong and Berg (2008) state: "The genetic structure of problem-solving—first determining the nature of the problem and then intervening—influences the content of the interaction between practitioners and clients" (p. 8). They go on to point out that most practitioners spend their time on the "who," "what," "when," "where," and "why" of problems; therefore, the interaction between the person being helped and the helper is mainly problem focused.

Problem Talk

Problem talk explores the past to "get to the bottom" of a problem in the present. Its primary purpose is to understand the "why" behind a problem situation, with the assumption that such an understanding will facilitate a solution. There is a seductive logic in trying to understand the problem, but for the types of situations and developmental issues that clients bring to a coaching session problem talk is not useful.

A Problem-Talk Conversation

Coach: How are things going in the world of quality?

Client: Oh, pretty well, but I've got a problem with Rafael.

Coach: What's going on?

Client: He's supposed to be a senior member of the team, but I just can't seem to get him to focus on some of the strategic projects that I would like to see implemented.

Coach: How long has this been happening?

Client: I'd say for several months now.

Coach: What have you tried so far?

Client: I've tried hinting that he should put some time in thinking about where we want our quality effort to be in three to five years. I've even offered to help him start thinking through it, even though that's his job, not mine.

Coach: It sounds as if you've made it clear that this is a priority for you. Why do think your suggestions haven't worked?

Client: I should probably have emphasized this aspect of his role when I first brought him on board. I talked about it but may not have emphasized it enough.

Coach: Why doesn't he see it for himself?

Client: I don't know. Maybe he's just caught up in his own world and doesn't feel comfortable doing things that are outside of his experience. I mean, it's not like he's not motivated. He puts a lot of energy into other aspects of his work.

Coach: What does he like to do?

Client: I think he enjoys the direct contact with the department heads and doing the actual teaching about quality. He's very good at it.

Coach: If he's good at that you'd think that he'd want to take quality to the next level here. Could it be he's just not wired to think that way?

Client: Possibly, he doesn't do very well when he has to lay things out conceptually. The last time he gave a presentation about where quality in our institution is going over the next several years he struggled with it, and I had to take over. He's good at teaching the content and interacting with the people, but not thinking about it strategically.

Coach: Why haven't you been more direct with him?

Client: I'm concerned that if I push him too hard, he'll get upset, and it will affect what he's currently doing. I can't afford that because he's too well-liked by the department heads. Plus, no one else can teach that stuff the way he does. I don't want to demotivate him.

As you can tell from this exchange, a conversation beset with problem talk goes nowhere. The coach is trying to help, and it is likely the client feels listened to and appreciates the coach's efforts, but there is no progress because the client's attention is on the problem and the history surrounding it. When you ask questions that focus the attention of clients on the problem, you elicit stories about what they don't want, things that are wrong, forces beyond their control, and the reasons things are as they are. This is a type of mental quicksand that prevents clients from escaping the stranglehold of their present situation. Although it is appropriate that you listen carefully and clarify their narrative as part of Support-for-Thought, you will certainly want to avoid problem talk, or you risk becoming mired in the minutiae surrounding their problem. Looking for root causes to problems or dissatisfying situations is not as fruitful as defining the client's preferred future and then helping them to take action in its pursuit.

Principle #2: Focusing on the Future Creates More Useful Energy than Focusing on the Past

Everybody has a preferred future. People who seek to be coached want something to be different in their lives. Why else would they be there? Thus, the most direct route to helping clients is to start talking about the future: their desired outcomes and what they can do to achieve them. Establishing the desired future in and of itself can be a motivating experience. The discrepancy created by the difference between one's current state and the desired future state creates pressure for change. People are motivated to reduce the incongruity between what currently exists and the picture in their heads of what they want (Glasser, 1984). Therefore, focusing on their desired future state will naturally generate more motivational energy than dwelling in the past.

Principle #3: Clients Have Skills, Strengths, and Resources They Have Used Before and Can Use Again

Focusing on the future is paramount, but there is one exception to this principle: using the past to discover resources that can be utilized in the present. Identifying personal strengths, skills, behaviors, and resources used successfully in the past to help achieve a current goal is a fundamental solution-focused tactic. Saleebey (2007), an advocate of helping people identify their strengths, says, "So what is of interest to us is how people have taken steps, summoned up resources, and coped. People are always working on their situations, even if just deciding for the moment to be resigned. As helpers, we must tap into that work, elucidate it, find and build on its promise" (p. 285). Listening for times when clients have experienced—even in some small way—what they want more of means something has worked and can be used again.

Principle #4: Small Steps Lead to Big Changes

Solutions are end-results. They are the product of clients taking beginning and intermediate steps to do something different that will move them toward where they want to be. Solution-focused practitioners believe that a little change in the right direction is better than trying to take steps that cause the client to feel overwhelmed by their magnitude. Small steps help overcome the inertia of doing nothing, provide an immediate sense of progress, and maximize the probability of success. For many clients, small steps are more realistic and sustainable, and certainly better than doing nothing.

Small steps also lead to stable solutions. The types of problems, challenges, and goals for which clients seek coaching have no textbook answers; therefore, a heuristic approach to problem solving or goal attainment is required. Heuristic solutions evolve from a series of small experimental steps, assessing their effectiveness, adjusting the next steps based upon what has been learned, and trying out the new approach until the desired results are achieved. Solutions that emerge from this process are more stable because each piece of a solution must survive the test of effectiveness before it is combined with other pieces that result in progress.

Principle #5: Differences Make the Difference

Gregory Bateson (2000), the famed semanticist, wrote that in the world of communication "effects" are brought about by differences and that what we call change is a difference which occurs across time. It stands to reason, then, that helping clients change means helping them discover what they want to be *different* in their lives and then what they are going to do or how they are going to think *differently* to achieve it. After all, it was no less than Albert Einstein who is proposed to have said, "Insanity is doing the same thing over and over again and expecting different results." While there is some debate as to whether it was indeed Einstein who coined this phrase, it does emphasize the fact that clients cannot work their way out of problem situations or grow personally or professionally by continuing to do the same things they have previously done. Helping clients to perceive their situations differently, think differently, and behave differently will indeed be the *difference that makes a difference.*

Following Solution-Focused Principles Has Several Advantages

- The coaching conversation is efficient. Concentrating on solutions, and only solutions, will enable clients to move toward action in less time. The more clients are mired in their problems, the slower the progress.

- Clients will find it easier to work out an appropriate solution if their thinking is not problem focused. Solution-focused thinking concentrates on what clients want and how to get it as opposed to the "what and whys" of the problem; the client's entire mental resources are devoted to identifying a solution.
- Clients will have an increased sense of responsibility and accountability. It is the client who thinks through his or her situation in such a way as to come up with what is really wanted, and what will be done to achieve it. The client owns the solution, and with ownership comes a felt responsibility and the pressure to follow through on ideas for action.
- Client confidence is increased. When clients begin to think and act with a solution-focused mindset, they become more optimistic about their ability to deal with problem situations and achieve their goals.

Solution-focused principles guide your coaching conversation and are the basis for the methods and practices used in Challenge-for-Thought and Challenge-for-Action.

Challenge-for-Thought

Challenge-for-Thought has two purposes: 1) designing the client's preferred future and 2) challenging self-talk and counterproductive beliefs interfering with either the creation of a preferred future or the ability to take action to achieve the preferred future. The remainder of this chapter describes how to help clients design their preferred future.

Designing the Preferred Future

> You've got to be very careful if you don't know where you are going because you might not get there.
>
> —Yogi Berra

Goal Hierarchies

The themes and issues for which clients seek coaching are many. They range from situational objectives (i.e., making a decision or handling a problem), a desire to better oneself (i.e., skill development or behavioral change), and even goals for self-actualization (i.e., finding meaning and increasing personal or professional satisfaction). These themes and issues represent a continuum of goals, otherwise known as a goal hierarchy. The concept of goal hierarchies was introduced by Bandura (1997). He argued that goals could be placed in hierarchical order according to their proximity—in other words, how far the goals are conceptualized into the future. Goals that can be reached in the immediate future he called proximal goals, while goals that are more distant in their achievability are termed distal goals.

Research has shown that goal hierarchy plays a fundamental role in human motivation (Bandura, 1997; Locke & Latham, 1990). While distal goals—long-term goals that represent personal importance and value, and define desired and enduring aspirations—attract individuals toward meaningful destinations, it is proximal goals that regulate immediate motivation and action. Proximal goals lend themselves to increased imagery that defines in detail a clear and vivid picture of one's desired future. The sharper the picture, the more attainable the goal is in the mind of the client. This has several advantages: It reduces anxiety by making the task of achieving the goal seem more manageable and enhances buy-in by rendering goals more real, thus energizing the coachee (Ives & Cox, 2012). Proximal goals also stimulate the search for or use of strategies to accomplish them. This enables clients to direct their attention and effort to relevant tasks that facilitate movement toward their goal (Locke & Latham, 1990). Proximal goals are what coaches most often work with, even if a client's ultimate desire is defined by a distal goal. Distal goals can only be achieved through the accomplishment of a series of proximal goals.

The distinction between goals and strategies warrants elaboration. A goal is *what* is to be accomplished, and a strategy is *how* it is accomplished. "Strategies do not define future outcomes, but rather they define behavioral or cognitive activities that, if employed, lead to the attainment of such outcomes" (Masuda et al., 2010, p. 223). This distinction is the differentiator between Challenge-for-Thought and Challenge-for-Action. In Challenge-for-Thought, the coach helps clients crystallize what they desire: to think clearly about what it is they want. That is to say, coaches help clients maintain a forward focus and *imagine* what their desired future state looks like when it is achieved. Challenge-for-Action, on the other hand, directs clients' attention to the specific, practical actions they can take in the near future to move forward toward what they want to accomplish. Obviously, the more well-defined the desired outcome, the easier it is to chart a path to that destination. To that end, there are two quadrant-related activities to help clients think about what they want in a very conscious and deliberate way so as to add specificity to their goal setting: developing discrepancy and constructing a well-formed outcome.

Developing Discrepancy

Locke and Latham (2006) state that "because goals refer to future valued outcomes, the setting of goals is first and foremost a discrepancy-creating process. It implies discontent with one's present condition and the desire to attain an object or outcome" (p. 265). Ives and Cox (2012) support this assertion and point out that without creating a discrepancy between the goal set (the client's desired outcome) and what currently exists in the client's world, there is nothing to reach for, and consequently no action is triggered. "Effective goal setting is therefore about *discrepancy production*" (p. 35). Asking clients to describe the difference between what they want in the future compared to what they are currently experiencing is a first step toward adding specificity to proximal goals. Developing discrepancy can be initiated by simply asking the person to answer a version of the question: "What do you want to be different from what you are experiencing now?" Let's revisit an example from Chapter 4. This conversation begins in Support-for-Thought but transitions to Challenge-for-Thought when the coach begins to develop discrepancy.

Developing Discrepancy

Coach: So, what would you like to talk about or work on today?

Client: Well, actually this is a very timely call because just this week—well, the past couple of weeks—I've gotten some new responsibilities. But we are in an unusual place in the organization where we haven't fully transitioned some people who are going to be on my team. So basically, I've gotten increased responsibility but not the people to accomplish what I need to. So I'm supporting two significantly large groups in the company from an HR perspective, and this includes doing coaching with the leaders and managers. I'm feeling stressed out because these leaders and managers are coming to me with all sorts of questions and issues, and frankly I'm not able to keep up with the activity. I'm even a little frustrated with my own management because they have announced my name as the person responsible, but they know I don't have the resources. I feel as if I'm in over my head.

Coach: Here's a question for you: Given the situation as you've described it, what would you like to get from our conversation today?

Client: I need to get a handle on my own emotions, my own stress level. I would also like to establish a plan that, even for the short term, will get me on track to managing my workload.

Coach: You've mentioned two things: getting a handle on your emotions and stress, and developing a plan for managing your workload, correct?

Client: Yes.

Coach: Which one would you like to focus on first in case we don't get to both of them during this session?

Client: My emotions, handling my stress.

Coach: When you are handling your emotions and stress the way that you want, how will it be different from what you are experiencing now?

Client: I would be enjoying the interaction with the leaders and managers. I would be building a relationship with them, gaining their trust. I would feel good and feel professional. I would feel like I was giving it my best.

The client began the coaching session by providing a set of information or facts in response to the coach's question "What would you like to talk about or work on today?" The client's answer does not answer this question. To set the agenda, the coach properly redirects the conversation with another question: "Given the situation as you've described it, what would you like to get from our conversation today?" The client ultimately concludes that getting a handle on his emotions and handling his stress is his top priority. The coach uses a discrepancy question to help the client imagine what success looks like when the client achieves his desired future. Next, the coach will recover some of the deletions in the client's portrayal to refine his description of what he wants, e.g., "You say that you would be building a relationship with them. What will that relationship look like? In other words, how will you know that you have the kind of relationship that you want?"

Do Not Mistake Actions for Outcomes

When developing discrepancy, it is not uncommon for clients to answer the question "What do you want to be different?" with an action they want to take, rather than a description of the desired future state that is to be gained by taking that action. To illustrate, a client might answer the question "When you are handling your emotions and stress in the way that you want, how will it be different from what you are experiencing now?" by saying "I will schedule my meetings with the managers during times when I'm able to relax and attend to the conversation." If clients answer the discrepancy question by stating a proposed action as opposed to describing what will be different, the conversation has moved into Challenge-for-Action. Redirect their thinking so they describe what they want to *accomplish* by taking that action, e.g., "If you take that action what will be different going forward?" In so doing, you remain in Challenge-for-Thought by linking the purpose of the action to their desired future state.

Turning Actions into Outcomes

Coach: You mentioned that you received some feedback on your leadership style. Based on what you learned, what do you want to be different about your leadership style from what it is now?

Chief Technology Officer: I want to do more listening than talking when I interact with my team.

Coach: If you were to do more listening than talking when you interact with your team, what goal will you accomplish?

Chief Technology Officer: I will be a better leader.
Coach: In what way will you be a better leader?
Chief Technology Officer: I will be the kind of leader that gets people involved. My team will feel like they have ownership in the changes that we are making around here.
Coach: What else will you see, hear, or experience that will let you know you are a better leader?

The process of developing discrepancy, when combined with the recovery of deletions, will sharpen the client's picture of success. However, there is another option, and that is to "go with the flow" and continue what the client initiated by moving to Challenge-for-Action. This means developing additional action steps the client can take to realize his goal. This path will create movement by inducing the client to think about *how* and *when* he is going to take action to get what he wants—even though what is wanted has not been well-defined.

Moving to Challenge-for-Action

Coach: You mentioned that you received some feedback on your leadership style. Based on what you learned, what do you want to be different about your leadership style from what it is now?

Chief Technology Officer: I want to do more listening than talking when I interact with my team.

Coach: What else can you start doing differently to change your leadership style in the way that you want?

Even though the "want" (what is to be accomplished by taking those actions) is not yet defined, the desired outcome can be revisited at some point by asking the question "If you start taking the actions you've identified, how will you know that they have worked? What is your picture of success?" Remember; the FsCF represents the "terrain" of a coaching conversation. Moving to different parts of the Framework is a fluid process. It is okay to leave the work of one quadrant undone if the client's thinking and dialogue naturally moves to another part of the terrain. The key is to avoid getting lost in the process by keeping the Framework in mind so that you always know where you are and, when appropriate, can return to those areas not yet fully discussed.

Developing Discrepancy: A Core Competency

Developing discrepancy, like recovering deletions or using reflection and summary, is a tool that serves a variety of purposes depending on the quadrant in which it is used. In Support-for-Action, it is used for its motivational value. By making the gap between what clients are currently experiencing and what they want to experience explicit, the motivation to change oneself or one's circumstances is increased. Developing discrepancy is used in Challenge-for-Action to prompt clients to think about what they need to *do* differently to get what they want. Finally, as explained above, in Challenge-for-Thought it is employed to induce clients to describe how their preferred future is different from the present, helping to create a picture of success in the process.

Constructing Well-Formed Outcomes

Clients often have only a vague idea of what they want in terms of their desired future. "Goals do not leap out fully formed" (Egan, 2010, p. 321). In fact, therein lies the value of coaching. Clarifying what a client wants is an iterative and multi-layered process. Ives and Cox (2012) argue that this activity solidifies the client's "fuzzy vision" in a way that enhances the probability of actually achieving it. Encouraging clients to talk about how they would like things to be different is a first step in helping them deal with their not knowing precisely what they want (Pemberton, 2006). However, helping clients make their vision of a preferred future actionable requires more than just developing discrepancy. It requires that you help clients convert their needs and wants into well-formed outcomes.

A well-formed outcome contains elements that make the difference between wanting something in theory and actually achieving it. The idea of a well-formed outcome is a construct of Neural Linguistic Programming (Cameron-Bandler, 1985) and can be defined as:

> A positive statement of what is wanted, which includes demonstrable indicators of success, the attainment of which is under the control or direct influence of the individual seeking that outcome.

A Positive Statement of What Is Wanted

Suppose you are helping a friend move some furniture into her new home, and you ask, "Where do you want this chair?" and she responds with, "I don't want it in that corner." That information does little to help you know where to put the chair. Similarly, when clients talk about what they do not want, it is of little value to you in helping them designing their preferred future. Consider this interchange:

> **Coach:** So, tell me, Carmen, what do you want to be different in the future?
> **Carmen:** I don't want to be perceived as unprofessional or not being able to respond and add value.

Carmen's response is a negative representation of a future state, which is inherently confusing when establishing a destination *toward* which one wants to move. To state it differently, thinking about what she does *not* want does little in the way of helping her achieve what she *does* want. Hoag (2012) refers to this type of thinking as *Away-From* thinking.

Away-From Thinking

Focusing on what is not wanted, or what is to be avoided, is *Away-From* thinking. It is quite common for clients to think and express themselves in terms of what they do not want; what they want to get *Away-From*. Even when asked for what they do want, many clients will often answer, "Well, I don't want this" or "I certainly don't want that." Iveson et al. (2012) explain,

> The problem with these negative outcome statements is that although they might be of use in a problem-solving model where the focus is on reducing the frequency or severity of the problem's manifestations, they are of little use in a solution focused approach where the coach concentrates on building the preferred future—what will be happening when the problem is not. They

give the coach no idea of what direction the client wants to take and, therefore, no way of knowing how to proceed.

(p. 44)

Changing Negatives to Positives

The conditions of a well-formed outcome require clients to state their goals or outcomes as a positive. If they begin with a negative outcome statement, their thinking can be redirected through the use of an *instead* question. An "instead" question is a restatement of what is not wanted, combined with the inquiry "What would you like instead?" or "What do you want instead?"

> ### An "Instead" Question
>
> **Coach:** So, tell me, Carmen, what do you want to be different in the future?
> **Carmen:** I don't want to be perceived as unprofessional or not being able to respond and add value.
> **Coach:** If you don't want to be perceived as unprofessional, or not being able to respond and add value, *what do you want instead?*

Away-From thinking will occur throughout the coaching session and is recognizable whenever the client answers a question with an "absence," e.g., "I wouldn't be looking at his work hoping there wasn't anything I needed to correct" or "I wouldn't feel anxious every time I have to speak in front of a group." Whenever you hear Away-From thinking, consider an "instead" question to help the client think about the presence of something rather than its absence.

Demonstrable Indicators of Success

Lewis Carroll wrote in his literary classic, *Alice in Wonderland,* "If you don't know where you're going, any road will get you there." While true, it is also true that if you don't know what it looks like when you arrive, you will never know that you have gotten there. Therefore, the second condition for a well-formed outcome is that it contains demonstrable indicators of success: a clear and concrete picture of what the client's world looks like when he or she has accomplished what is needed or wanted. Simply put, it answers the question, "What will clients see, hear, or experience when they have gotten what they want?" The more specific clients can be in describing what they want, the more noticeable it becomes when they have achieved it. Equally important is that once a person has spelled out a concrete picture of success, it is easier to construct a path to that end state than if the outcome is vague and ill-defined.

Finally, clients rarely achieve what they want in one giant leap. Change takes place over time; therefore, to keep from getting discouraged, clients have to know that they are moving in the right direction. Having concrete, behavioral, and measurable indicators of success enables them to measure their progress and reinforces the fact that they are moving in the right direction. As the saying goes, "Success creates success," so when clients can see evidence of their progress, it stimulates their continuing efforts toward their preferred future. This, of course, assumes that their indicators of success are realistic. Allowing clients to establish unrealistic indicators of success sets them up for failure. Well-formed outcomes must be achievable given clients' capacities and the context in which they operate.

Defining Success

As discussed in Chapter 4, each client has a unique model-of-the-world, a particular perception of reality. Within that map, there is an intuitive picture of what success is for any desired outcome. However, the client's intuitive definition of success must be translated into concrete indicators of what will be seen, heard, or experienced when the desired outcome is attained. There are two frames of reference that the client can use to define the demonstrable indicators of a successful outcome: self and other. Both frames of reference enable clients to sharpen their picture of success. Defining success from the "self" perspective is your starting point. Asking questions that elicit descriptions of what clients, themselves, would see, hear, or experience if their future state existed in the present is common practice for extracting demonstrable indicators of success. In fact, any question that prompts clients to visualize, in detail, what the attainment of their desired outcome looks like is a legitimate question. There are, however, two particular methods derived from solution-focused therapy and coaching that are particularly helpful for this purpose: scaling and the miracle question.

Scaling

Scaling is a solution-focused assessment method by which clients convert their intuitive thoughts and feelings into something more concrete and usable. It stems from the premise that we do not live in an either-or world but experience things in degrees or increments. Scaling uses a simple zero-to-ten structure that allows clients to assess where they are now as compared to where they want to be relative to some measure.

| 0 | 1 | 2 | 3 | 4 | 5 | 6 | 7 | 8 | 9 | 10 |

Since each scaling question is crafted to the situation, it can be used to access clients' perception of almost anything. In Challenge-for-Thought, the scaling technique is used to identify the client's starting point and then pinpoint what success would look like when he or she has achieved a place on the scale a few points higher. Your client's answers to questions such as "What will tell you that you have moved one point up the scale?" or "How will you know when you have reached a seven or eight on the scale?" define the indicators that help to quantify signs of progress and demonstrable indicators of success.

Introducing the Scale

Scaling is introduced, in general, by using the following directive:

> *"Imagine a scale from zero to ten with ten being when you have* (insert their desired outcome), *even if it is not perfect, and zero being the opposite. Where on the scale would you say you are now?"*

While ten represents the end state, it should not be presented as a state of perfection but as a realistic description of their preferred outcome. Moreover, it is best to leave zero relatively vague, thereby allowing clients to define what it means for their individual situation, hence the phrase "with zero being the opposite." Once you have a point of reference, ask clients to specify what they would see, hear, or experience when they arrive at one or two points higher on the scale.

Scaling in Challenge-for-Thought

Coach: You've mentioned two things: getting a handle on your emotions and stress, and developing a plan for managing your workload, correct?

Client: Yes.

Coach: Which one would you like to focus on first in case we don't get to both of them during this session?

Client: My emotions, handling my stress.

Coach: Okay. Now, I have a question for you: *On a scale of zero to ten, with ten being that you are handling your emotions and stress in the way that you want, even if it's not perfect, and zero being the opposite, where on the scale would you say you are now?*

Client: As I think about it, I guess I would have to say that I'm probably at a six on the scale.

Coach: A six, that's pretty good. *What would it look like if you were at an eight on the scale? In other words, what will you see, hear, or experience that will tell you when you have moved up the scale to an eight?*

When asking the client to describe what success will look like when he has moved up the scale, the coach is only asking him to describe incremental progress. Because clients often perceive ten as perfection (even though it is not introduced as such), it is usually best to ask them to describe demonstrable indicators of success that are only slightly higher on the scale than where they are now to be consistent with Solution-Focused Principle #3: Small steps lead to big changes.

The Miracle Question

Despite your best efforts, some clients have difficulty articulating what success looks like. The miracle question is a way of eliciting success indicators using the client's imagination while, at the same time, removing any pressure associated with taking action to bring about their described outcome. "The miracle question has become almost a trademark of solution focused coaching and is one of the most useful and creative starts to the process of eliciting a description of the preferred future" (Iveson et al., 2012, p. 39). The precise language may vary, but the basic set up and wording for the question is as follows:

> *I'm going to ask you a question that will challenge your imagination [pause]. Suppose that while you are sleeping tonight, a miracle happens [pause]. The miracle is that [state the client's desired outcome] has been realized; but, because you are asleep, you don't know that this miracle has happened [pause]. When you wake up tomorrow morning, what will be the first thing you would notice that tells you that something is different: that a miracle has occurred, and you have [state the client's desired outcome]?*

Clients have a variety of reactions to this scenario: puzzlement, confusion, and even amusement. However, if you set up the question correctly and present it in a serious way, given some time to think about it, they usually come up with some very specific things that describe a successful outcome. Because the miracle question has a future focus, it moves the thinking of clients away from their current situation to a positive picture of goal attainment and expands their thinking about what is possible. In the example below, the conversation moves from Support-for-Thought to Challenge-for-Thought where success indicators are elicited using the miracle question.

Miracle Question

Coach: So, what would you like to talk about today?

Client: Well, I need to discuss my situation at work. It is just becoming unbearable.

[The conversation begins in Support-for-Thought. The client responds to the question with a subject statement.]

Coach: Really? In what way is it becoming unbearable?

Client: Recently, they have reorganized the company, and I was appointed as an assistant to not one but two managers. So I mean, I've got more to take on. I can deal with that, but what's frustrating is that they are so preoccupied with their own changes in their job that they are not paying any attention to what I am doing. They're only worried about increasing their own influence.

[The coach attempts to recover an unnamed reference, but the client answers with a set of information and then a story. The coach repeats his original question.]

Coach: You mentioned earlier that the situation was unbearable; how is that situation unbearable for you?

Client: Well, I just don't have any autonomy, and I was really used to that. I can't make independent decisions because they have taken away the authority I had before. It just seems they are more interested in themselves and in micromanaging. I am really frustrated by this.

Coach: So, what would you like to be different going forward?

Client: Well, I would like a new job that is at least as good or maybe even better. But honestly, at my age and given the job market, I think the chances of getting another job are probably close to zero. Plus, I'm so busy I am not able to look for another job. I don't want to start something at the bottom again and work my way up. I just don't want to do that.

[The coach tried to move the conversation to Challenge-for-Thought by using a discrepancy question. The client states a goal that, by her own admission, is unreasonable. The coach returns to Support-for-Thought.]

Coach: Okay, so what would you like to take away from our session today?

Client: I don't think it is realistic for me to find another job. At least, that's not an option right now. So, I guess I want to know how to deal with this. How am I going to tolerate this situation better?

Coach: That sounds like a reasonable goal. So, to help you think about this further, I have an interesting question for you. In fact, it's going to challenge your imagination. Suppose that while you are sleeping tonight a miracle happens. The miracle is that you are dealing with and tolerating your situation in the way that you want; but, because you are asleep, you don't know that this miracle has happened. When you wake up tomorrow morning, what will be the first thing you notice that tells you something is different: that a miracle has occurred, and you are dealing with it and tolerating the situation in the way that you want?

[The coach first reinforces the client's positively stated goal. He then moves into Challenge-for-Thought by using the miracle question to begin defining demonstrable indicators of success.]

Client: That's a very interesting question; I would love a miracle to happen. I guess I would wake up and notice that I was looking forward to going to work.

Coach: What else will you notice?

Client: That I was more assertive with my bosses. Actually, that is why I would be looking forward to the day because I would be more assertive with them.

Coach: How will you know that you are more assertive with them? What will you see, hear, or experience?

Client: I guess that I am not just blindly accepting what they're saying to me.

Coach: So what is happening instead?

[Changes Away-From thinking to a positive.]

Client: Speaking up when I think that what they are asking me is unreasonable. Also, I would be clarifying or confirming with them what the priorities are so that I'm not getting caught in the middle of what the two of them want; that would be really helpful.

Coach: What else will you see, hear, or experience?

Client: That I'm making some decisions on my own when it involves what I do and how I do it. I'm not checking with them on everything I do, for heaven's sake. So it would seem that I am clarifying what my boundaries of authority are.

Coach: If this picture were to come to life, will it help you to achieve your goal of dealing with and tolerating your situation better?

[Reality-tests whether the success indicators do in fact describe the client's desired outcome.]

Client: Absolutely, I'm feeling better already.

[When clients focus on a positive future, it is motivating and positively affects their emotional state.]

Coach: That's good. So, given the picture you've just painted, let's talk about what you can do in the near future to make it a reality, okay?

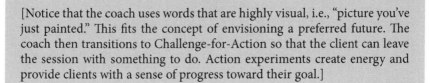

[Notice that the coach uses words that are highly visual, i.e., "picture you've just painted." This fits the concept of envisioning a preferred future. The coach then transitions to Challenge-for-Action so that the client can leave the session with something to do. Action experiments create energy and provide clients with a sense of progress toward their goal.]

In addition to illustrating the use of the miracle question, this example demonstrates the future-focused, goal-directed approach that typifies solution-focused coaching. Very little time was spent analyzing the problem or listening to the frustrations the client has with her current situation. Future-oriented questions are used to help the client focus on how she would like her life to be and how she can take action to get what she wants. This is an iterative process. As the client takes action, she will revise her picture of success based on what she experiences and then realize further actions she can take to achieve it. Present-oriented questions can also be employed to direct the client's attention to what she is already doing to deal with or tolerate her situation so that the coach can gently nudge her to do more of what is currently working. This approach works well because the client is already familiar with these behaviors. During this session, the coach may also choose to spend time in Support-for-Action to test and then strengthen the client's motivation surrounding her goal and what she is going to do to achieve it.

Using the "Third-Party" Perspective

Sometimes, asking clients to provide a picture of success from their perspective will elicit a response such as "I don't know. I'm not sure." When clients do not seem to know how to describe demonstrable indicators of success, changing their frame of reference can help. The solution-focused approach has roots in systems theory, and specifically the family therapies of the 1950s and 1960s. From a systems theory point of view solutions are interactional; that is, they involve other people such as colleagues, subordinates, managers, friends, and even family members (de Shazer & Dolan, 2007). For that reason, asking clients to define a successful outcome from the perspective of what other people might see, hear, or experience is another way of eliciting concrete indicators of success. For the client who wants to become a better leader, asking her to tell you what her staff might notice that is different when she is the type of leader she wants to be can overcome mental blocks that prevent her from defining success from a "self" perspective. In fact, it is often helpful to ask for both the self and other perspectives in the same conversation, even if no such block exists.

Using Self and Other Perspectives to Define Success Criteria

The Situation:

Greg is a new supervisor and needs help. His recent promotion has put him in the position of supervising an employee who is a good friend. He often finds himself in a situation where he needs to deliver a tough message to his friend as part of his supervisory role, but he does not want to endanger their friendship. This has caused him to tolerate behavior that he would not accept from others on the team. He now believes that others on the team are noticing this, and he feels like he is losing their respect as a leader. In this coaching session, Greg has explained his situation (Support-for-Thought) to his coach and now the conversation is moving into Challenge-for-Thought.

Coach: Greg, based upon what we've talked about so far, what would you like to be different in the future?

Greg: I'd like to find a way to become a more responsible leader in this situation rather than being viewed as a friend first.

Coach: If you were a more responsible leader, rather than a friend first, what will it look like; what will you be seeing, hearing, or experiencing?

Greg: Well, I'd be coming to work thinking more objectively about what needs to be done. If there were a problem with someone, I would be able to put aside my personal feelings.

Coach: Think for a moment about your friend Kim. How will you know if you are thinking objectively about what needs to be done and are putting aside your personal feelings?

Greg: I guess I'd be focusing more on what we have to do as a team. That would be my priority.

Coach: OK. What else will you be doing?

Greg: I would not be looking at his work hoping there wasn't anything I needed to correct. [Stated in the negative.]

Coach: What will you be doing instead?

Greg: Well, if there is a problem, I'd be taking it in stride.

Coach: How will you know that you are taking it in stride?

Greg: If I noticed a problem, I'd be talking to him about it and offering feedback on how he could improve his work. I would still be giving him positives, but I wouldn't be afraid to challenge him if I thought it would improve the outcome.

Coach: What else would let you know that you are a responsible leader rather than a friend first?

[The coach returns to the original question.]

Greg: I would think that this is something that I'd do with anybody on the team. I'm not just singling him out and that this isn't personal. We can still be friends, but this is what I need to do as the leader of the team.

Coach: What will other people on the team notice when you are a responsible leader in the way that you want?

[The coach asks for an "other" perspective.]

Greg: I think they will see that I am treating everyone fairly and that no one is getting special treatment just because I've known them longer or have a personal relationship with them. Also, they will notice that I'm spending more time with each of them than I have in the past.

Coach: And this friend that you are talking about, what will he be noticing?

Greg: I think he would notice that I'm more serious in my work interactions with him and that I'm not thrown off by our friendship. He would notice that I'm drawing a clearer boundary between our interactions on the job and our interactions off the job. I wouldn't blur the lines as much as I do now.

Coach: You said that you wouldn't be thrown off by your friendship with him; such as what, specifically?

[Recovers an unnamed reference.]

Greg: I wouldn't be thrown off by jokes, or by him wanting to talk about personal things from off the job. For example, if he brought up something about going to a ball game, I wouldn't wander off into that conversation. I'd keep it focused on work. I'd keep it focused on the job.

Coach: It seems like you have a good picture of what success looks like for you if you were a more responsible leader in the way that you want. So let's talk about the first steps you are going to take over the short term to move toward this picture.

[Moves to Challenge-for-Action.]

Greg: Okay, that sounds good to me.

During the conversation, the coach does several things that prepare Greg to take action:

1. When Greg speaks in general terms, she asks him to focus on the specific situation with his friend.
2. She asks, "what else?" questions to encourage expansive thinking rather than accepting his first answer.
3. When he states what wouldn't be happening, she uses the *instead* question to elicit what *would* be happening.
4. She elicited both self and other success criteria.

Translating "Feeling" Goals to External Indicators

Sometimes, desired outcomes are stated as internal states, i.e., descriptions of how clients want to *feel* generally, or how they want to feel in response to a specific situation. As an example, a partner in a big four financial consulting firm wanted to "feel more confident" when he made presentations to C-suite clients. Not only is it impossible for you to know what he means by feeling more confident, it may be difficult for *him* to know as well—unless you help him identify external indicators that are the equivalent of "feeling more confident." Translating feeling-goals to outer actions is an essential skill in your solution-focused repertoire (Iveson et al., 2012). In the case of the partner who wants to feel more confident, the following questions can help him translate his feeling-goal to external indicators:

*   How will you know when you are feeling more confident?
*   What will you be doing differently that will tell others that your confidence is growing?
*   What will others see, hear, or experience when you are feeling more confident?
*   When you are feeling more confident in the way that you want, what will be the first thing you notice?

Under the Client's Direct Control or Influence

A well-formed outcome is one that is dependent only on factors the client can manage and control. The test for this is to pose a simple inquiry to your client: "To achieve what you want, is it yours and only yours to control?" Placing the attainment of one's outcome at the mercy of others is to invite failure. Accordingly, when a client's outcome is for others to change or behave differently, the goal must be reframed so that it consists of a change in the *client's* behavior for the purpose of influencing other people to some end. A well-formed outcome, then, signifies that its realization is within the locus of control of the individual who desires it.

Fostering an internal locus of control is essential for the coaching process to work. The belief that clients can determine their own internal state, direct their own behavior, and influence their environment sufficiently to achieve desired outcomes is a prerequisite for self-directed change and problem solving. Locus of control theory (Lefcourt, 1982; Rotter, 1954) states that people either believe they are in control of their life (internal locus of control) or that their life is controlled by environmental factors over which they have no influence (external locus of control). An internal locus of control has been determined to correlate positively with a variety of success factors. It can be argued that one of the real benefits—and purposes—of coaching is to increase the client's internal locus of control not only to assist in goal achievement but also to contribute to identity transformation.

Chapter Summary

In Challenge-for-Thought, coaches assist clients in creating a picture of their desired future state. The solution-focused principles that underlie both Challenge-for-Thought and Challenge-for-Action are simple, but powerful. The concept of a goal hierarchy was introduced, emphasizing the importance of proximal goals in regulating motivation and action. Proximal goals lend themselves to increased imagery that defines, in detail, a clear and vivid picture of the client's preferred future. To help clients think about what they want and to add specificity to their goal setting, the method of developing discrepancy and the practice of constructing well-formed outcomes were explained and illustrated. The technique of scaling and the use of the miracle question can be employed to elicit demonstrable indicators of success as part of creating a well-formed outcome.

It may be tempting to simplify the purpose of Challenge-for-Thought by thinking of it as merely challenging clients to design and set goals. However, for most clients their proximal goals are an ill-defined, fuzzy vision of what they want (assuming they know what they want at all). Challenging clients to envision their desired end states as the presence of something rather than its absence, and with enough specificity and concrete indicators of success to realize its attainment through self-initiated actions, will improve the probability of their success. However, accomplishing this end is not always as simple as it seems.

The ICF competencies (ICF Core Competencies—International Coach Federation, n.d.) addressed by the content of this chapter are:

- **Active Listening**
    - Attends to the client and the client's agenda and not to the coach's agenda for the client.
    - Integrates and builds on client's ideas and suggestions.
    - "Bottom-lines" or understands the essence of the client's communication and helps the client get there rather than engaging in long, descriptive stories.

- **Powerful Questioning**
  - Asks questions that reflect active listening and an understanding of the client's perspective.
  - Asks questions that evoke discovery.
  - Asks open-ended questions that create greater clarity, possibility, or new learning.
  - Asks questions that move the client toward what he or she desires, not questions that ask for the client to justify or look backward.
- **Direct Communication**
  - Reframes and articulates to help the client understand from another perspective what he/she wants or is uncertain about.
- **Creating Awareness**
  - Invokes inquiry for greater understanding, awareness, and clarity.
  - Identifies major strengths vs. major areas for learning and growth, and what is most important to address during coaching.
- **Managing Progress and Accountability**
  - Engages the client to explore alternative ideas and solutions, to evaluate options, and to make related decisions.
  - Advocates or brings forward points of view that are aligned with client goals and, without attachment, engages the client to consider them.

CHAPTER 6

Challenge-for-Thought

Eliciting Self-Talk and Beliefs

Coaching, at its core, is a cognitive process. As such, it is incumbent on coaches to help clients think with greater specificity, clarity, depth, and with less distortion about the things that are important to them. Clients may have a very clear idea of what they want to achieve, but erroneous conclusions, limiting assumptions, maladaptive self-talk, and impoverished beliefs will sabotage their ability to construct their preferred future or take action toward its realization. As a catalyst for a better future, it is the coach's role to challenge clients to change ways of thinking that keep them mired in problem situations or prevent them from identifying and developing opportunities. This chapter focuses on the cognitive methods and practices used in Challenge-for-Thought for this purpose.

Cognitive Coaching

Coaches are thinking partners, and they have become more attuned to the role of metacognition (thinking about thinking) and its part in fostering more benefi-cial methods of internal communication for their clients to help overcome self-defeating or self-limiting beliefs and assumptions. In fact, this type of coaching is labeled *cognitive coaching*. The term "cognitive coaching" was originally coined by Art Costa and Robert Garmston (1994) for use in education. It refers to a method of instruction that prepares new teachers to think more reflectively and foster independent learning. When applied to coaching, however, it is an app-roach derived from the practice of cognitive-behavioral therapists to change patterns of thinking that interfere with people's ability to attain successful out-comes in their lives and experience a higher level of life satisfaction. To be

Informed Practitioners, coaches must have a working knowledge of the tenets of cognitive-behavior therapy (CBT), its methods, and techniques for helping people manage their thoughts effectively, and understand how to utilize those methods and techniques within the process of coaching.

The Cognitive-Behavioral Approach

Cognitive-behavioral therapy (CBT) is an evidence-based discipline that seeks to help clients analyze and reality-test existing patterns of thinking and their effect on feelings and behavior. The cognitive component of CBT was developed by Aaron Beck in the early 1960s as a structured, time-limited approach for helping clients overcome depression (Beck, 1964). Various forms of CBT have been developed, most notably Albert Ellis's rational-emotive therapy (Ellis, 1962) and Donald Meichenbaum's cognitive-behavioral modification (Meichenbaum, 1977). Interest in the cognitive component affecting feelings and behavior came about, in part, due to the view that behavior therapy—a dominant approach in the mid-twentieth century—reflected a narrow, mechanistic view of the human condition and therefore an integration of the work of cognitive semantic therapists was merited. Over time, practitioners of CBT have placed increased emphasis on the cognitive component, which is more in agreement with Beck's original work. "Under the banner of CBT many practitioners have adopted an approach that might more accurately be called **Cbt**, just as an earlier generation clung to the known effectiveness of what amounted to cBt" (Sheldon, 2011, p. 5). Currently, the use of the **Cbt** approach is broadening and is increasingly being used by practitioners from different professional backgrounds, not the least of which is coaching.

The Cbt Model

The **Cbt** model is based on the proposition that people's emotional and behavioral responses are influenced by their *perception* of (thoughts about) situations and not the situation in and of itself. In other words, it is the way people *construe* a situation that determines their reactions to it (Beck, 1964; Ellis, 1962). Imagine, for example, two drivers, each sitting in their car waiting to make a legal right turn on a red light. In front of them is another car stopped at the light with its right-turn blinker on and not making the turn, even though the way forward is clear. One of the drivers in the cars behind is feeling frustrated, even angry at the delay, and honks his horn in an attempt to get the car in front to move. Another driver, by contrast, waits patiently with no negative feelings and accompanying behavior. Both drivers are in the same situation but have different emotional and behavioral responses. What is different between the two? According to the **Cbt** model, the situation itself does not directly determine how these two drivers feel. For the angry driver, the situation activates beliefs and thoughts that produce an emotional reaction (frustration and anger), which is then followed by a behavioral response (honking the horn). For the second driver, there are no such "hot cognitions" and, therefore, no elevated feelings and acting-up behavior.

Core Beliefs

In Chapter 4, it was explained how our experiences, beginning in childhood, shape our perception of reality and create our personal model-of-the-world (M-O-W). Contained within our M-O-W are beliefs about ourselves, other people, and the world in general, which were shaped by those experiences. The most fundamental of these beliefs are called *core beliefs*. Core beliefs are so primary and concealed within our Deep Structure that they often operate outside of our awareness. Consequently, we rarely articulate these core beliefs, even to ourselves. They are accepted as "just the way things are"—unquestionable truths that are rarely challenged. Core beliefs are unconditional and take the form of simple, blanket statements such as "No one cares about me." Core beliefs can be enabling (e.g., "I'm smart. I'm capable.") or they can be debilitating (e.g., "I'm incompetent. I'm not good enough.").

Most of the time core beliefs lie dormant within our M-O-W, but when pertinent to a situation they awaken. As an example, if a client has the core belief, "I'm incompetent," it will become activated when this belief is relevant to the situation at hand, such as when confronted with a new challenge at work. Since core beliefs serve as a basis for screening, categorizing, and interpreting our experiences, clients will unconsciously construe their situations through the lens of their core beliefs. When rationally examined, their interpretation may be demonstrably untrue. However, this does not stop people from selectively focusing on information that confirms their core beliefs while at the same time ignoring or discounting information that is to the contrary. Selective perception is one reason core beliefs developed in childhood survive into adulthood—even those that are detrimental to our well-being.

Intermediate Beliefs

Intermediate beliefs, like core beliefs, affect our thinking and ultimately our emotions and behavior. They typically take two forms: assumptions and rules. Assumptions are conditional beliefs that exist in an "If . . . then . . ." format, e.g., "If I always say yes, then people will like me." Rules are general beliefs about how things *should* be or how people *should* act, e.g., "People should respect those who are in positions of authority." Intermediate beliefs stem from our core beliefs. For example, the core belief "I'm incompetent" might produce the intermediate belief "If I make a mistake, then I am a failure." What is of particular interest to coaches is the idea that intermediate beliefs interfering with the achievement of client goals can be unlearned and new beliefs that are more reality-based and functional inserted in their place.

Automatic Thoughts

Automatic thoughts are the most superficial level of cognition and, therefore, are the closest to conscious awareness. At the other end of the spectrum are core beliefs, the most deep-seated and elemental of our beliefs; they are universal and rigid. In between are intermediate beliefs: conditional assumptions and rules for living. Just as intermediate beliefs emanate from core beliefs, automatic thoughts spring from intermediate beliefs. Because they are so much a part of our view of ourselves and the world, automatic thoughts are believed as both plausible and valid because they arise by reflex without any reflection or reality-testing on our part:

> It generally does not occur to a person to question the validity of his thoughts. He tends to regard ideas as though they were a microcosm of the outside world. He attaches the same truth value to his thought as he does to his perception of the external world.
>
> (Beck, 1976, p. 245)

Automatic thoughts also include mental pictures: images in our "mind's eye" that accompany internal dialogue. To illustrate, think about the driver in the example above who is frustrated and angry. If his thoughts are captured at that moment, they would probably consist of internal dialogue and mental pictures such as, "Why isn't he turning? I've got to get going, or I'm going to be late to my meeting with my boss [mind's eye: imagining how far he has to go by a certain time]. That guy is probably talking on his cell phone and not paying attention. He shouldn't be doing that. Some people just don't care about what other people have to do. If I'm late to this meeting, I'm going to be really embarrassed [mind's eye: picturing his boss's reaction]. Doesn't he know people are waiting to make the turn?"

Automatic thoughts can be triggered by any internal or external event that is personally meaningful (Beck, 2005). There are several common triggers for automatic thoughts:

- Discrete events (such as the one described above).
- Memories or other images because they are like discrete events except that they occur in our inner world as opposed to the external world.
- Distressing thoughts that, when people become aware of them, become a trigger for subsequent automatic thoughts.
- Emotions or physical sensations that generate automatic thoughts in response to what is being felt.

To summarize, incoming information from an event, situation, or condition trigger automatic thoughts (and mental pictures), which are evaluated according to a set of intermediate beliefs. The interaction between our thoughts and beliefs produces an emotional response that creates an inner urge to act out of that emotional state. The driver honks his horn (behavior), which stems from his frustration and anger (emotions) evoked by what he is thinking and picturing (automatic thoughts). For shorthand, I will use the term "Cognitive-Behavioral Cycle" to refer to this process.

Cognitive Therapy versus Cognitive Coaching

Cognitive-behavioral therapy was developed for the therapeutic setting and is used in the treatment of a variety of personality disorders. Cbt terminology, such as rational versus irrational thoughts, reflect its clinical roots. The cognitive therapist attempts to modify the entire Cognitive-Behavioral Cycle, including automatic thoughts, intermediate beliefs, and eventually core beliefs. The Cbt therapeutic process consists of examining how core beliefs originated and then restructuring early memories so as to modify those beliefs, which creates change throughout the Cognitive-Behavioral Cycle. Clearly, many of the ideas and techniques of Cbt have found their way into the field of self-help psychology and eventually to coaching.

It is important to keep in mind, though, that coaches are not therapists, and coaching is not therapy. Coaches deal with different issues and a different category of clients. Consequently, it is appropriate that Cbt terminology and methods fit the practice of coaching rather than the aims of therapy. To that end, only the parts of the Cognitive-Behavioral Cycle that fit the purpose of coaching will be highlighted in this book. With regard to terminology, it has been the author's experience that clients respond better to "self-talk"—a term devised by Maultsby (1986)—than to "automatic thoughts," even though understanding the concept of automatic thoughts can be useful. Clients intuitively feel that they can change how they talk to themselves easier than they can change their thoughts since, by definition, those thoughts are "automatic." Focusing primarily on self-talk—with some emphasis on intermediate beliefs—is sufficient for most coaching issues. Challenging and changing core beliefs are generally left to therapists.

Transactional Analysis and Cognitive Coaching

In Chapter 3, the phenomenon of ego states (i.e., Parent, Adult, and Child) was briefly discussed as to their effect on rapport in Support-for-Thought. Transactional Analysis (TA), however, has more to offer than a theory of interpersonal interaction. It is also a theory of personality that teaches us how ego states affect our inner experiences—including the way we talk to ourselves. While it is beyond the scope of this chapter to provide a comprehensive explanation of TA, it is worthwhile to discuss those elements of the TA model that can help identify, challenge, and change counterproductive self-talk and intermediate beliefs.

Ego states are defined as "coherent systems of thought and feeling manifested by corresponding patterns of behavior" (Berne, 1972, p. 11). From a cognitive-behavioral perspective, Berne is saying that each ego state—Parent, Adult, and Child—is defined by a particular cognitive structure (each ego state is given a capital letter to signify the difference between actual parents, adults, and children). This structure is composed of self-talk and beliefs unique to that ego state. At a deeper level, it also includes the memories of events, past and present, which are the source of those beliefs. The feelings and behavior that correspond to each ego state flow naturally from its cognitive structure.

The Parent Ego State

The cognitive structure of the Parent ego state contains all of the admonitions, rules, and "laws" that we learn growing up. Most are learned from our parents as we are taught how we should be and how we should behave from their point of view, e.g., "You have to do your best if you want to succeed!" When experienced often enough, these pronouncements translate into generalized rules, e.g., "People should do their best at all times." In addition to what we learn from verbal declarations, we also absorb rules through inference: what we extrapolate from the behavior of our parents. For example, seeing a frown or look of parental disappointment upon seeing a "B" on a report card instead of straight As can be interpreted by the young person as, "I wasn't perfect. Therefore, I failed." Later this becomes a rule (i.e., "Unless I'm perfect, I'm a failure"). We also learn the "shoulds of life" from sources other than our parents, including relatives and other people in positions of authority, e.g., teachers, religious figures, etc. "Any external situation in which the little person feels himself to be dependent to the extent that he is not free to question or to explore produces data which is stored in the Parent" (Harris, 1969, p. 24). Even a small child sitting in front of the television set is being taught a concept of life that provides content for the Parent ego state. To summarize, through directives, inferences, and observations absorbed while we are growing up, we learn what we are "supposed" to do and how we "should" be. These beliefs are treated as facts and stored within the cognitive structure of the Parent ego state.

Having a well-functioning Parent ego state is important because it helps us to be moral, responsible human beings. "Do not steal"; "Look both ways before crossing the street"; and "Do a good job" are useful admonitions. When the Parent ego state is *integrated* with the Adult, it helps us by setting limits, defining values, and providing structure and even support. When the integrating Adult intervenes, rules and value judgments made by the Parent are reality-tested and, if necessary, modified so that they are reasonable and flexible. A problem arises, however, when we respond to situations with Parent self-talk that is the result of exaggerated, overgeneralized, and absolute rules and beliefs. According to Harris (1969):

> Many of these edicts are fortified with such additional imperatives as "never" and "always" and "never forget that." . . . These rules are the origins of compulsions and quirks and eccentricities that appear in later behavior. Whether Parent data is a burden or a boon depends on how appropriate it is to the present, on whether or not it has been updated by the Adult.
>
> (pp. 23–24)

To put it another way, the Parent becomes a burden when it turns into a critical Parent that unleashes a stream of disparaging self-talk causing us to judge, unfairly, ourselves and others using a set of unrealistic rules and beliefs learned as children but which are untested and unchallenged by the Adult ego state. When this happens, our Parent ego state is said to be *contaminated* (Stewart & Joines, 1987). It is as though our immature Parent intrudes into the boundary of the Adult and we mistake it for Adult reality—which it is not—contaminating our self-talk in the process.

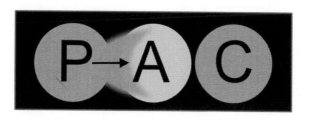

The Child Ego State

The Child ego state is similar to the Parent in that its cognitive structure contains echoes from the past. While the Parent harbors beliefs in the form of rules and value judgments copied from parents and parental figures, the cognitive structure of the Child ego state is filled with beliefs and associated self-talk derived from an *emotional evaluation* of early experiences. At the outset, children do not have any other way to evaluate and learn from their experiences except through emotional reasoning because they have no vocabulary with which to construct meanings; feelings are facts. "In emotional reasoning, a person makes an inference about himself, the world, or the future on the basis of an emotional experience" (Persons, 1989, p. 107). For example, a sour look turned in the direction of a child can only produce negative feelings within the child. These feelings are data that—in a child's mind—leads to emotionally based conclusions, e.g., "I feel bad. Therefore, I am bad." When added to a reservoir of similar conclusions, a belief forms within the child about his or her worthiness, e.g. "I'm just no good." This belief (and the self-talk generated by it) is recorded in the cognitive structure of the Child ego state waiting to be triggered by a situation that, even remotely, simulates the early experience. As Harris (1969) explains it, "[T]he Child is a state into which a person may be transferred at almost any time. . . . There are many things that can happen to us today which recreate the situation of childhood and bring on the same feelings we felt then" (p. 26).

Emotions in and of themselves can be a trigger for self-talk. Suppose a client is anxious about giving a presentation in front of her peers. If she is operating from her Adult ego state, she will be able to interpret her anxiousness in different ways (e.g., excitement), but if her Child ego state takes over without the "supervision" of her Adult ego state, her emotional reasoning will attribute the anxiety to incompetence and produce counterproductive self-talk, e.g., "I'm feeling anxious. Therefore, I must not be prepared." This kind of self-talk can generate more anxiety and negative fantasies, such as imagining herself stumbling through the presentation and being ridiculed by her peers. This thought process began when—unconsciously—her Child ego state produced automatic self-talk based on assumptions and beliefs stored from early childhood experiences similar to the one she now comes across as an adult, i.e., "If I feel anxious it is because I'm not prepared." This Cognitive-Behavioral Cycle is propelled by a *contaminated* Child ego state. In other words, she is talking to herself from her Child ego state while presuming she is doing so from her Adult.

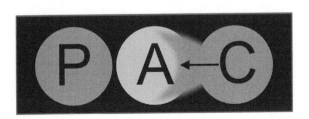

As with the Parent, there is a positive side to the Child ego state. It is through the mature expression of the Child that we exhibit creativity, curiosity, and the desire to know and explore. From the Child comes spontaneity, intuition, and joy; we "feel" life through our Child ego state. We also appropriately adapt and comply with the expectations of others from our mature Child. We demonstrate to others that we know how to behave properly, e.g., we apologize when we bump into someone, and we say "please" and "thank you." We are polite, considerate, and accommodating when the Child is integrated with our Adult so that it expresses itself sensibly.

Parent and Child Contamination

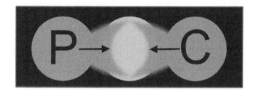

The contaminated Parent and Child ego states contain "of all the outdated, distorted beliefs a person holds about himself, other people and the world" (Stewart & Joines, 1987, p. 52). These ego states are said to be contaminated because of the characteristics of the beliefs and because the person is acting on those beliefs while thinking he or she is responding to the situation from the Adult ego state. The contaminated Parent and Child work together to reinforce each other. For example, a Parent rule exists (e.g., "You should respect other people") and the Child agrees to it with a corresponding assumption (e.g., "If I can't respect someone, I have to keep quiet"). The two ego states talk to each other so much that most people hardly hear it. People merely accept their automatic self-talk without realizing that it is contaminated and, therefore, debilitating. While a distinction can be made between contaminated Parent and contaminated Child self-talk, in truth, it is not always necessary to differentiate between the two in order to advance the coaching process. It is enough for the coach to discern that the client is engaging in some form of Parent-Child contaminated self-talk and move to the Challenge-for-Thought quadrant to examine its validity and usefulness.

The Integrating Adult

The cognitive structure of the Adult ego state is a rational, reality-based thinking process. It provides us with the ability to process incoming information uncontaminated by the Parent and Child. The Adult accumulates data about what is different about life from the "taught concept" of the Parent and the "felt concept" of the Child so that we can respond logically and objectively to the here-and-now:

One of the important functions of the Adult is to examine the data in the Parent, to see whether or not it is true and still applicable today, and then to accept it or reject it; and to examine the Child to see whether or not the feelings there are appropriate to the present or are archaic and in response to archaic Parent data.

(Harris, 1969, p. 30)

To rephrase, it is the role of the Adult to take the best from the past and use it appropriately in the present. In so doing, there is an integration of the positive aspects of both the Parent and Child ego states. The *integrating* Adult continually updates our self-talk and beliefs so that they are appropriate to the moment—and to the situation, event, or condition we are experiencing.

The integrating role of the Adult is illustrated by the First Order Structural Model of TA.

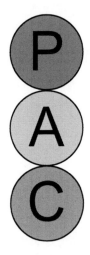

In this diagram, the Adult is placed in the middle of the three ego states just touching the Parent and the Child to show that its function is to intervene between the Parent and the Child so as to stop any negative dialogue between the two. Its purpose is to help us see reality as it is, instead of viewing it through the distorted lenses of the contaminated Parent and Child. The Adult monitors both ego states to determine what is valid and what is not and helps us deal with situations and events without negative self-talk influenced by our past.

Identifying Contaminated Self-Talk

How can you determine whether your client's self-talk (thinking) is contaminated? Pucci (2008) proposes three questions adapted from Maultsby's (1986) Five Criteria for Rational Thinking to assess whether a person's thoughts are healthy (Adult driven) or contaminated (P-C driven). I have adapted them for use in coaching. Here are the "Three Rational Questions" to ask yourself when gauging your client's thinking:

1. Is my client's thinking coming from his or her integrated Adult?
2. Does my client's thinking help him or her achieve his or her stated goals?
3. Does my client's thinking help him or her feel the way he or she wants to feel?

The answer to all three questions must be *Yes*. If there is a *No* answer to any of them, your client's thinking is not serving him or her well and is probably contaminated. When you suspect contaminated thinking, it is appropriate to move to Challenge-for-Thought and employ the methods and practices discussed below and in Chapter 7 to help clients examine their self-talk from an Adult perspective. Modifying their self-talk is the secret to achieving a shift in your clients' thinking because when their self-talk changes for the positive, their beliefs move in the same direction.

Eliciting Self-Talk

Self-talk coexists within a person's natural stream of thinking and, therefore, often requires little effort to retrieve because it emerges spontaneously and frequently as part of the client's speech (Persons, 1989). In other words, it is a matter of listening for clues in the client's language that signal the presence of any contaminated self-talk preventing a *Yes* answer to the Three Rational Questions listed above. All contaminated self-talk shares a common theme: It consists of automatic thoughts that are *exaggerated*, *overgeneralized*, and *absolute* that:

•   are always negative,
•   make the person feel bad,
•   are self-sabotaging, and
•   stem from contaminated P-C beliefs.

Listen for Spontaneous Expressions of Self-Talk

No matter which quadrant the coaching conversation is in, always listen for outward expressions of contaminated self-talk.

Client Procrastination Example

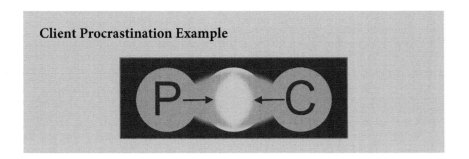

Client: I sit down to start a project and find myself just staring at the work . . . (Long pause) . . . I don't know what's wrong with me.

["I don't know what's wrong with me" is a vocalization of his self-talk.]

Coach: So, you are saying to yourself that there's something wrong with you.

[Reflection]

Client: Yes, because if there wasn't something wrong I would be able to get started.

[An "if . . . then . . . " conditional assumption]

Coach: What else do you say to yourself when you are sitting there?

[Eliciting more self-talk]

Client: I'm thinking that I should be able to get to work on this, and I start imagining what's going to happen if I don't get it done—which makes me even more anxious.

Coach: What do you imagine is going to happen?

Client: If I don't get this done my boss will be upset. He won't trust me and I won't get the opportunity to do future projects that will advance my career. Then I'll be stuck because I won't have any career options, while everyone else will be getting ahead of me.

In the above example, it is easy to imagine the client's Child ego state feeling that "There is something wrong with me," while at the same time his Parent is declaring, "You should be able to get started (and you're not)," which prompts the Child to imagine all kinds of negative consequences. The integrating Adult is not part of the equation, so the client ends up feeling anxious (and probably guilty) as a result of his contaminated Parent-Child self-talk.

Negative Feelings Signal Contaminated Self-Talk

A client's self-talk is not always evident in his or her Surface Structure language. However, there is another way it can be brought to light: Pinpoint the negative feelings the client had in response to a situation or an event and then ask the client what thoughts produced those feelings. (The words *thoughts* and *self-talk* are used interchangeably because thoughts manifest themselves as internal dialogue—even though technically speaking, they include mental images.) There are at least five ways to elicit the self-talk from a specific situation:

1. **Ask for their thoughts directly.** Summarize the situation and the feelings experienced and inquire as to what was going through the client's mind when he or she felt the negative feelings, e.g., "What was going through your mind when you felt . . . ?"

> **Client:** I've got this project at work and every time I sit down to work on it I feel anxious. It's like things go fuzzy and I feel weighed down by it. I've got to work through this.
>
> **Coach:** Okay, so you sit down to work on this project and all of a sudden you get this sense of anxiety, and then things kind of go fuzzy, and you feel weighed down. Is that right?
>
> **Client:** Yes.
>
> **Coach:** What is going through your mind when you first feel anxious?

As illustrated above, it is usually best to summarize the client's description of the situation before asking for self-talk, e.g., "So, you sat down to work on the project and all of a sudden you felt fuzzy and weighed down. What is going through your mind when that happened?" Sometimes the client answers by describing a feeling instead of his or her self-talk. If that happens, simply restate the question using the new information.

> **Client:** I've got this project at work and every time I sit down to work on it I feel anxious. It's like things go fuzzy and I feel weighed down by it. I've got to work through this.
>
> **Coach:** Okay, so you sit down to work on this project and all of a sudden you get this sense of anxiety, and then things kind of go fuzzy, and you feel weighed down. Is that right?
>
> **Client:** Yes.
>
> **Coach:** What is going through your mind when you first feel anxious?
>
> **Client:** I feel overwhelmed.
>
> **Coach:** And when you feel anxious and overwhelmed, what is going through your mind?
>
> **Client:** I'm thinking that I should be able to get to work on this, and there must be something wrong with me because I can't seem to get started. Then, I start imagining what will happen if I don't get it finished.

Sometimes, it works well to ask the client to provide images, instead of words. For example, "When you sit down to work on this project and all of a sudden you get this sense of anxiety, and then things kind of go fuzzy, and you feel weighed down, what mental images come to mind?" The images themselves may reveal associated thoughts, e.g., "I get a picture of this giant hill that I have to climb, and I say to myself, 'This is going to be an impossible task.'"

2. **Recreate the situation in real-time.** If verbally describing the situation is insufficient to elicit the client's self-talk, ask the client to relive the situation at the moment.

Client: I've got this project at work and every time I sit down to work on it I feel anxious. It's like things go fuzzy and I feel weighed down by it. I've got to work through this.

Coach: Okay, so you sit down to work on this project and all of a sudden you get this sense of anxiety, and then things kind of go fuzzy, and you feel weighed down. Is that right?

Client: Yes.

Coach: What is going through your mind when you first feel anxious?

Client: I don't know. Nothing really.

Coach: Okay, would you be willing to try something?

Client: (The client nods his head.)

Coach: All right, imagine yourself sitting at your desk right now. What's on your desk? Who else is there, if anyone? What exactly are you doing? Tell me when you have that pictured.

Client: I've got it.

Coach: Now, while you are mentally experiencing that, what are you saying to yourself right now?

Client: I'm saying to myself, I should be able to get to work on this. Why can't I get things done on time? What's wrong with me?

3. **Ask the client to make a guess.** If the client is still stuck, hypothetically thinking about what he *might* have said to himself in that or similar situations may open the door to his self-talk.

Client: I've got this project at work and every time I sit down to work on it I feel anxious. It's like things go fuzzy and I feel weighed down by it. I've got to work through this.

Coach: Okay, so you sit down to work on this project and all of a sudden you get this sense of anxiety, and then things kind of go fuzzy, and you feel weighed down. Is that right?

Client: Yes.

Coach: What is going through your mind when you first feel anxious?

Client: I don't know. Nothing really.

Coach: Okay, think about it hypothetically. If you were to guess, what might you say to yourself in a situation like this?

Client: I would probably say, "I should be able to get to work on this. Why can't I get things done on time? What's wrong with me?"

4. **Ask the client what thoughts most people would have if they felt that way.** After the client answers, ask, "Is it possible you are saying these things to yourself in this situation?"

> **Coach:** Okay, so you sit down to work on this project and all of a sudden you get this sense of anxiety, and then things kind of go fuzzy, and you feel weighed down. Is that right?
> **Client:** Yes.
> **Coach:** What is going through your mind when you first feel anxious?
> **Client:** I don't know. Nothing really.
> **Coach:** Okay, what kind of thoughts do you think most people would have if they felt anxious in this situation?
> **Client:** Probably something like, "I won't be able to get this done, and then I'll look bad."
> **Coach:** Is it possible you are saying this very same thing to yourself?

Depersonalizing it may make it easier for him to reveal something about his own thinking. In fact, you are actually asking the client to engage in projection. The thoughts he ascribes to others may very well be his own. If he disagrees with the idea that he is saying the same things to himself, it opens the door to inquiring as to how his thinking is different.

5. **Make some suggestions about what you or other people might say to themselves in that situation.** You can always draw upon your personal experience as a basis for suggestions as to what might be going through your client's mind, e.g., "When I've felt the same way in similar situations I had thoughts such as. . . ." This approach adds a degree of self-disclosure on the part of the coach. In addition to stimulating the client's thinking, it makes it easier for the client to admit to the thoughts he or she may have had but is embarrassed to say out loud. Even better, if you have a sense of your client's underlying belief system, base your suggestions on the kind of self-talk that might be generated by those beliefs. Of course, the common method of making a suggestion in this way is to state what most people are likely to be thinking in that situation. Right or wrong, it gives the client an opportunity to agree with you or correct the record.

> **Coach:** Okay, so you sit down to work on this project and all of a sudden you get this sense of anxiety, and then things kind of go fuzzy, and you feel weighed down. Is that right?
> **Client:** Yes.
> **Coach:** What is going through your mind when you first feel anxious?
> **Client:** I don't know. Nothing really.
> **Coach:** You know, it's not uncommon for people who are anxious to be thinking about not being able to get it done and the negative consequences might follow. Does that ring a bell for you?

Thought Records: Teaching the Client to Become Self-Aware

Teaching clients to learn to identify their self-talk is an essential step in the cognitive coaching process. Until the thoughts and images stimulated by external events are put into words, it is difficult for clients to change counterproductive self-talk and the negative emotions and behavior that emanate from them. Remember: The fundamental premise guiding cognitive coaching is that the thoughts clients have about their experiences determine how they feel and behave in response to those thoughts. Many clients, however, are surprised or at least under-aware of the fact that their emotional and behavioral responses to situations and events are the result of how they think (what they say to themselves), and that by modifying their self-talk they can have very different responses. A guiding principle in coaching is to empower clients to have control over their lives. To this end, teaching that: 1) thoughts and feelings are distinct phenomena and 2) thoughts create feelings and drive behavior, are vital concepts for clients to understand if they want more control over the way they experience situations, events, or conditions.

Developing awareness is the first step in changing contaminated self-talk, or if needed, challenging the counterproductive beliefs producing the self-talk in the first place. Self-talk can be elicited by moving into Challenge-for-Thought during the coaching conversation and employing the methods described above. Sometimes, however, clients are not able to recall or re-create the self-talk that is triggering their feelings and subsequent behavior, even if you use the techniques described above. Their self-talk is so programmed that they are not able to remember it for very long past the time it occurs. Therefore, becoming aware of those thoughts as they occur *in situ* may be a required step in the learning process for the client.

How to Create a Thought Record

A Thought Record is a fundamental tool in Cbt. It is used to give clients practice in identifying the link between their emotions and the self-talk that is producing those emotions as they are happening. Frequently, it is a necessary step before clients can move on to challenging their contaminated self-talk and correcting counterproductive beliefs. Sampling self-talk from a variety of situations is also useful for the purpose of identifying themes and patterns in the client's thinking. Thematic self-talk makes it easier to extract intermediate beliefs.

Although it may not be immediately apparent to clients, practicing self-awareness is an action step. Clients are often eager to *do* something to make a change, but before experimenting with new behaviors or new ways of thinking, self-observation and reflection may be needed. In fact, such an undertaking is called an *Observation Experiment* in the Challenge-for-Action phase of the FsCF (Chapter 9). Suggesting that the client construct a Thought Record moves the conversation from Challenge-for-Thought to Challenge-for-Action.

In Cbt, there are several different types of Thought Records, but they are all designed to do one thing: identify *hot cognitions*. Hot cognitions are the automatic thoughts (self-talk) that arise during a triggering event and produce a change in emotion (Beck, 1995). Creating a Thought Record is a simple process. It is merely a matter of providing the client with a few basic guidelines:

1. **Be aware of the unwanted emotion at the exact moment it is felt and note the circumstances surrounding it.** This is when the emotion is first felt in the body (e.g., a sinking feeling when the manager gives a disapproving look). What is the feeling? What is the situation or event that triggered it? Sometimes this must be done upon reflection until the client becomes more skilled at making the association between the event and the emotion in real time. Occasionally, there seems to be no apparent triggering event; the feeling appears out of nowhere. This might occur, for instance, when the client is just sitting around thinking. In this instance, the triggering event is the ruminations of the client that led to the feeling.

2. **Label the feeling.** Was it anxiety, anger, depression, sadness, guilt? Whatever the feeling, express it as a primary feeling and not a sentence, e.g., "depressed" versus "I felt down because when my manager looked at me that way I knew that I had done something wrong." Sentences mix thoughts and feelings together. Thought Records require that self-talk be separated from the emotion generated by it. Keep in mind that the client may feel more than one emotion. If so, insist that they label each one.

3. **Rate the strength of the emotion using scaling.** Rating the strength of the emotion teaches that feelings are not just turned off or on, but that they appear with different degrees of intensity (Cbt practitioners typically use a scale from 0% to 100%). Additionally, using scaling will allow the person to notice when the intensity of a feeling is lessened by the substitution of alternative self-talk.

4. **Identify the self-talk that is generating the feeling.** We all have an ongoing stream of self-talk that occurs throughout the day, but not all of it is linked to the feelings we want to change. The aim of the Thought Record is to isolate the self-talk (hot cognitions) most closely associated with negative feelings and the behavior they produce.

5. **Write down the information you have collected in steps 1, 2, 3, and 4 for each activating event.** It is the hope that the clients will have several events recorded in their Thought Record prior to their next coaching session because cognitive themes and patterns will become more apparent.

The advantages of Thought Records are summarized nicely by Greenberger and Padesky (1995) in their book *Mind Over Mood: Change How You Feel by Changing the Way You Think*:

> There are two advantages to completing Thought Records regularly. First, a Thought Record can help you broaden your perspective on troubling situations so that you react in ways that are consistent with the big picture rather than a narrow and possibly distorted view. Second, Thought Records actually help you learn to think automatically in more flexible ways. After completing 20 to 50 Thought Records, many people report that they begin to think alternative or balanced thoughts in distressing situations without writing out a Thought Record. When you reach this point, you will experience fewer and fewer situations as truly distressing, and you can spend your energy on solving what problems remain and on enjoying yourself in more situations.
>
> (p. 108)

The coach, armed with information from the Thought Records, will be able to help clients think about and evaluate contaminated self-talk. When contaminated self-talk takes over, it causes clients to neglect information that does not fit with what they are telling themselves. In a way, it acts as a filter that excludes "friendly facts." If the veracity of the contaminated self-talk can be tested by the integrating Adult ego state, a change in perspective often occurs, which frees up coping and problem-solving skills. At any rate, once clients are cognizant of the self-talk that produces their unwanted feelings and behavior, the coach can help them design *thought experiments* as part of Challenge-for-Action. These experiments will test alternative ways of thinking about the triggering event, situation, or condition by substituting self-talk from the integrating Adult ego state to help clients achieve their emotional and behavioral management goals.

Chapter Summary

Whether it is by helping clients increase their professional competence, think through decisions, work through problem situations, or find meaning and personal satisfaction, coaching facilitates the goal attainment of clients. Frequently, this involves helping clients change their emotional and behavioral responses to situations. Cognitive coaching is a means to that end. Challenging the thinking of clients as a precursor to facilitating a change in feelings or behavior resides in the Challenge-for-Thought quadrant of the Foursquare Coaching Framework.

Feelings are a physiological response to a mental stimulus. The mental stimulus is, of course, our self-talk (thoughts) about a situation or an event. We feel anxious, depressed, angry, afraid, happy, exhilarated, helpless, or sad because of the things we say to ourselves and then act or behave in response to our feelings. Our internal conversations are affected by the interaction of the Parent, Adult, and Child ego states. When the Parent and Child interact without being mediated by the integrating Adult, the internal dialogue frequently becomes contaminated and produces self-talk that is exaggerated, overgeneralized, and absolute.

During Challenge-for-Thought, coaches help clients become aware of and correct any contaminated self-talk (thinking) and counterproductive beliefs standing in the way of goal attainment. This task is accomplished by eliciting the self-talk linked to undesirable feelings and behavior. Contaminated self-talk is reflexive, and most clients need help in bringing it to the surface. The coach can help by listening for contaminated self-talk in the client's Surface Structure language, and then educating the client about the thought-feeling connection. Additionally, when your client's self-talk produces unwanted emotions and behavior, it is a clear signal that it is worth examining. There are several ways of eliciting self-talk during the coaching session, and these are described in this chapter. Finally, there are times when a more structured approach to identifying contaminated self-talk is needed. For this, creating a Thought Record as part of an observational experiment stemming from Challenge-for-Action is very useful. Once identified, the next step in the cognitive coaching process is to change the contaminated self-talk and counterproductive beliefs that interfere with goal attainment.

The ICF competencies (ICF Core Competencies—International Coach Federation, n.d.) addressed by the content of this chapter are:

- **Active Listening**
  - Hears the client's concerns, goals, values, and beliefs about what is and is not possible.
- **Powerful Questioning**
  - Asks questions that reflect active listening and an understanding of the client's perspective.
  - Asks questions that evoke discovery, insight, commitment, or action (e.g., those that challenge the client's assumptions).
  - Asks open-ended questions that create greater clarity, possibility, or new learning.
- **Creating Awareness**
  - Invokes inquiry for greater understanding, awareness, and clarity.
  - Identifies for the client his/her underlying concerns; typical and fixed ways of perceiving himself/herself and the world; differences between the facts and the interpretation; and disparities between thoughts, feelings, and action.
  - Helps clients to discover for themselves the new thoughts, beliefs, perceptions, emotions, moods, etc., that strengthen their ability to take action and achieve what is important to them.
  - Communicates broader perspectives to clients and inspires commitment to shift their viewpoints and find new possibilities for action.
  - Helps clients to see the different, interrelated factors that affect them and their behaviors (e.g., thoughts, emotions, body, and background).
  - Expresses insights to clients in ways that are useful and meaningful for the client.
  - Identifies major strengths vs. major areas for learning and growth, and what is most important to address during coaching.

CHAPTER 7

Challenge-for-Thought

Changing Contaminated Self-Talk and Counterproductive Beliefs

It usually does not occur to clients to question the validity of their thoughts. As Beck (1976) points out, people tend to regard their thoughts—and the ideas they represent—as though they were a miniature version of the outside world. In doing so, they attach the same truth, accuracy, and validity to those thoughts as they do to objective reality. From a Transactional Analysis (TA) perspective, that is what transpires when the Parent and Child ego states become contaminated. Detours of logic and arbitrary inferences emanating from these ego states have the same truth value as the thoughts and beliefs that have been updated and reality-tested by the integrating Adult. Thus, the core strategy for changing contaminated self-talk and counterproductive beliefs in clients is to re-engage the Adult ego state in separating fantasy from facts. This process is called *distancing* in the Cbt community. "Distancing involves being able to make the distinction between 'I believe' (an opinion that is subject to validation) and 'I know' (an 'irrefutable' fact)" (Beck, 1976, p. 243).

Patterns of Contaminated Self-Talk

Coaching is a form of transformative learning. One feature that makes transformative learning applicable to coaching is that critical self-reflection is a part of the growth process. Critical self-reflection promotes awareness, and there is no doubt that awareness and change go together. In fact, it has been said that awareness is 80% of change, and so helping clients label mistakes in their self-talk by understanding the distorted pattern it fits can be all that is needed to promote a positive change in their self-talk.

Contaminated self-talk can be classified according to their particular biases or distortions (Leahy, 2003). Beck (1976) noted several patterns of "irrational ideation" such as personalization, polarized thinking, catastrophizing, and overgeneralization. Burns (1980) added mental filters, disqualifying the positive, jumping to conclusions (mind reading and fortune telling), emotional reasoning, should statements, and labeling and mislabeling to the list of patterns he named *cognitive distortions*. Pucci (2006) expanded the list even further to twenty-six patterns. Bandler and Grinder, in their book *The Structure of Magic* (1975), identified classes of Surface Structures indicating impoverished models-of-the-world that echo the patterns identified by cognitive therapists. Rather than presenting an exhaustive list, the cognitive distortions discussed in this chapter are accepted as being the most common and are nicely defined by Judith Beck (1995), David Burns (1999), and Aldo Pucci (2008). These distortions are products of the contaminated Parent and Child ego states. The self-talk generated by these thinking patterns typically produces negative feelings that usually result in counterproductive behavior.

Thirteen Cognitive Distortions

1. **All-or-Nothing Thinking** (also called black-and-white, polarized, or dichotomous thinking). The client views life in only two categories instead of on a continuum. Things are black or white, good or bad, perfect or a failure, wonderful or horrible. *There is no middle ground.* The hallmark of this distortion is an insistence on dichotomous thinking when confronted with troubling situations. This thinking pattern creates a world with no nuance or shades of gray; reactions to events swing from one extreme to another. This distortion is typical of both the contaminated Parent and Child ego states.

> **Client:** Either my presentation is perfect, or I'm not going to do it at all. If I can't make everybody happy, then I have failed.

2. **Victimization** (also called blaming or external control fallacy). Blaming is when clients ascribe to other people or circumstances the cause for their plight or feelings, e.g., "My boss made me angry." In the process they overlook their contribution to the situation and ignore what is under their control. It is the opposite of overpersonalization where the client blames him- or herself inappropriately. In this case, clients avoid taking responsibility for their contribution to their predicament, leaving themselves helpless to do anything about it. This distortion is typical of the contaminated Child ego state.

> **Client:** I can't help it if the quality of my work is poor; my boss demanded that I work overtime, and it stressed me out.

3. **Catastrophizing.** The client predicts the future negatively without considering other, more likely outcomes. In this way, it is similar to fortune telling. However, catastrophizing differs from fortune telling in that, when clients catastrophize, they start with a present situation, anticipate the worst possible outcome, and then engage in a spiral thinking process that produces self-talk containing increasingly negative "what if" and "if-then" statements. In a nutshell, the client is making a catastrophe out of a present situation by giving it an adverse spin based on nothing more than negative projections. This cognitive distortion leads to unnecessary worrying about the future and is typical of the contaminated Child ego state.

> **Client:** What if I don't do well in this presentation; I could lose the account. If I can't keep my accounts, then management will lose their confidence in me. Then what will happen if there's another layoff? I could lose my job. . . . What if I lose my job? Then . . .

4. **Emotional Reasoning.** Emotional reasoning is allowing feelings about an event to override a rational evaluation of that event. Clients assume that because they feel a certain way, that is the way things really are. For example, if the client *feels* guilty, then he or she must have done something wrong. It is the client's feelings that guide their interpretation of a situation. The problem with emotional reasoning is that emotions, by themselves, have no validity; they are byproducts of thoughts and images. Believing that emotion tells the truth is like believing that if it's on the Internet, it must be true. This distortion is typical of the contaminated Child ego state.

> **Client:** I know I get things done, but I still feel like a failure so it doesn't really matter.

5. **Fortune Telling.** Clients believe they know what is going to happen in the future without any facts to back it up. In essence, fortune telling causes clients to render negative assumptions about the future and then make decisions or take actions based on those assumptions. The result is that it stops clients from doing something even before they can start. If clients look to the future and take their fortune as fact, they will strike out in their minds before even getting to the plate. This distortion is typical of the Child ego state.

> **Client:** There's no point in applying for the position; I won't get it anyway.

6. **Global Labeling**. Clients put a fixed overall label on themselves or other people without considering that the evidence might point to a different conclusion, e.g., "The person who refused to help me is a jerk." Labeling makes the clients' views of themselves and others stereotypical and one dimensional. While the label may have a grain of truth, it is highly colored and emotionally loaded. Labeling is a type of polarized thinking that only references the negative traits and characteristics of oneself or other people. This distortion is typical of the contaminated Parent ego state.

Client: I'm incompetent. He's overbearing.

7. **Magnification**. Clients blow things out of proportion and, in the process, make a mountain out of a molehill. Magnification has been described as looking at problems, mistakes, and weaknesses through binoculars, but when examining contradictions, the binoculars are turned around, so the client sees contradictory evidence as smaller than it actually is. This process can easily lead to catastrophizing. This distortion is typical of the contaminated Child ego state.

Client: I really mishandled my conversation with the CEO. I couldn't say anything right [magnification]. It was really bad, and it will affect my ability to get promoted in the future [fortune telling].

8. **Mental Filter** (also called selective perception). The client pays undue attention to one aspect of a task or situation such that he or she cannot see anything else. It is a form of tunnel vision—a single detail is picked out, and the client's interpretation of the whole event or situation is colored by this detail. Mental filters are also involved when clients only perceive or acknowledge information that reinforces a preexisting attitude or belief, discarding information to the contrary. This distortion is typical of both the contaminated Parent and Child ego states.

Client: I received one low rating on my performance evaluation [ignoring the high ratings that are also there]. I'm doing a lousy job.

9.   **Mind Reading.** Clients believe they know what people are thinking while failing to consider other, more likely possibilities. Mind reading also includes making assumptions about the intentions and motivations of others. These assumptions are born of intuition, hunches, vague misgivings, or one or two past experiences; nevertheless, they are taken as fact. This distortion is typical of both the contaminated Parent and Child ego states.

> **Client:** He believes that I don't know the first thing about this project. He's acting that way because he's jealous of my success.

10.   **Overgeneralizing.** To overgeneralize is to exaggerate unintentionally. The client makes a sweeping negative conclusion that goes far beyond the current situation. General conclusions are reached based on a single incident or piece of evidence. Overgeneralizations are often couched in the form of absolute statements, "*Nobody* cares what I have to say . . . I'll *never* be able to trust anyone again . . . I could *never* get a better job." The most commonly used words when clients overgeneralize are *always* and *never*. However, other cue words that indicate overgeneralizing are *all*, *every*, *none*, *everybody*, and *nobody*. This distortion is typical of both the contaminated Parent and Child ego states.

> **Client:** When I go to these social events, I can never interact comfortably with the people who are there. Everybody is always trying to be something they're not.

11.   **Overpersonalizing.** Automatically accepting blame when something bad occurs even though the client has little or nothing to do with the cause of the negative event. In other words, it is the tendency for the client to relate everything to himself and what he did wrong. "If I had not done . . . then . . . [the negative event or reaction from others would not have occurred]." The client believes everything is his fault without considering more plausible explanations for what happened. This distortion is typical of the contaminated Child ego state.

> **Client:** My teammates were rather curt today. I wonder what I did wrong.

12. **Irrational Shoulds**. Clients have a precise, fixed idea of how they or others should behave and overestimate how bad it is when their expectations are not met. Underlying irrational shoulds are a set of rules about how the client and other people *should* act, and how the world *must* work. The rules are rigid and indisputable. As a result, the person is often in the position of judging and finding fault. Cue words for this distortion include imperatives, such as *should, ought*, or *must*. This distortion is typical of the contaminated Parent ego state.

> **Client**: I should feel confident in every situation. I should always be under control. They shouldn't be going around me.

13. **Irrational Definitions**. The client has an unrealistic and rigid personal definition of some concept, e.g., "John didn't always keep me informed about the project; he's not trustworthy." In this case, the client's definition of trustworthiness apparently means "always being kept informed" with no exceptions. While being kept informed may be a legitimate part of the definition of trustworthiness, the exaggerated nature of the definition makes it unrealistic for use in the real world and, therefore, irrational. This distortion is typical of both the contaminated Parent and Child ego states.

> **Client**: I'm lazy if I don't complete my "to do" list every day.

Techniques for Challenging Contaminated Self-Talk

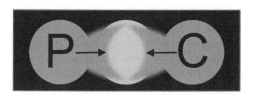

Contaminated self-talk will contain any number of cognitive distortions. In fact, it is common to hear more than one type of cognitive distortion present in the dialogue of your clients.

Contaminated Self-Talk with Distortions

Client: I'm angry that I have to report to Bill rather than Mike.
Coach: What are you thinking about that is causing you to feel angry?

Client: Bill doesn't even understand what we do [mind reading]. He always goes around me and talks to my people while I'm away [overgeneralizing]. He shouldn't be doing that. He should always come to me first if he has questions [irrational shoulds]. It's obvious he doesn't trust me [mind reading]. If he did he wouldn't go around me to get the answers to his questions [irrational definition]. I think I'm going to have to draw a line in the sand.

In this example, the contaminated Parent and Child ego states are in full control of the client's self-talk. The result is a highly agitated emotional state that drives the client's decision to "draw a line in the sand." Now, suppose the client decides to set a goal of changing her emotional reaction to the situation (i.e., "I'm not happy. I want to feel better about my situation now that I'm reporting to Bill and not Mike"). The client has stated a coaching goal that involves an *internal* change; an adjustment in how she *feels* about the situation. In other words, she wants to feel different about the situation than what she feels now.

Given the client's goal, the coach will help the client identify the self-talk that is producing her current negative emotional response. Following that, a variety of techniques can be used to enable the client to formulate a more adaptive response that is in line with her desired goal state. The techniques used to challenge contaminated self-talk and counterproductive beliefs are all designed to engage the integrating Adult ego state. These techniques range from simply increasing client awareness by labeling the contaminated P-C self-talk using the above distortion patterns to diligently contesting their validity and usefulness through Socratic inquiry.

1)   Name That Distortion

Teaching clients to identify specific distortions in their self-talk is one way to help them recognize patterns in their thinking that may be producing unwanted emotional and behavioral responses. Given that clients may come to coaching with the goal of feeling different about themselves or their situation, their path to goal achievement frequently involves monitoring and modifying their self-talk. Becoming aware of the mental habits that result in contaminated self-talk is an important first step in this change process. Furthermore, some clients like the intellectual challenge of labeling distortions in their thinking. Here is an example that illustrates how to employ this technique with a client who wants to improve his patience and demeanor when interacting with peers.

Name That Distortion

Coach: We've been talking about how people's emotional states and behavioral reactions are a result of their thoughts about a situation. In other words, how their self-talk causes them to feel and act the way they do. Right?

Client: (Nods his head.)

Coach: Okay, you said that during your interaction with Rajiv last week you let your emotions get the best of you, and we have identified some of your self-talk that contributed to your response, correct?

Client: Yes.

Coach: When your self-talk is not helpful, it is the result of some common thinking mistakes that everyone makes from time to time. It might be helpful if you can figure out what mistakes you made in your self-talk during your interaction with Rajiv. If you can do this, you'll be more aware of how to think differently the next time. Are you interested in trying this?

Client: Sure.

Coach: Here is a list of thirteen common thinking mistakes. Let's see if we can identify any that you made during that interaction. The first one is all-or-nothing thinking where you see things in very black and white terms, instead of shades of gray.

The coach and client continue down the list of cognitive distortions, and the client identifies two or three that had the biggest effect on his self-talk during his interaction with Rajiv. When clients are labeling their distortions, they are operating from their Adult ego state. Just becoming aware of their distorted thinking patterns can lead to self-correction because their Adult ego state is in charge. Whether or not you use "name that distortion" with your clients, it is important that you are able to label distorted thinking patterns as they occur in your clients' speech so that you can challenge them appropriately.

2)   Evaluate the Utility of the Self-Talk

Self-talk may represent thoughts that are entirely valid, or it may contain cognitive distortions *believed* to be valid by the client, but that are not! The coach is not in a position to judge what is or is not true in the client's thinking. The coach must keep in mind that automatic thoughts manifesting themselves as self-talk are rarely completely erroneous. Usually, they contain a "grain of truth"—and it is important to acknowledge what is true. It is through Socratic questioning that the coach and client, in concert, examine the self-talk and its underlying beliefs to test their *validity* and *utility*. This process is called *collaborative empiricism* by Beck (1995). During this process, it is the coach's role to 1) help clients determine the effect of their self-talk on their emotions and behavior and 2) explore the advantages and disadvantages of continuing the self-talk.

What Is the Effect of the Self-Talk?

Coach: Okay, you said that during your interaction with Rajiv last week you let your emotions get the best of you.

Client: That's right. He should have been more respectful to me during the meeting. After all, I'm in charge, even if he doesn't think so.

Coach: You may be right. Rajiv should have been more respectful in the meeting given your position, and maybe he doesn't think you are in charge—even though you are. My question to you is what happens when you're saying those things to yourself during the meeting?

Client: What do you mean?

Coach: You have those same kinds of thoughts running through your mind during the meeting, correct?

Client: Correct.

Coach: How do you feel when you have those thoughts?

Client: I'm angry. I shouldn't have to put up with that.

Coach: I understand. On a scale of 0 to 100%, how angry do you get?

Client: Probably around 80%.

Coach: When you're that angry what do you do?

Client: I let him have it.

Coach: How so?

Client: Well, I make sure that he, and everyone else, understands that I'm in charge and won't tolerate that from anyone.

Coach: Okay. So that is what happens when you have that conversation with yourself, right?

Client: Right.

Once the effect of the self-talk on the client's emotions and behavior has been determined, the client is in a position to think about the advantages and disadvantages of continuing the self-talk brought about by the situation. Clearly, if clients come to understand that the disadvantages of their situational self-talk outweigh the advantages, then they will be amenable to constructing alternative ways of thinking about the situation.

Advantages and Disadvantages of the Self-Talk

Client: Well, I make sure that he, and everyone else, understands that I'm in charge and won't tolerate that from anyone.

Coach: Okay. So that's what happens when you have that conversation with yourself, right?

Client: Right.

Coach: What's the advantages of telling yourself he should be more respectful, that you should not have to put up with that, and that he doesn't even appreciate the fact that that you are in charge during the meeting?

Client: Well, it makes it easy to tell him what I think?

Coach: And what's the disadvantage of saying those things to yourself over and over?

Client: The disadvantage?

Coach: Does saying those things help you keep your emotions under control? Does it help you get what you want from Rajiv? Does it enhance your reputation as a leader?

Client: I guess not.

Coach: So, is it fair to say that having that kind of conversation with yourself during the meeting has its disadvantages?

Client: Yeah, I guess so.

Coach: What could you say to yourself that might be more useful? In other words, what kind of dialogue could you have with yourself to avoid the disadvantages and actually help you manage your emotions?

Client: Well, I guess I could remind myself that, regardless of what he might think, I have the ultimate say. Therefore, I don't have to worry about what he is saying in the meeting.

Coach: Great. What else?

Client: Maybe it would be helpful if I calmed down a bit.

Coach: And what could you say to yourself to help you to calm down?

Client: That I don't have to let him push my buttons. I'm bigger than that. Also, that this is not a life or death situation. When someone disagrees, it's not a personal challenge.

In addition to listing the advantages and disadvantages of the situational self-talk, Leahy (2003) suggests asking the client to do a cost-benefit analysis. He recommends apportioning 100% between the advantages and disadvantages of the self-talk producing the negative emotions, i.e., "How would you split 100% between the advantages and disadvantages of what you are saying to yourself in this situation? Would it be an even 50/50, meaning the advantages and disadvantages are equal, or would it be skewed in one direction or another?" Alternatively, ask the client to do the same for self-talk that might produce a more positive or constructive emotional response, and then compare that analysis to the results of the original cost-benefit analysis. The point is to give the client the opportunity to convince him- or herself of the value of modifying his or her self-talk.

A similar approach is to ask the client to evaluate the *personal costs* of continuing to think the way he or she does when it is producing unwanted feelings and behavior. Here is an illustration using a different client example. The conversation is picked up mid-session.

What Is the Cost of the Self-Talk?

Coach: Let me see if I understand what you are saying. You're saying that telling yourself that you have to be perfect in every way works for you. Is that right?

Client: Right. If I didn't think this way, I would not be successful.

Coach: Okay. Obviously, you're entitled to believe anything you wish. So, if you are committed to this way of thinking, then I assume that you are willing to absorb the costs of your thinking.

Client: What do you mean?

Coach: I mean that you're willing to live with the anxiety, overwork, and self-criticism that you described earlier that is the byproduct this way of thinking.

Client: But I don't want to feel that way.

Coach: I know you don't like the costs, but if that's the way you need to think to be successful, there's no way of getting around the costs.

This approach might seem counter to the supportive role of the coach, but remember, to help clients, sometimes you have to make them uncomfortable. In this case, the coach is merely challenging the client to think about what she wants and the price she is willing to pay for it. This line of questioning is consistent with the *challenge* component in Challenge-for-Thought. The coach is ensuring that the client is clear about the cost of her thinking and is making a conscious choice about how she wants to be, going forward.

3)   *Engage the Adult Ego State*

Self-talk is the verbal manifestation of thoughts that arise out of the interpretation of one's experience. Self-talk can be rational (objectively valid) or irrational (contaminated) because it is disconnected from reality since the thinking stems from Parent and Child ego states *unsupervised* by the integrating Adult. Fortunately, the client's thinking can be submitted to reality checks by engaging the client's Adult ego state through a process of rational inquiry designed to assess the validity of the client's self-talk and the beliefs that are supporting it. When self-talk fits one or more of the distorted patterns described above, the goal is to introduce constructive self-doubt about its validity so that more adaptive thinking can be substituted in its place. There are several Cbt methods and techniques for accomplishing this.

A.   *Test for Accuracy (How True Are Their Statements?)*

Testing the accuracy of self-talk is akin to assessing the degree of truth about what clients are saying to themselves. Many of the distortions described above have the potential for being extremely inaccurate. If a client says, "I'm upset because my manager doesn't trust me. He doesn't even understand what we do. He always goes around me and talks to my people while I'm away" she is engaging in mind reading and overgeneralization (not to mention having an irrational definition). Testing these statements for accuracy is a straightforward process. It is a matter of asking clients to provide evidence for and against the thoughts they have expressed. You might say: "Now that you've become aware of what you are saying to yourself in that situation let's step back and take an objective look at any evidence that would support the validity of those thoughts. [After doing so, look at it from the other side.] Now, what is the evidence that would suggest there are inaccuracies in what you are thinking?"

Leahy (2003) points out that there are a few things to keep in mind when testing the evidence for and against your clients' self-talk.

1) Self-talk must be in the form of a *proposition*; that is, a statement of what the person believes is true before it can be tested (e.g., "My boss doesn't trust me.").
2) Avoid statements that refer to feelings because these are not thoughts that can be tested (e.g., "I'm really angry at my boss.").
3) Rhetorical statements cannot be tested (e.g., "Isn't it awful when a boss doesn't trust you?"), but the statement, "My boss doesn't trust me" is testable because it is a proposition.
4) "What if" questions are not clear statements about reality and cannot be tested (e.g., "What if I don't take this promotion, and I never get another opportunity?"). Beliefs stated as a question must be rearticulated as a statement prior to collecting and examining the evidence for and against the proposition (e.g., "If we were to change your question into a statement, then you believe that if you don't take this promotion, you will never get another opportunity. Correct?").

When evidence for or against their statements can be found, it makes it easy to determine whether their thinking is accurate or distorted. However, people exaggerate, and the evidence is not always clear. When this is the case, it is appropriate to ask the client to step back, think about what he or she is saying, and then ask the question, "How much do you believe that thought right now? (use the 0–100% scale)" Upon reflection, it is not uncommon for clients to revise their degree of belief to a lower percentage. After that, the coach can elicit reasons for the decrease, which prompts clients to argue against their distorted thoughts.

B. Challenge Their Reasoning (Does Logic Support the Conclusion?)

Just because clients can justify their self-talk does not mean their reasoning is solid, legitimate, or even relevant when looked at objectively. Challenging their thinking means subjecting their self-talk to cross-examination by the Adult ego state. If their reasoning is valid, it will withstand the challenge; if not, the rationality of the integrating Adult will help clients reexamine its legitimacy and substitute more situationally correct thinking. There are three techniques commonly used by Cbt practitioners for challenging the reasoning behind distorted thinking: the Defense Attorney, Rational Role-Play, and the Double-Standard Technique.

The Defense Attorney: This is a game of "Would this stand up in court?" Ask clients to imagine that they are presenting the reasoning for their self-talk to a jury as evidence for its validity. Now, play the defense attorney by asking questions that challenge the credibility of the client's case, or have the client play defense attorney by contesting the statements he or she has previously made. Would the jury accept the type of evidence the client is using to justify his or her thinking? Would the criteria the client is using apply to everyone (or are they singling him or her out)? Is there an alternative explanation for what the client is concluding? Here is an illustration of this technique applied to the earlier scenario in which the client is angry because of the change in her reporting relationship.

The Client as Defense Attorney

Client: I'm really angry that I have to report to Bill rather than Mike.

Coach: What are you thinking about that is causing you to feel angry?

Client: Bill doesn't trust me.

Coach: And you know this, how?

Client: He always goes around me and talks to my people while I'm away. He shouldn't be doing that. He should come to me if he has questions. If he trusted me, he wouldn't go around me to get the answers to his questions. I need to get over this anger if I have any chance of making this work.

Coach: Okay. Are you willing to try something for a minute?

Client: Sure.

Coach: Imagine that you are presenting what you just said to a jury as evidence of the case you are making against Bill. What would Bill's defense attorney say if you said, "Bill always goes around me and talks to my people while I am away"?

Client: He would probably challenge the fact that I said Bill always does this.

Coach: And you would answer . . . ?

Client: Well, he doesn't always talk to my people while I'm away, but he seems to do it a lot.

Coach: So it's not as extreme as you first stated. And what would the defense attorney say to your assertion that because he talks to your people directly—it means he doesn't trust you?

Client: He would probably ask me for different reasons Bill might be doing that.

Coach: Right. Can you see where we are going with this? If we kept this up, do you think the jury would convict Bill of not trusting you?

Client: No.

Coach: I would agree. So, what do you think would be another way of thinking about this situation that would be more realistic?

As you can tell, the purpose of this line of inquiry is to engage the Adult ego state in challenging the thinking that is leading to the client's strong emotional response. The goal is not to eliminate any emotional response on the part of the client to what she is experiencing, but ensuring that it is proportional to the realities of the situation. In this case, it may be totally legitimate for the client to feel frustrated by Bill's behavior, but that is a far cry from engaging in contaminated self-talk and distorted beliefs that spark feelings of anger.

Rational Role-Play: This technique is a variation of the Defense Attorney; it asks the client to argue against his thinking while the coach takes on the role of the client.

Rational Role-Play

Coach: Okay. Are you willing to try something for a minute?

Client: Sure.

Coach: Okay, I'm going to be you and say the very same things you have said during our discussion. You be me and try to counter what I'm saying. Does that make sense?

Client: Yep.

Coach: You know; Bill just doesn't trust me. He is always going around me and talking to my people when I'm away.

Client: He always talks to your people while you are away? I mean, all of the time?

Coach: Well, maybe not all of the time, but a lot.

Client: So he doesn't always go around you?

Coach: No, but he doesn't trust me.

Client: How does the fact that he talks to your people sometimes mean that he doesn't trust you?

Coach: Okay, let's stop there. What have you learned from this?

Client: Maybe I'm overreacting a bit.

Coach: Exactly. So what could you say to yourself about this situation that would be more reasonable?

With this technique, clients take on a different role to distance themselves from the distortions in their self-talk. By stepping outside of themselves, they are better able to look at the situation from their Adult ego state rather than their contaminated Parent or Child.

The Double-Standard Technique: This technique is particularly useful when the self-talk of clients includes an unfair and unwarranted critical evaluation of themselves. Many clients are reasonable and fair when considering other people but harsh and critical when thinking of themselves—particularly when the contaminated Parent ego state takes over. This technique examines the client's rationale for applying one standard to herself and a more lenient and tolerant standard to others.

Double-Standard

Coach: You said that you feel like a failure because you were in a team meeting and were caught off guard by your manager's request to comment on one of your projects. You said that you felt like you were unprepared and just stumbled your way. And then you said you kind of beat yourself up over it that night [use of summary]. Well, suppose you had a colleague who was also your friend and that you cared about say that he was a failure upon having a similar experience as you. Would you think he was a failure?

Client: No. I'd probably be very supportive of him.

Coach: What kind of supportive things would you say?

Client: I'd tell him that he needs to keep it in perspective. Just because he felt unprepared and stumbled his way through, it doesn't mean he was a failure. I'd tell him he is probably overreacting a little bit.

Coach: Do you hear the double standard you are applying to this situation? You're more critical of yourself than you are to your colleague and friend. What would happen if you held yourself to the same standards that you would use with others?

Client: I'd feel a lot better.

C.   *Alternative or Balanced Thinking*

Alternative or balanced thinking occurs when additional information shifts the client's interpretation of a situation such that it is viewed from the integrating Adult ego state as opposed to the contaminated Parent or Child; the goal of which is to find a more positive, or, at least, neutral view of the situation. This is also termed cognitive reframing. The result of this process is that the *hot thoughts* that cause the initial reaction are replaced by thoughts that are more consistent with the evidence and, therefore, emotionally neutral. Alternative thinking results in a more positive view of the situation, while balanced thinking, at the very least, produces a fair and balanced perspective that takes into account the evidence supporting and contradicting the client's original emotion-producing thoughts and beliefs.

Alternative or balanced thinking is made possible when a client has an expanded view of him- or herself, or of the triggering event. One source of information that has the potential to increase the client's perspective is what is learned from Thought Records—specifically, the self-talk (hot thoughts) being sparked by various situations. Greenberger and Padesky (1995) suggest a series of questions that challenge the validity of the client's self-talk, and also allow for perspective-taking about the situation itself. The answers to these questions may shift the client's interpretation of the situation, resulting in alternative or more balanced thinking. These questions are paraphrased below:

- Has the client had any experiences that show that his or her specific thoughts are not completely true all the time?

- If his or her best friend knew what he or she was thinking, what would that person say to the client? What evidence would the friend point out that would suggest the client's thoughts were not 100% true?
- When the client is not feeling the way he or she does, does he or she think about this type of situation differently? How?
- When he or she has felt this way in the past, what did he or she think about that helped him or her feel better?
- Has he or she been in this situation before? What happened? Is there anything different about this situation and previous ones? What has he or she learned from prior experiences that could help now?
- Are there any small things that contradict his or her thoughts that he or she might be discounting as not important?
- Five years from now, if the client looks back at this situation, will he or she look at it any differently?
- Are there any positives in the situation that the client is ignoring?

After thinking through their answers to these or similar questions, if the evidence does not support the validity of the client's self-talk, then have the client express (or write) an alternative view of the situation that reflects a more realistic interpretation. If the client cannot come up with a more affirmative view, then have him or her express (or write) a more *balanced* interpretation that takes into account evidence that both supports and contradicts his or her original thinking. Finally, using scaling, have the client rate his or her degree of belief in the new alternative or balanced viewpoint.

D. Thinking in Shades of Gray

It is a fact that thoughts that produce strong emotional responses are, by definition, intense. That is why they are called *hot cognitions*. Another method for scaling back the intensity of strong emotional responses produced by hot cognitions is to identify a less extreme version of the emotion and then ask the client what he or she could say differently to him- or herself to produce a lesser—but not zero—reaction. Anger, for example, exists on a scale that goes from irritation to rage (irritation-frustration-anger-rage). To change the self-talk associated with feelings at the high end of the scale, ask the client to define less intense versions of the emotion and then ask for the self-talk that would be consistent with that version of the emotion.

Thinking in Shades of Gray

Client: I'm really angry that I have to report to Bill rather than Mike.
Coach: What are you saying to yourself that causes you to feel angry?
Client: Bill doesn't trust me. He always goes around me and talks to my people while I'm away. He shouldn't be doing that. He should come to me if he has questions. If he trusted me, he wouldn't go around me to get the

answers to his questions. I need to get over this anger if I have any chance of making this situation work.

Coach: Okay, let me ask you a question. If anger was a ten on a scale from zero to ten, what would you be feeling if you were at a six or seven on that scale?

Client: I don't know, maybe irritation or frustration.

Coach: Good. So let's suppose you want to be irritated but not angry. What could you say to yourself that would be different from what you are saying to yourself now that causes you to feel angry?

Client: Gee, I guess I could say that I don't like it when he goes around me, but maybe he has a reason for doing it that I don't know about.

Coach: Great, what else?

Client: Just because he is talking to my people without me present doesn't necessarily mean he doesn't trust me. He does share a lot of information with me that, if he didn't trust me, he would probably keep to himself.

Coach: Now you're getting somewhere! Let's talk about how you can use this approach to modify your self-talk the next time this happens, and what you might want to do—or not do—when you feel irritated rather than angry. Okay?

Client: Okay.

Thinking in shades of gray, naming the distortion, evaluating the utility of the self-talk, and engaging the Adult ego state in testing for accuracy and reasoning are all techniques to be used in Challenge-for-Thought when modifying contaminated self-talk (automatic thoughts). The above examples are meant to demonstrate the use of these techniques, but during actual coaching sessions, the process of changing self-talk may be somewhat more complicated. Nevertheless, if you follow the principle of collaborative empiricism, with persistence and skill, you will no doubt be able to help clients challenge—and change—their contaminated self-talk and counterproductive beliefs. After all, if these techniques work in clinical settings, they most certainly will combat the distorted thinking displayed by coached clients. There is, however, one cognitive distortion that deserves special attention because it is so pervasive and can be very debilitating: *irrational shoulds*.

Irrational "Should" Statements

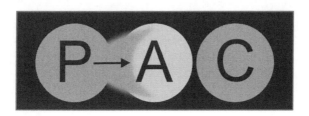

What does the word "irrational" mean? There are many synonyms for the word irrational, e.g., unreasonable, illogical, unjustifiable, absurd, ridiculous, ludicrous, silly, foolish, and senseless. Many of these words aptly describe the irrational "should" statements that stem from the contaminated Parent ego state. Irrational "should" statements represent internal rules, but unlike rules that have been reality-tested by the Adult ego state and applied appropriately to situations with a degree of flexibility, irrational "shoulds" are extreme, rigid, and blindly followed. Aaron Beck (1976) speaks of the power of these rules and the blindness people have to them when he writes that "a person has a program of rules according to which he deciphers and evaluates his experiences and regulates his behavior and that of others. These rules operate without the person's being aware of his rule-book" (p. 95). Irrational "should" statements are part of a rule-book filled with flawed beliefs and assumptions, and yet clients are unaware of its existence.

Inward-Pointed "Should" Statements

"Should" statements can be pointed in one of two directions: inward or outward. Should statements that are pointed inward (e.g., "I should/I have to/I need to/I must") are based on a formula, equation, or premise about how one is supposed to be, or how one is supposed to act, so as to live up to one's internal rule-book of shoulds. "Should" statements pointed inward do not refer to natural and logical cause and effect conditions like, "I should mail this letter today if I want it to get there by next week." Instead, they indicate the presence of an internal imperative that, when violated, leads to emotional distress in the form of guilt.

Guilt is an emotion that we experience when we are angry, irritated, or disappointed in ourselves. For example, a client that regrets not taking another person's feelings into account when he or she "should have" will feel guilty for violating his or her internal rule about how people are supposed to be treated. It would be reasonable to ask the question, "What's wrong with a rule that says one should take other people's feelings into account?" On the surface, this rule seems to be a good one; but irrational "should" statements often appear innocuous on the surface even though they can be very troublesome. Karen Horney (1950), in her classic book, *Neurosis and Human Growth*, wrote about the tyranny of irrational "shoulds." She points out that irrational "shoulds" are a set of inner dictates that are altogether too difficult and too rigid. She proposes three reasons for why inward-pointed "shoulds" are so troublesome.

First, there is a *disregard for feasibility*. The expectations imposed upon the individual by the requirements of these underlying rules are simply unrealistic. A client once said, "I should be able to finish every project I start." This illustrates Horney's (1950) point that "[m]any of these demands are of a kind that no human being could fulfill. They are plainly fantastic, although the person himself is not aware of it" (p. 66). The second reason that inward-pointed "shoulds" are problematic is that there is a *disregard for the conditions* under which the demands can be fulfilled. This was recently illustrated by a client when she said that she *should* be able to handle all the responsibilities of her new job while still performing her old job. Her former position had not yet been filled by someone else, and she was temporarily doing both jobs. This was an unrealistic expectation, but her "should" statement revealed that she was ignoring this reality. Naturally, this inevitably led to feelings of disappointment and discouragement (a topic of one of her coaching sessions). Finally, inward-pointed "shoulds" are troublesome because they *disregard the person's present state or abilities.* An excellent coach once confided in me that she was feeling guilty because she was not giving her clients her complete, undivided attention—even though she *should.* Upon further discussion, it was revealed that one of her friends had discovered that she had a glioblastoma—a very aggressive brain tumor. The coach was naturally very concerned and distracted during coaching sessions; however, this did not stop her from saying to herself, "I should be fully present for my clients" and feeling guilty when she was unable to do so.

Challenging Inward-Pointed "Should" Statements

Inward-pointed "shoulds" and their derivatives such as "have to/need to/must/ought to" are imperatives that pressure a person to be or act a certain way. *Pressure words* have the power to control, direct, or restrain the individual. Recovering the deletions related to pressure words can help shed light on underlying rules or beliefs that are untested by the Adult ego state.

- **Ask clients to explain what they think would happen if they did or didn't follow their linguistic directive.** For example, an "I shouldn't" statement can be challenged by asking, "What would happen if you did . . . ?" or an "I have to" statement can be challenged by asking, "What would happen if you didn't . . . ?"
- **Ask clients to explain what a violation of the rule** *means* **for them, or what it indicates** *about* **them.** Their answer can surface an underlying belief upon which the rule is built. This line of questioning is known as the *downward arrow technique* (Burns, 1999) or the *vertical descent procedure* (Leahy, 2003). The coach cycles through a series of increasingly penetrating inquiries about what it means to the client if his or her imperative is not obeyed until an underlying rule or belief surfaces that can be examined by the integrating Adult ego state.

Vertical Descent Procedure

Client: I'm feeling stuck right now. I'm also feeling really guilty. I'm happy with what I'm doing, but I shouldn't be so complacent. I have to challenge myself.

Coach: What would happen if you didn't challenge yourself?

Client: If I don't challenge myself, I'll never get ahead.

Coach: And by challenge you mean . . . ?

Client: I have to work harder than everyone else.

Coach: So if you don't work harder than everyone else, you'll never get ahead.

Client: That's right.
Coach: And if you don't get ahead, what does that say about you?
Client: It means I'm a failure.

In this short example, the client has the underlying belief, "If I don't get ahead, then I'm a failure." It is the intensity of this underlying belief that creates the strong emotion (i.e., guilt) when, in the perception of the client, she has violated the "should" that stems from this belief (i.e., when she hasn't worked as hard as she *should*). The coach can stop the vertical descent at the point when a counterproductive belief emerges that is significant enough to subject to rational analysis.

Underlying beliefs create the rules by which we live. These beliefs are often in the form of a conditional statement, i.e., "If I don't get ahead, then I'm a failure." Once a belief has power over an individual, it is natural for him or her to form a rule such as, "I should work harder than everyone else." A complete statement of this equation might look like this: "*If* I don't get ahead, *then* I'm a failure; *therefore*, I should work harder than everyone else." Sometimes it is easier for clients to see the distorted reasoning in the "if . . . then" portion of the equation than in the rule itself. In other words, a rational evaluation of the conditional belief, "If I don't get ahead, then I'm a failure" creates greater cognitive dissonance according to Beck (1995) than does the rule, "I should work harder than everyone else"—which, on the surface appears reasonable. Beck identifies three questions that can be used to help decide whether to challenge an underlying belief:

1) *What is the belief?*
2) *How strongly does the client believe it?*
3) *If strongly, how frequently or how deeply does it affect the client's personal or professional life?*

If the answers to these questions suggest that it would be helpful to challenge a counterproductive belief, Socratic questioning is used to engage the client's Adult ego state in testing the validity or usefulness of the belief—just as it is done with contaminated self-talk. In fact, the very same methods employed to challenge contaminated self-talk can be used to challenge counterproductive beliefs, i.e., assessing the utility of the belief (advantages, disadvantages, and cost) and questioning its logic (Defense Attorney, Rational Role-Play, and the Double-Standard Technique).

Outward-Pointed "Should" Statements

"Should" statements pointed outward are an insistence that the world (and other people) conform to one's personal standards. Without question, many rules exist because they are good for society, organizations, or people in general, but these rules become irrational when they are in the form of moralistic demands (Pucci, 2006). How do you know when an outward-pointed "should" statement may stem from a rule based on an irrational belief? The person feels angry when the world does not comply with his rule!

Remember the example of the client who said that her boss should talk to her before talking to her subordinates—and she was angry because he did not? She had a belief about the way bosses "should" behave with their direct reports, and when life did not align itself with her world-view, she became angry. For her, the world was not operating as it "should." When the world does not meet the imperatives imposed by clients, they get angry. When clients fall into this trap, they are taking one problem and creating two. Not only are they experiencing the discomfort of not getting what they want, but they have also added the experience of unpleasant, angry feelings—which stimulate even more anger-producing self-talk.

Challenging Outward-Pointed "Should" Statements

Challenging "should" statements does not mean that you are eliminating the rule or its underlying belief entirely. There is usually an element of truth embedded within any "should" statement; however, it is the extreme and inflexible nature of the rule that is limiting. Challenging outward-pointed "should" statements is often nothing more than removing the all-or-nothing thinking accompanying them.

- **Change "Shoulds" to "Preferences."** Thinking and speaking in terms of *preferences* rather than *shoulds* decreases the emotional intensity surrounding the rule and underlying belief. Note the difference in your emotional response to these two statements: "People should never be late to meetings!" versus "I would prefer that people not be late for meetings." It is easy to understand why people would have less of an emotional attachment to a preference than they would to a "should." This simple change in wording softens the demand people place upon the world, resulting in a concomitant decrease in the intensity of their emotional response.

Changing Shoulds to Preferences

Coach: I notice that you are really upset about this, even angry.

Client: Of course I am. What would you expect? This nonsense has been going on far too long, and it has to stop.

Coach: What would you like him to do instead?

Client: He should know that a good leader doesn't just go around his manager and talk to her subordinates without, at least, letting her know. He shouldn't use his position to circumvent appropriate lines of communication.

Coach: Ah, I see. This really pushes your buttons.

Client: Yes, it does. Why wouldn't it?

Coach: Okay, let me ask you a question. If you were to rate your anger on a scale from zero to ten, with ten being extremely angry, how would you rate your anger?

Client: I'd have to say it's a pretty high rating. I'd probably set it at an eight or nine.

Coach: Is it helpful to try and deal with this situation when you're so angry?

Client: No. Probably not.

Coach: Perhaps there's a way to express your displeasure with the situation while not becoming so upset.

Client: How?

Coach: What if you were to say to yourself that you would "prefer" that your boss talks to you before talking to your direct reports rather than thinking of it as something he "should" do. What would that do for you?

Client: Well, it seems less severe if I think of it that way.

Coach: If it seemed less severe, do you think it might cause you to be less angry?

Client: Probably.

Coach: So, if you think about it as something you would prefer, but not a "should," where would you rate your level of anger on that scale?

Client: Probably more at a five.

Coach: So, would it be fair to say that you would be more annoyed than angry?

Client: I think that would be accurate.

Coach: If you were merely annoyed, rather than angry, how would that help you?

Client: If I were annoyed, rather than angry, it might help me talk to him about the situation in a way that would allow him to understand my perspective. Maybe he will do things differently going forward.

Coach: Is this something you're willing to try?

Client: Sure, I think it will probably help.

- **Change the significance of the outcome.** As Pucci (2008) so aptly states, "Irrational, magical should statements insist that reality conform to one's desires, demands, or ideas of right and wrong, rather than our desires conforming to reality. However, reality does not conform to our mere desires or ideas of right and wrong" (p. 73). Simply put, our "shoulds" are frequently violated by the realities of life. That is not necessarily a problem; however, our *reaction* can be. The client who asserts that "people should never be late to a meeting" became extremely upset when it happened. His attitude would spill over into the meeting, and eventually his behavior became a problem (or to put it in coaching terms a "growth area"). This is only one of the many "shoulds" included in his internal rule-book. As a result, he lived in a good or bad, right or wrong world.

Rather than challenge the "shoulds" or rules that clients have, sometimes it is best to help them understand that there are "big shoulds" and "little shoulds" and a whole array of "in-between shoulds." Clients who have problems with outward-pointed "shoulds" generally treat all "shoulds" as if they are all terribly significant and have the same degree of impact on their lives. For example, the driver who overreacts because the car in front of him "should" be turning at a red light when it is not, is elevating the significance of that "should" out of proportion with what is warranted by the situation.

You can help clients maintain their perspective when their "shoulds" are violated by asking them to judge the length of time they will be affected by the situation. For example, in the case of the driver who is furious because the car in front is not turning right, the question could be asked, "How long will the fact that he is not turning affect you? Years? Months? Weeks? Days? Minutes? Seconds?" The rational answer is certainly no more than a few minutes—at most. So the question is whether the emotional response is commensurate with the significance of the event. In this case, the answer is obviously no. In fact, this type of question was posed to the client who became upset when people were late to meetings. Upon reflection, he came to be aware that, in the scheme of things, the impact was relatively insignificant, and he was able to scale back his emotional and behavioral reactions. Learning to place his "shoulds" on a continuum from big to little enabled him to respond more appropriately when the world did not meet his expectations.

Chapter Summary

This chapter introduced methods and tools to be used in Challenge-for-Thought when challenging contaminated self-talk and counterproductive beliefs interfering with goal attainment, or when the regulation of emotions and behavior is, in and of itself, the client's goal. Whether it is refuting patterns of distorted thinking present in their self-talk or uncovering and disputing counterproductive beliefs, the basic strategy is the same: Engage the integrating Adult ego state through the process of collaborative empiricism to reality-test the client's thinking. Socratic questioning guides the client in this reality-testing process. The thoughts and beliefs of clients not only affect their mood and behavior but also their motivation to take action in support of their goals. Strengthening their motivation to act is the focus of the Support-for-Action quadrant in the Foursquare Coaching Framework.

The ICF competencies (ICF Core Competencies—International Coach Federation, n.d.) addressed by the content of this chapter are:

- **Active Listening**
    - Hears the client's concerns, goals, values, and beliefs about what is and is not possible.
    - Encourages, accepts, explores, and reinforces the client's expression of feelings, concerns, beliefs, suggestions, etc.

- **Powerful Questioning**
    - Asks questions that reflect active listening and an understanding of the client's perspective.
    - Asks questions that evoke discovery, insight, commitment, or action (e.g., those that challenge the client's assumptions).
    - Asks open-ended questions that create greater clarity, possibility, or new learning.
- **Direct Communication**
    - Is clear, articulate, and direct in sharing and providing feedback.
- **Creating Awareness**
    - Invokes inquiry for greater understanding, awareness, and clarity.
    - Identifies for the client his/her underlying concerns; typical and fixed ways of perceiving himself/herself and the world; differences between the facts and the interpretation; and disparities between thoughts, feelings, and action.
    - Helps clients to discover for themselves the new thoughts, beliefs, perceptions, emotions, moods, etc., that strengthen their ability to take action and achieve what is important to them.
    - Communicates broader perspectives to clients and inspires commitment to shift their viewpoints and find new possibilities for action.
    - Helps clients to see the different, interrelated factors that affect them and their behaviors (e.g., thoughts, emotions, body, and background).
    - Expresses insights to clients in ways that are useful and meaningful for the client.
    - Identifies major strengths vs. major areas for learning and growth, and what is most important to address during coaching.
- **Designing Actions**
    - Challenges client's assumptions and perspectives to provoke new ideas and find new possibilities for action.

CHAPTER 8

Support-for-Action
Strengthening Motivation for Change

When clients come to coaching, it is assumed that there is a desire for change and that they are committed to making that change. However, as most coaches are aware, even when clients describe what they want and express commitment to it, it is not a given that they will take action, or if they do, that their efforts will continue. As Hettema et al. (2005) point out, "Anyone who aspires to help others change will quickly discover that people are often less than 'ready, willing, and able' to do so" (p. 92). Since there is no change without action and no action without motivation, the coaching process must address motivational support for action. Motivation is determined by the *importance* of the goal, the *confidence* people have in their ability to make it happen, and their *readiness* to go after it. It is in Support-for-Action that client motivation is tested, reinforced, and strengthened.

Importance: Do I Want to?

Motivation always precedes committed action. According to the expectancy-value model of motivation (Eccles, 1983; Fishbein & Ajzen, 1975; Wigfield, 2000), intrinsic motivation is, in part, a function of people's beliefs and values about the goal toward which they are working. For *willingness* (the motivational force) to be present, the goal must have *attainment value* (DeBacker & Nelson, 1999). To put it differently, it must be personally *important* so that there is some value to succeeding. Importance creates a bond or attachment to the goal that generates determination and persistence in its pursuit. Importance is a function of self-concordance. Self-concordance refers to the degree to which a goal is aligned with a client's enduring intrinsic or identified interests, motivations, and values. Goals that are self-concordant are more likely to be engaging and associated with a willingness to make greater effort to accomplish those goals.

Importance inflates the discrepancy between what one has and what one wants. Developing discrepancy was introduced in Chapter 5 as a first step in creating specificity for proximal goals, but discrepancy also has motivational value. William Glasser (1984), the founder of *Control Theory*, uses the analogy of a thermostat to explain how discrepancy generates motivation. Thermostats operate by sensing the difference between the set temperature (the temperature it "wants") and the air temperature in the room (what currently exists). When an out-of-range value is detected, a change process kicks in. He argues that people are similar; once they have attached *importance* to a goal, a discrepancy exists between the goal and current reality and there is greater motivation (*willingness* to put forth the effort) to reduce the difference.

Confidence: Can I Do It?

Sometimes clients want to pursue a goal because it is personally important but do not have faith in their ability to make it happen and, therefore, do not act. The expectancy-value model of motivation explains this phenomenon by hypothesizing that, in addition to goal attainment value, people must believe that success is possible and that there is a causal relationship between what they do and their success. In short, they must have *confidence* that they can succeed.

Confidence stems from self-efficacy: the conviction that one has the ability to execute a course of action to achieve valued outcomes (Bandura, 1982). Self-efficacy does not refer to actual abilities per se, but rather to the two-fold *belief* that one has the capability to undertake the needed actions for goal attainment and the requisite control or influence over those variables that can affect the outcome of one's efforts. Individuals with high self-efficacy are more likely to set goals that are challenging, respond with renewed efforts to setbacks, and to discover successful action strategies for goal accomplishment (Locke, 1996). Conversely, individuals who perceive themselves as less able or less in control of outcomes more easily succumb to external factors that may be considered roadblocks and tend to show lower goal commitment (Hollenbeck & Klein, 1987). Confidence, as a function of self-efficacy, varies depending on the goal and the circumstances surrounding the goal.

When a person has confidence in the fact that they are able to act and succeed, it affects four major psychological processes that influence success (Bandura, 1994): cognitive processes, motivational processes, affective processes, and selection processes.

1. Cognitive Processes

When people have confidence in their ability, they are able to visualize success scenarios that support their change efforts. When people lack such confidence, they are more likely to visualize failure and dwell on the many things that can go wrong. It is difficult to carry out the actions needed to achieve well-formed outcomes while fighting self-doubt.

2.   Motivational Processes

Intrinsic motivation is self-generated, and since people form beliefs about what they can or cannot do, their commitment to a planned course of action will be affected by the confidence they have in being able to carry out the plan and its associated activities. Confidence determines the goals one sets, how much effort is expended toward those goals, how long one perseveres in the face of difficulties, and one's resilience to failure.

3.   Affective Processes

Whether people perceive a situation as a "threat" or a "challenge" is determined by their belief in their ability to cope effectively with that situation. If people lack confidence in their ability to cope or succeed, then they will perceive the situation as threatening and experience the stress and anxiety that accompanies such an appraisal. On the other hand, confidence dispels anxiety and facilitates emotional responses that positively support one's efforts.

4.   Selection Processes

People avoid activities and situations they believe exceed their coping capabilities. The greater the belief a person has in their capabilities, the wider the range of options they will consider *selecting* in pursuit of their desired goals. Since success is achieved through choice-related processes, it makes sense that the more choices a person will consider, the greater the chances they have in achieving success. If a person refuses to experiment with different actions to gain what they want, their paths to accomplishment are limited. One of the main goals of any coaching process is to increase the choices a person perceives as available to them.

Readiness: Am I Ready to Take Action?

Importance and confidence are not enough to ensure action; action requires *readiness*. When clients are less than ready, it indicates that they are ambivalent about either the importance of what they want in relation to other things in their life or that they have doubts about their capability. Merriam-Webster's Online Dictionary defines ambivalence as "1: simultaneous and contradictory attitudes or feelings (as attraction and repulsion) toward an object, person, or action; 2a: continual fluctuation (as between one thing and its opposite) 2b: uncertainty as to which approach to follow." These definitions capture the mixed thoughts and feelings people often have about taking action. By way of illustration, Kimberly, a manager who has a problem with one of her direct reports, reveals during a coaching session her ambivalence about confronting the person.

> I have an issue with Chris, my IT manager. I spend what seems like much of my day dealing with the fallout of his interactions with clients. He just doesn't seem to understand that he is there to serve them, not just have them comply with his edicts. I've talked to him multiple times, to no avail.

I think it's time for me to write him up, but if I do that he will be difficult to deal with, and may even decide to move on—which I can't afford right now. Still, he can't keep making clients angry such that I have to intervene constantly.

Kimberly's ambivalence is analogous to standing on the edge of a cliff, but not making the leap. Some people stand on the edge of the cliff for days, others for weeks, and still others for months and years until their ambivalence is resolved.

The Ambivalence Appraisal Process

Cognitive appraisal has long been at the heart of many psychological theories. One of the first theorists to advance the idea of cognitive appraisal is Richard Lazarus, who, with his colleague Susan Folkman, proposed that stress and other emotional responses were the product of an automatic, often unconscious, intuitive appraisal of an individual's real-time experience and the meaning attached to it (Lazarus & Folkman, 1984). Building on this idea, clients who are considering whether to take the next step in pursuit of their change goals likewise undergo an appraisal process, most of which is also unconscious, dynamic, and intuitive. However, unlike the cognitive appraisal process described by Lazarus and Folkman, this appraisal process involves conflicting feelings about their readiness to take action.

Prochaska et al. (2005) address ambivalence in their transtheoretical model of change (TTM). They propose five stages of change through which people pass: precontemplation, contemplation, preparation, action, and maintenance. Ambivalence is viewed as a natural characteristic of the contemplation stage. In this stage, people are on a teeter-totter, weighing the pros and cons of moving forward until they can conclude that the investment of time and effort is justified given other demands or valued activities.

Just as a decision is a bridge between wishing and acting, resolving ambivalence is the bridge between the stated desire for change and the motivation to act in its pursuit.

Are the Costs and Possible Consequences Acceptable?

It is human nature to seek equity. Equity theory was first proposed several decades ago by John Stacy Adams (1965) as a variable in determining employee job satisfaction. According to Adams, equity is the perception that one is treated fairly relative to comparable others within the organization. As equity theory evolved, it became evident that perceptions of equity are not only evaluated through comparisons with others but are determined by one's internal standards as to what is the appropriate ratio of inputs (e.g., effort, time, education, experience) to outcomes: anything received in return that has tangible or psychological value (Porter et al., 2002). Simply put, equity exists when the benefits gained are equal to or greater than the costs of attaining those benefits. It is, therefore, reasonable to expect that when there is ambivalence, the question of equity has not been answered in the affirmative. The costs and possible consequences of pursuing one's goal may not match the importance of that goal, and until equity perception exists, there will be ambivalence and motivational readiness will suffer. To the extent that ambivalence exists, it is resolved during Support-for-Action. However, a word of caution is in order. Ambivalence exists for a reason; it may be a sign that importance and confidence are not where they need to be or that there are other priorities competing for the client's time and attention. Whatever the cause, ambivalence must be addressed and resolved to ensure sufficient readiness.

Motivational Interviewing

The motivational process is automatic, often unconscious, and very intuitive. Given the nature of this process, it raises the question, "How can you help your clients when their motivation is unclear, even to them?" The answer: Use the methods and techniques of Motivational Interviewing. Motivational Interviewing (MI) is an off-spring of client-centered psychotherapy. It was initially developed by William Miller (1983) from his experience in the treatment of problem drinkers. Moyers (2004) points out that the client-centered roots of MI have influenced it in two important ways: 1) the emphasis on Motivational Interviewing as a way of being with clients as opposed to a series of techniques and 2) the use of reflection as a core competency for provoking self-exploration in clients. She also describes the impact of another significant psychological model on the development and practice of MI: Bem's (1972) self-perception theory. As Moyers explains it:

> Bem's self-perception theory focused Miller's thinking on how a client's perception of him or herself could be shaped by language as it emerges through a social interaction. The current focus on client commitment language in MI and how such language can be recognized, reinforced, and elicited in order to influence behavior change owes an intellectual debt to Bem's work.
>
> (Moyers, 2004, p. 292)

Motivational Interviewing, then, can be described as a collaborative method of communication with particular attention to the language of change. Its purpose is to strengthen the client's motivation for and movement toward a specific goal by eliciting and exploring Change Talk: the client's own arguments for change.

Change Talk

Change Talk is client speech that favors movement in the direction of change (Miller & Rollnick, 2002). Conversely, *Sustain Talk* is client speech that favors the status quo. Since MI was originally developed to help clients overcome problem behavior, Change Talk has been traditionally directional, i.e., focused only on speech that strengthens motivation for behavioral change. Coaching clients differ somewhat from clinical clients in that they may have wants and outcomes distinct from personal change—as in Kimberley's example about wanting to confront her direct report. The good news is that Change Talk is effective in strengthening motivation regardless of the target of that motivation. For the purposes of the FsCF, and specifically Support-for-Action, Change Talk, then, is considered to be any client speech that increases importance, confidence, and readiness to act in pursuit of one's goals and desired outcomes.

The French mathematician, physicist, and religious philosopher Blaise Pascal (1623–1662) is credited as saying, "People are generally better persuaded by the reasons which *they* have themselves discovered than by those which have come into the mind of others." Change Talk is based upon this very idea: that people can talk themselves into making a change or taking action when they hear themselves acknowledge the value of what they want and express belief in their capabilities to achieve it (Rollnick et al., 2008). Since clients are more likely to do what they have genuinely spoken in favor of during their coaching session, encouraging clients to make the argument for their own readiness, willingness, and capability is a worthwhile and practical coaching strategy.

Types of Change Talk

"Change Talk consists of statements reflecting desire, perceived ability, need, readiness, reasons, or commitment to change" (Arkowitz & Miller, 2008, p. 8). These statements are generally reduced to five categories of Change Talk that strengthen importance, confidence, and readiness. Importance-related Change Talk consists of statements about the desire for change (wants and wishes), advantages of change (goal attainment value), and disadvantages of the status quo (need to change). Confidence-related Change Talk consists of affirmative statements about the ability to change (optimism and capability). Readiness-related Change Talk consists of statements of personal commitment (strong intention). While these categories are presented as discrete groupings, in truth there is overlap. Still, it is useful to have a structure for recognizing different types of Change Talk and differentiating it from other types of language occurring within the coaching session.

Desire for Change (Wants and Wishes)

Desire-for-change statements indicate that the client wants something different from what he or she is experiencing now. They signal that the client is, in some way, unhappy with the status quo. For ease of remembering, desire-for-change statements can be thought of as statements of "wants" and "wishes." These statements frequently surface in Support-for-Thought, often in response to the coach's inquiry about the client's agenda for the session (e.g., Coach: "What would you like to work on today?" Client: "*I want* to become more proactive in following through on things that I know need to get done."). A "want" or a "wish" is analogous to the tip of an iceberg; it reveals that there is more beneath the surface. To put it in the language of deletions (Chapter 4), this kind of statement contains unstated reasoning about what makes the "want" or "wish" important. In addition to requests for topics of discussion, desire-for-change statements are frequently inserted as part of the client's narrative about his or her present situation.

> **Client**: The other day I was in a team meeting, and my manager asked me to comment on one of the projects my team is working on. I was caught off guard because this wasn't on the agenda. I wasn't prepared and just stumbled through it. I felt embarrassed. This isn't the first time this sort of thing has happened. *I really wish* I was more assertive so that I could talk to him about this, but it's hard for me to bring it up because he has such a dominant personality. This is something I want to work on.

The exact wording of the stated desire may indicate the strength of its importance. Notice how the wording of the following statements suggest different intensities of desire: "*I definitely want* to become a better leader," "*I really wish* I could become a better leader," "*I'd like to* become a better leader," "*I mostly want to* become a better leader," "*I guess I'd like to* become a better leader." The more definite, strong, emphatic, and absolute the statement, the more it suggests stronger commitment and, therefore, more support for action.

Statements of *wants and wishes* provide you with a couple of choices as to where you might go in the Foursquare Coaching Framework. One choice is to develop discrepancy between the status quo and their stated desire as a step toward creating a well-formed outcome (Challenge-for-Thought). The second choice is to regard *wants and wishes* as Change Talk and move into Support-for-Action. The choice is up to you and whichever path you take will be acceptable, as long as you are conscious of which quadrant you are moving into and why.

Advantages of Change (Goal Attainment Value)

Client speech that articulates the good things to be gained from achieving the desired goal state strengthens importance. It also has the potential to increase readiness because enhancing goal attainment value can reduce ambivalence. When clients express how life might be better than it is, they experience a form of cognitive dissonance as they think about what is versus what could be. The dissonance tips the motivational scale toward change, which builds momentum for action. Examples of statements advocating the advantages of change are:

- "One thing that could come out of this is that I would have a lot more time to think strategically about what needs to be done in our department, rather than just firefighting problems."

- "I think that by improving my teaming skills, I will be seen more positively by my director, not just my colleagues."

Disadvantages of the Status Quo (Need to Change)

Statements about the disadvantages of the status quo express concern or discontent with one's present circumstances. By underscoring what is currently not working and why, discomfort mounts and pressure for change increases. Often, client statements of dissatisfaction with the status quo are the first type of Change Talk to emerge in a coaching conversation. Clients bring problem situations to their coaching sessions to figure out ways to resolve them. The mere statement of a problem, however, is not enough to motivate action because it does not paint a complete picture of the discomfort produced by the unwanted situation. The more that clients talk about their dissatisfaction with the status quo, the more attractive the alternative becomes. Examples of statements pointing out the disadvantages of the status quo are:

- "I can see that, in the long run, the pace that I'm working is going to do me in if I don't make a change."
- "I'm getting things accomplished, but not in a way that's going to make me a better leader."

Need-to-change statements are another type of Change Talk that signal dissatisfaction with the status quo. Need-to-change statements are general imperatives for change (i.e., "*I have to* . . ." "*I need to* . . ." "*I've got to* . . ."). When clients use this type of language in expressing their desire to change (in contrast to the use of these imperatives as a form of irrational "shoulds"), it is a powerful statement of dissatisfaction with the way things are. Need-to-change statements signal that there is clear recognition on the part of clients that aspects of their current situation are untenable. Exploring what is behind these statements induces clients into adding more specificity about the disadvantages of their current situation. By voicing aloud their displeasure, the push toward changes or action is bolstered.

> **Client**: I need to have a better work-life balance. [Expression of need]
> **Coach**: You need to have a better work-life balance because . . . ? [Inducing elaboration by recovering the unstated reasoning]
> **Client**: I can see that, in the long run, the pace that I'm working is going to do me in if I don't make a change. [States a disadvantage of the status quo]
> **Coach**: So, you see no upside in continuing at your current pace. In fact, you think that it will cause you even more problems down the road. [Complex reflection]

Statements about the disadvantages of the status quo and the advantages of change are two sides of the same coin. Both work hand in hand to heighten client awareness of the *importance* of their change goals while simultaneously reducing ambivalence, thereby increasing *readiness* to take action.

Ability to Change (Optimism)

Statements about the desire for change, the advantages of change, and the disadvantages of the status quo are a type of Change Talk that strengthens motivation by elevating importance, and to some degree, readiness. Equally significant is when clients speak optimistically about their capability to be successful in attaining what they want because it builds confidence. "These statements may include knowing what or how to make the change as well as beliefs that they can do it, if they make up their mind to do so" (Rosengren, 2009, p. 92). Confidence-related Change Talk includes (1) declarative affirmations about present ability; (2) references to past successes; and (3) statements of possibility.

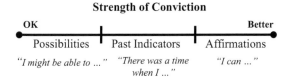

Declarative affirmations are easy to recognize because they are direct statements of self-efficacy. They are the strongest expressions of confidence and include statements such as:

- "I can be very assertive when I want to."
- "I'm certainly capable of creating a plan of action and sticking to it."

Past indicators of success inspire confidence because they are proof that clients have, at some point, demonstrated their capability. When people assert that they can do something now because they have done it before, it is obviously a sign of confidence.

- "This is something I know I can do because I had a similar situation in the past where I had to be very assertive, and I had no problem with it."
- "I was in a similar situation once where I was being bombarded with questions that I couldn't answer because I was new to my job, but I was able to deflect them without making the other person feel as if I were putting her off."

Statements of possibility are statements that suggest something is possible or likely to happen. Even though statements of possibility reflect confidence, they are not as strong as declarative affirmations or references to past successes. Inherent in a statement of possibility is an expression of optimism that change or action is conceivable.

- "I might be able to start delegating tasks that, even though I enjoy doing them, can be done by others who are just as capable."
- "I think I can start pulling back in some of the meetings, so I don't come across as a know-it-all by appearing as if I have all the answers."

Personal Commitment (Strong Intention)

Statements of personal commitment and strong intention include phrases such as "I will," "I am going to," and "I intend to." By making those types of declarations, clients are not only implying that they have the capability to act in pursuit of their desired outcomes, but they are *ready* to do so. Readiness-related Change Talk indicates that ambivalence was never an issue or, if it was, it has been resolved.

- "I'm going to manage my emotions so that my personal stress doesn't bounce all over the place."
- "I will be more assertive with my teammates in meetings so that I don't get stuck with all of the tasks that no one wants to do."

Magnifying and Reinforcing Change Talk

Change Talk strengthens motivation to act by either confirming or increasing the client's perception of importance, confidence, and readiness. Whether a person will continue to engage in Change Talk or veer away from it will depend on the coach's response to it. Responding to Change Talk is contingent, first, on the coach's ability to recognize it, and, second, on his or her ability to magnify and reinforce it.

Recognizing Change Talk is analogous to going on a treasure hunt. The treasure hunter is hyper-aware of anything that might be valuable and learns to recognize objects of worth that others may miss. Change Talk is like treasure to a coach. So, as with the treasure hunter, the coach learns to be watchful for valuable "nuggets" of Change Talk that can be used to strengthen motivation. When Change Talk surfaces, you have the option of moving directly to Support-for-Action to magnify and reinforce it or, alternatively, of making note of it and moving to Support-for-Action at a later point. Magnifying and reinforcing Change Talk employs four techniques: Elaboration, Affirmation, Reflection, and Summary. These techniques are easy to remember if you think of the phrase "Use your **EARS** when you hear Change Talk." The techniques of reflection, summary, and clarification (recovering deletions) were explained in Chapters 3 and 4, but not as to their use in magnifying and reinforcing Change Talk.

1) Elaboration

In Support-for-Thought (Chapter 4), the methodology of recovering deletions was introduced as a means to assist clients in restoring a fuller linguistic representation of their experience as a part of clarifying their narrative. Open-ended "what" and "how" questions constructed from the client's idiosyncratic language were used to recover unnamed references, unspecified actions, and unstated reasoning occurring in surface-level language. This same methodology is used in Support-for-Action to magnify and reinforce Change Talk. Recovering deletions force clients to *elaborate* on their change statements thereby amplifying their own arguments for change.

Elaboration

Client: I want to do more delegating of tasks.

Coach: How does that help you? [Recovering unstated reasoning: advantages of change]

Client: I would have a lot more time to think strategically about what needs to be done in our department, rather than just firefighting problems.

Coach: What else does it do for you? [Recovering unstated reasoning: advantages of change]

Client: I think it would help with my work-life balance.

Coach: How, specifically, would it help with your work-life balance? [Recovering unnamed references: advantages of change]

Client: I wouldn't be staying at work after hours because I would be focusing on what's important, and letting go of less important, time-consuming tasks.

Coach: What would be a concern for you if you don't do more delegating of tasks? [Direct inquiry: disadvantages of the status quo]

Client: I'm afraid that some of my good people will get frustrated because they're not getting a chance to show what they can do.

Coach: And that's a problem because? [Recovering unstated reasoning: disadvantages of the status quo]

Client: They might start looking for other opportunities.

2)   *Affirmation*

"Affirmations are statements of appreciation for the client and his or her strengths" (Rosengren, 2009, p. 62). Affirmation strengthens confidence by building client feelings of empowerment and self-efficacy. According to Rosengren, affirmations are strategically designed to anchor clients to the strengths and resources they have available for change and the pursuit of goals. Although they do not have a particular structure, affirmations are positively stated and usually take the form of clear and genuine words of approval for any Change Talk that signals confidence.

Affirmation

Client: I know this is something I can do because I'm pretty stubborn. Once I set my mind on something I stay with it.

Coach: A lot of people would view stubbornness as a weakness, but you're able to see the strength of it and how it can help you in this situation. [Affirming an attribute]

Client: I try to focus on the positive.

Coach: Well, you're certainly doing that now. [Affirming the client's behavior]

Client: Yeah, that's right. I hadn't thought of it that way.

Whether with animals or people, reinforcement works. Miller and Rollnick (2002) have the view that commenting positively on *any* type of Change Talk is beneficial. When you affirm Change Talk, two things happen. First, it produces a favorable reaction in people, making it more likely that they will make similar comments in the future. Second, it strengthens their belief in what they said, regardless of whether it boosts importance, confidence, or readiness. However, positively reinforcing Change Talk is analogous to adding seasoning to food; too little of it and the food will lack flavor, but too much of it spoils the taste. Therefore, affirming should be used judiciously and genuinely lest it lose its impact.

3) *Reflection*

Reflection is used throughout the Foursquare Coaching Framework, but for different purposes. When used in Support-for-Thought it is part of the Empathy Cycle as the coach expresses or shows felt awareness of what the client is experiencing. During Challenge-for-Thought and Challenge-for-Action, reflection confirms the accuracy and practicality of what clients want and what they will do, respectively. During Support-for-Action, reflection is used to put a spotlight on Change Talk. Reflecting Change Talk has two advantages: First, clients hear echoes of their expressions of importance, confidence, and readiness, which multiplies the effect of those expressions; and second, it encourages people to elaborate on the Change Talk itself. Reflection is much like a Swiss Army knife in that it has several uses all contained within a single tool.

In its most simplistic form, reflection is the process of restating what another person is saying, using your own words. The importance of this skill, however, demands that coaches become more expert in its use, particularly as it is used with Change Talk. Practitioners of Motivational Interviewing employ several types of reflection: simple reflection, complex reflection, amplified reflection, understated reflection, double-sided reflection, and metaphoric reflection (Rosengren, 2009).

Simple reflection is a restatement of the client's words in a way that is very close to, but not exactly, what was originally said. A simple reflection of the phrase "I know this is something I can do because I'm pretty stubborn. Once I set my mind on something I stay with it" would be "Knowing that you will stick with it makes you convinced that you can do it." This statement adds little to the client's message, but it does reinforce this confidence-related Change Talk and encourages elaboration.

Complex reflection goes beyond the client's words. It infers additional meaning from what the client has said. A complex reflection of the previous statement might be, "This goal is so important to you that you're not going to let anything stand in your way. And there's no problem with confidence because in your heart you know you can do it." Even though the client did not say this, it can be *inferred* from what was said. Complex reflections can embellish motivation by introducing elements from the client's message that he or she may not have considered or are there but unexpressed, e.g., the client's implication that the goal is so important he will allow nothing to get in his way. Complex reflection forces clients to reflect on the hidden message in their communication. Essentially, the difference between simple and complex reflections is the *depth* of the reflection.

Amplified reflection is an exaggeration or overstatement of what the client has said. It is useful in helping a person to back away from a statement that may be inaccurate, unreasonable, or extreme. Suppose a client says, "I should have known that what I tried wasn't going to work." An amplified reflection might be, "So, you should be able to tell the future." The coach uses an amplified reflection to press on the extreme element in the client's message in such a way as to cause the client to reflect on the accuracy of what he or she has said. Amplified reflection causes the client to reconsider a more accurate or appropriate view of the situation. If for some reason, the client does not reconsider, then the reflection may, indeed, be accurate.

Understated reflection is the opposite of amplified reflection; it involves emphasizing statements at or below the intensity with which they were originally expressed. It is a useful means of using the corrective aspect of reflections to your advantage. In other words, when a reflection is inaccurate, clients instinctively will respond with a correction. For example, if a client makes a statement of possibility like, "I might be able to find time to meet with my manager to discuss this," an understated reflection would be, "So, it's really not important enough to make the time." If the client reaffirms the importance of what he or she wants, the coach can point out the contradiction between the stated importance of the goal and the lukewarm commitment to action.

A *double-sided reflection* is used to draw attention to the client's ambivalence. It is a reflection that presents both sides of the client's conflicting thoughts or feelings. It is usually stated as follows, "On one hand you feel as if your plate is full right now, and on the other hand, you feel as if you should be more proactive in pursuing your career." When using a double-sided reflection, Rosengren (2009) recommends that you start with the statement that favors the status quo and end with the statement that favors the goal statement. He believes that this approach leads to a natural discussion about the importance of the goal, which can help resolve the ambivalence. It is also helpful to connect the two sides of the reflection with an *and*, instead of *but*. As Rosengren points out, "*But* tends to dismiss everything that precedes it, whereas *And* acknowledges both sides as having merit" (p. 37).

A *metaphoric reflection* is a form of complex reflection. It goes well beyond what the client has said by painting a *word picture* of the client's message. Referring again to a previous example, the client says, "I know this is something I can do because I'm pretty stubborn. Once I set my mind on something I stay with it." A metaphoric reflection might be, "So, you're like a dog with a bone, once you get a hold of something you don't let go" or "So, you're like one of those icebreakers that plow through the thick ice no matter what." Metaphoric reflections bring a visual element to the conversation that provides clients with a new way to understand and think about what they have said. In so doing, it magnifies Change Talk.

Reflections, regardless of type, are statements—not questions. Statements have a stronger impact than questions and do a better job of highlighting Change Talk. Some coaches find that an introductory phrase is helpful, e.g., "It seems that . . .", "So, you're wondering if . . .", or "If I understand you correctly. . . ." For the purposes of Support-for-Action, *selectively* reflect *only* those statements that you deem most influential in reinforcing or magnifying importance, confidence, or readiness.

4)   *Summary*

Summarizing was introduced in Chapter 3 for use in the Empathy Cycle as part of Support-for-Thought. When used in Support-for-Action, summary allows people to hear, yet again, their own Change Talk. It reinforces the importance of the material you have chosen to summarize and subtly encourages clients to elaborate on the Change Talk being summarized. Normally, summaries are delivered in "bullet-point" fashion and use as much of the client's exact language as you can recall. To ensure that you are accurate with your summary, you may conclude with a question such as "Does that sound right to you?", "Have I got this right?", or "Have I missed anything?" These questions provide clients with the opportunity to confirm, correct, or elaborate on what they have just heard.

Summarizing Change Talk

"Based on what you've said so far, let me see if I can capture your main points and you tell me if I'm correct. It sounds like it's important to you that you start delegating tasks for several reasons. First, it will give you more time to think strategically, instead of just firefighting. Second, it will help your work-life balance. Third, you're afraid that if you don't start delegating more often, your good people will seek other opportunities because they will not feel challenged. Not only do you believe that doing this is important, but you're also confident in your ability to do it because you've done it before. Have I got this right?"

Eliciting Change Talk—Direct Inquiry

As a treasure hunter looking for gold, you may unexpectedly find nuggets lying on the ground in full view. Otherwise, you will have to dig for them. By the same token, Change Talk may occur spontaneously in the narratives of clients, but if not, you will need to elicit it using direct inquiries. If you have explored the other quadrants in the FsCF and have not yet spent time in Support-for-Action, then eliciting Change Talk is more than appropriate; it is necessary. Direct inquiries to elicit Change Talk use the same rules as other powerful questions: They are open-ended "what" and "how" questions using the client's idiosyncratic language; however, they are restricted to the motivational determinates of importance, confidence, and readiness. For example, if confidence has not been addressed during the discussion, the coach might say: "You have said that overcoming procrastination is something that you want to do. What makes you confident that you can overcome this?" This question will evoke affirmative statements about the client's capability.

Scaling

Scaling, discussed in Chapter 5, is a very effective technique for directly evoking Change Talk. Use the simple zero-to-ten structure previously introduced to assess importance, confidence, and readiness directly.

- "On a scale from zero to ten, with ten being very important and zero being the opposite, how important is it for you to . . . ?"
- "On a scale from zero to ten, with ten being very confident and zero being the opposite, how confident are you that . . . ?"
- "On a scale from zero to ten, with ten being very ready and zero being the opposite, how ready are you to take action now?"

For there to be enough motivation to support action, estimates for all three scales must be at seven or above. A lower number signals that eliciting, reinforcing, and magnifying Change Talk for that motivational factor is something that needs to be done. In the example below, scaling is used to elicit change talk about goal attainment value (importance).

Scaling for Change Talk

Coach: You've mentioned that you want to get a handle on your emotions and stress, correct?

Client: Yes.

Coach: Okay, I have a question for you, on a scale of zero to ten, with ten being that handling your emotions and stress is the highest priority for you, and zero being the opposite, where on that scale are you now?

Client: I'm at least a six.

Coach: A six, that's pretty good. It seems that your emotions and stress are causing a lot of problems for it to be that high [Complex reflection]. What would be some of the specific advantages of getting your emotions and stress under control? [Importance: advantages of change]

Success Experiences

Success experiences provide opportunities to strengthen confidence if they are used to uncover strengths and resources that can be called upon to assist clients in their current efforts for goal attainment. Furthermore, merely remembering that one has been previously successful in similar endeavors increases self-efficacy.

Success Experiences

Coach: You've mentioned getting a handle on your emotions and stress, correct?

Client: Yes.

Coach: Have you ever experienced a time when you were able to get a handle on your emotions and stress in the way that you want to now—even in some small way?

Client: Actually, yes, now that I think about it.

Coach: What strengths or attributes helped you be successful in that situation that will help you now?

The use of success experiences will be discussed in more detail in Chapter 9 as a means to find out what has worked in the past that might be used as a basis for action experiments in the future.

Support-for-Thought, Challenge-for-Thought, and Support-for-Action

By focusing on a specific quadrant, it is easy to lose sight of the fact that, in practice, a coaching conversation moves rapidly from one quadrant to another in a natural flow. It is this very fluidity that makes the use of a schema (a knowledge structure that guides information processing) invaluable for tracking the conversation so that you have control over the process. Master-level coaches do this intuitively, but when you use the FsCF as your schema, the process becomes explicit and, therefore, facilitates both non-linear thinking and reflection-in-action. By way of illustration, the following example begins in Support-for-Thought and moves to Challenge-for-Thought. However, the conversation primarily alternates between Support-for-Action and Challenge-for-Thought before moving to Challenge-for-Action.

Navigating the Quadrants

James has been in the role of Operations Manager for six months. During that time, he has begun to realize that it is more difficult than he thought it would be. He is beginning to wonder if he has the personality for the job. His colleague, Alvaro, whom he has known for many years, has made the leap from supervising ten employees to being responsible for sixty employees in his role as Sales Manager. James attends several company meetings with Alvaro and notices how well he is adapting to the change in responsibility. James wonders what he is doing wrong and what Alvaro is doing right. He brings this up in his coaching session.

James: I've been watching my colleague Alvaro, and he seems to be making the transition to his new role easily, but things are not going as smoothly for me.

Coach: What's not going as smoothly for you?

Clarifying his Narrative

James: Let me give you an example. I attended the leadership team meeting the other day, and it was very contentious. Emotions ran high; people became very partisan when discussing their areas of responsibility and in my opinion, disingenuous. I felt uncomfortable; I don't handle those situations very well, but I need to be able to because I'm going to run into this a lot as Operations Manager.

Coach: What else is not going "as smoothly" as you would like?

Clarifying his Narrative

James: I think I internalize things too much.

Coach: In what way?

Clarifying his Narrative

James: If I'm in a conversation and the person complains about something that's happening, I feel responsible; in fact, I tend to take it personally. I've also noticed that when I offer my solution to a problem and people push back, I see it as some kind of slight. I know that I'm probably overreacting, but that's what happens. I guess, in some ways, I'm just too sensitive.

Coach: So what do you want to be different in the future?

Developing Discrepancy

James: I think the main thing is I want to stop overreacting.

Coach: If you weren't overreacting, what would you be doing instead?

Creating a Well-Formed Outcome

James: Good question. I'm not sure.

Coach: OK, let me ask you this: What's the downside of overreacting? When you overreact, what problems does it create for you?

Eliciting Change Talk

James: The biggest problem is that it causes people to want to be even less cooperative, but it's their cooperation I want. So I kind of create a vicious cycle; the more I push for them to cooperate, the more they resist, and then the more I push.

Coach: So what you're doing now is not working because you're pushing too hard, but when you don't get what you want you're just doing more of it instead of doing something different.

Reflecting Change Talk

James: Yeah, that's exactly what's going on.

Coach: So what does that tell you about what you want to be different in the future?

Developing Discrepancy

James: Now that I think about it, I guess what I want to be different is how I interact with people so that I can build better relationships. If I had those relationships, then I don't think I'd get the resistance I do now, or at least, I'd have a better chance of gaining some cooperation. I think that would smooth things out.

Coach: How specifically would that "smooth things out" in a way that helps you?

Elaborating Change Talk

James: I would have less conflict, and so I would feel less stress. I think that's part of the problem; I feel tense all of the time, and this might help me go about things in a more relaxed way.

Coach: What would people notice when you are going about things in a more relaxed way?

Creating a Well-Formed Outcome

James: I think they would see me giving up some things and not just trying to have everything my way. Also, I have a tendency to try and go directly from point A to point B without letting people know my reasoning. I just assume that it's obvious, and they'll agree. So they would hear more of the thinking behind what I'm requesting or the conclusions I've reached.

Coach: So, you would be tipping the scales in their direction more often, and they would feel like they're winning once in a while. Also, you're going to share a little more of your reasoning for your requests so that they have a better understanding of why you are making the request.

Summarizing Demonstrable Indicators of Success

James: Exactly! (A recognition reflex)

Coach: Do you have an opportunity coming up where you could experiment with doing these things in the near future?

Pushing for a "When and Where"

James: As a matter of fact, I do.

Commentary

This conversation won't make everything go smoothly for James, but it's a start. By thinking about how he is going to approach his conversations differently, and improve his relationships in the process, he is beginning to head in the right direction. Notice that while some time was spent in Support-for-Thought building a platform of understanding about his current situation, the conversation proceeded quickly to Challenge-for-Thought in an attempt to develop discrepancy and build a well-formed outcome. However, the first effort failed. James's initial response to the question "What do you want to be different in the future?" produced an Away-From answer ("I want to stop overreacting"), and so the coach attempted to generate a positive statement of what James wants ("What would you be doing instead of overreacting?"). The conversation stalled when James responded with "I'm not sure." Instead of trying to force the issue, the coach moved to Support-for-Action to elicit Change Talk about the disadvantages of the status quo ("What's the downside of overreacting? When you overreact what problems does it create?"). After reflecting James's answer to these questions, the coach was able to return to Challenge-for-Thought and develop discrepancy by asking James what he wants to be different in the future. Moreover, by going to Support-for-Action first, and asking about the problems his current behavior is creating, the coach is able to highlight the importance of change.

As the conversation progresses, there is recurring movement between Challenge-for-Thought and Support-for-Action. This is not uncommon because the establishment of a well-formed outcome naturally leads to a discussion of its goal attainment value (importance) and the client's confidence in his or her ability to achieve it. Finally, the indicators of success listed by James in response to the question "What would people notice when you are going about things in a more relaxed way?" can be used as a springboard for developing action experiments in Challenge-for-Action (Chapter 9). Using the Foursquare Coaching Framework as a map, the course of the conversation was as follows:

This simple example illustrates the fluid nature of the coaching conversation and how it can be tracked (in real time) using the FsCF as your guide. As you might expect, there are other paths that could have been followed in this conversation. For example, suppose James began the conversation with the statement "I would like to start building better relationships so that I can have more productive conversations with the people I interact with in my new role." The coach might respond with "How would those relationships be different from what you're experiencing now?" [Developing discrepancy]. In this instance, the conversation moves quickly to the Challenge-for-Thought quadrant where a well-formed outcome can be generated and then would move to other quadrants from there. The salient point is that you have a choice of many paths within the Framework. As long as you know where you are, you can navigate any course that will help your client experience success. You just have to be skillful enough to do it, and that begins with knowing the map.

Chapter Summary

There is no change without action, and there is no action without the motivation to act. The purpose of Support-for-Action is to strengthen the client's motivation to follow through with the actions needed to achieve what is wanted. Motivation does not exist by accident. It is the result of the beliefs and values clients hold about their goals, themselves, and their priorities. To be motivated, clients must believe that success is possible, that there is a relationship between what they do and the achievement of what they want, and that there is some value to succeeding. Additionally, ambivalence in the form of mixed thoughts and feelings about moving forward must be resolved so that they are ready to act—and act now! Simply stated, motivation is a function of importance, confidence, and readiness.

Change Talk can occur spontaneously at any point in the conversation and can be amplified by responding appropriately to it. However, before you can respond, you must recognize it. Change Talk can take different forms: statements of desire ("I want to . . ."), statements that trumpet the advantages of change (goal attainment value), expressions of frustration with the status quo (need to change), acknowledgement of capability ("I can . . ."), and verbalizations of intent ("I am ready . . ."). Upon hearing Change Talk, four techniques are used to magnify and reinforce importance, confidence, and readiness: Elaboration, Affirmation, Reflection, and Summary (**EARS**).

Change Talk emerges spontaneously from the narratives of clients, but not always. Sometimes you must make an effort to elicit Change Talk. One method of eliciting Change Talk is to ask for it using open-ended "what" or "how" questions that target the three motivational factors. A second method is to use scaling. Asking clients to specify a number on the scale that represents the degree of importance, confidence, and readiness allows you to discern the client's level of motivation by factor. Finally, eliciting past success experiences reassures clients that they have the capability to succeed.

The activities of Support-for-Action are intended to assist the coach in evaluating and strengthening the client's motivation to take action in support of goal attainment. Whether the goal is personal change or something different matters not. What matters is that clients are ready, willing, and able to act in pursuit of their desired future.

The ICF competencies (ICF Core Competencies—International Coach Federation, n.d.) addressed by the content of this chapter are:

- **Establishing Trust and Intimacy with the Client**
    - Provides ongoing support for and champions new behaviors and actions, including those involving risk taking and fear of failure.
- **Coaching Presence**
    - Is present and flexible during the coaching process, dancing in the moment.
- **Active Listening**
    - Hears the client's concerns, goals, values, and beliefs about what is and is not possible.
    - Summarizes, paraphrases, reiterates, and mirrors back what the client has said to ensure clarity and understanding.

- **Powerful Questioning**
  - Asks questions that reflect active listening and an understanding of the client's perspective.
  - Asks questions that evoke discovery, insight, commitment, or action (e.g., those that challenge the client's assumptions).
  - Asks open-ended questions that create greater clarity, possibility, or new learning.
  - Asks questions that move the client toward what he or she desires, not questions that ask for the client to justify or look backward.
- **Direct Communication**
  - Is clear, articulate and direct in sharing and providing feedback.
- **Creating Awareness**
  - Invokes inquiry for greater understanding, awareness, and clarity.
  - Identifies for the client his or her underlying concerns; typical and fixed ways of perceiving himself/herself and the world; differences between the facts and the interpretation; and disparities between thoughts, feelings, and action.
  - Helps clients to discover for themselves the new thoughts, beliefs, perceptions, emotions, moods, etc., that strengthen their ability to take action and achieve what is important to them.
  - Communicates broader perspectives to clients and inspires commitment to shift their viewpoints and find new possibilities for action.
  - Expresses insights to clients in ways that are useful and meaningful for the client.
  - Identifies major strengths vs. major areas for learning and growth, and what is most important to address during coaching.
  - Asks the client to distinguish between trivial and significant issues, situational vs. recurring behaviors, when detecting a separation between what is being stated and what is being done.

CHAPTER 9

Challenge-for-Action

Generating Movement

Helping too often entails too much talking and too little action.

—Gerald Egan

Goals without action are mere pipe dreams. Action does not take place within the coaching session, it takes place in the real world, but the coaching session *prepares* the client for action. According to the Transtheoretical Model (TTM) of change developed by James Prochaska and Carlo DiClemente (1983), once clients have moved out of the contemplation stage, they are ready and willing to take action in the immediate future. They are now asking the question, "What do I do?" in an attempt to identify small steps that will move them toward goal accomplishment. In TTM terminology, they are in the *preparation* for action stage:

> Preparation for action represents a decision-making stage of change. The client is literally gearing up for action. The gearing-up process is demonstrated by decisions actually being implemented to take constructive steps, make inquiries, check things, and incorporate a need to do something about one's life situation in the near future (e.g., within the next month).
>
> (Mozdzierz et al., 2014, p. 98)

The preparation stage is as far as the coaching process can take clients. The coaching process is analogous to helping clients make ready for a solo sailing cruise. Throughout the coaching process, the coach has helped the client specify the destination, eliminate internal roadblocks, ensure that the trip is worth the energy and effort, build his or her confidence, identify resources needed for success, and chart a course to his or her desired destination. Now, the client must get on the boat and sail off alone. The only difference is that even though the coach is not on the boat with the client, she can communicate with him, track his progress, and support him throughout his journey. The coach's continued support will help him adjust to unexpected weather conditions, mechanical failures, and constant course corrections. It will help him remain optimistic in the face of obstacles, see his progress when it may not be apparent from his view inside the boat, and learn from both success and failure.

Challenge-for-Action is all about the preparation for the journey—for action. The conversation that takes place in this quadrant is designed to answer four questions:

1. *What* do clients have to *do* to get what they want?
2. *How* are they going to go about it?
3. *When* and *where* are they going to start doing it?
4. What have they *learned* from their previous actions that will help them take new actions?

The Heuristic Process

"How do I create better relationships with my peers?" There is no one correct answer to this question. There are as many different action possibilities as there are viable answers. Determining the actions that will accomplish the goal embedded within this question requires a heuristic approach. The word *heuristic* is derived from the Greek word *heuriskein*, meaning to "find" or "discover." A heuristic method is one "which on the basis of experience or judgment seems likely to yield a good solution to a problem, but which cannot be guaranteed . . ." (Foulds, 1983, p. 929). In practice, a heuristic approach means to use a good guess, educated trial and error, and common sense in deciding how to proceed in reaching a change goal or solving a problem; but success is not assured because there is no prescription as to what to do. Feedback from action experiments is used to refine one's efforts until the desired results are achieved. Most of life's goals and problems require the heuristic approach because they contain too much ambiguity and uncertainty to yield to a schoolbook solution.

The heuristic approach is much like encountering dense fog on the way to a destination where you have never been. The fog makes it difficult to see what's ahead, and since you can't predict what's there (e.g., road construction, detours, etc.), you go forward based upon what you *can* see. As you progress, new stretches of the road become visible, and you modify your driving to fit the circumstances. Similarly, when clients take action by following the heuristic method, they choose their path forward based on their best guess (judgment) as to what to do. The results of their actions provide new data that informs their future choices. The heuristic approach provides the template for the methods and practices used in Challenge-for-Action.

Action Experiments

Actions derived from the heuristic approach are, in effect, experiments. Clients speculate on what to do and then test their ideas through action. Because success is not guaranteed, it reduces psychological risk if clients think of their actions as experiments rather than an action plan. As Neenan and Palmer (2012, p. 97) affirm, "Experiments are a very effective way of gathering information, testing hypotheses, re-evaluating previous conclusions, responding to 'I don't know.'" Reframing an action idea as an experiment rather than a step in an action plan reduces the pressure to be perfect the first time. It sends a "let's try this and see what happens" message, thereby reducing paralysis by analysis so that the person can start doing something instead of waiting to figure out a flawless approach. Action, not perfection, is the goal because, as Churchill said, "Perfection is the enemy of progress" (Humes, 1997).

Action Experiments

Coach: So, tell me, what do you want to be different from what you're currently experiencing?

Developing Discrepancy

Client: I want to get a better handle on my emotions and my stress level. My stress level bounces all over the place day to day.
Coach: How would you know if you had a better handle on your emotions and stress?

Creating a Well-Formed Outcome

Client: I would be enjoying the interaction with the people. I would be building a relationship with them, gaining their trust, maybe even using a sense of humor. It would be a dynamic interaction where they walked away feeling good, and I walked away feeling good. We would have made a nice connection, even if I couldn't answer all of their questions at that time, and I had to defer them to a meeting next week, or whatever. I would feel good. I would feel like a professional. I would feel as if I was giving it my best.
Coach: What might you *experiment* with that will help you begin handling your emotions and stress so that you achieve the kind of outcomes that you've just mentioned?

Challenge-for-Action

Three Types of Experiments

There are three types of experiments, or action steps, that put clients on the path to reaching their goals: informational experiments, cognition experiments, and behavioral experiments.

Informational Experiments

Informational experiments are actions clients can take without changing their thinking or behavior. These experiments gather information that will help clients decide what to do next. Information gathering is an important part of the preparation stage as described by the TTM model. In an attempt to answer the question, "What can I do?" clients may need to do some research. This can include self-reflection about different possibilities for action, finding out what strategies and resources are available to them by talking to others, as well as collecting data about their own thinking and behavior. Too often, clients skip this activity and move directly from contemplation to action, only to fall flat on their faces because they have not adequately thought about what they can do, researched the various alternatives available to them, or collected enough data about themselves to proceed in an enlightened way.

In Chapter 6, Thought Records were introduced as a method for clients to become aware of the self-talk (thinking) that is driving their feelings and behavior in certain situations. It was explained that before clients can change their thinking, they must become aware of their current self-talk. Thought Records are a form of information gathering. The client collects data by focusing his attention on what he is thinking or doing in a particular situation, with the intent that the information will help him design some cognitive or behavioral experiments in the future. Noticing something different can lead to trying something different.

Informational experiments are a worthwhile first step for several reasons. First, they are a low-risk action. They do not require clients to change their behavior or thinking, and yet clients will still feel a sense of progress toward their goals as they gain insight into themselves. Second, informational experiments can be a vital source of information. By engaging in self-reflection and observation, talking to others and discovering additional resources, clients may discover strategies for action they have not previously thought about. Although clients think they know what they want to try, imposing a period of information gathering may sharpen their perspective. Finally, informational experiments can forestall ill-considered actions. For some clients, their problem is not that they refuse to act, but that they act hastily, and possibly imprudently. This tendency may be unwittingly reinforced by coaches (particularly Level I and Level II) who feel the need to have their clients leave with an "action plan" other than gathering information for later decision making. A sense of urgency is important but beware false urgency (Kotter, 2008). False urgency may lead to taking action but going nowhere because it is action for its own sake. Informational experiments can fend off the impulsiveness that false urgency may inspire. Sometimes it is necessary to go slow, to go fast.

Cognitive Experiments

Cognitive experiments are conscious intellectual acts. Their purpose is to encourage clients to try out different ways of thinking and understanding that will facilitate goal attainment. Sometimes cognitive experiments are designed to open up new ways of perceiving situations, even though there is no inherent problem with the client's thinking. A good example is reframing (see also Chapter 7). Reframing is a form of cognitive restructuring that helps clients change the meaning of events. The meaning or "frame" that clients attach to their experience has a significant impact on how they respond to it. Suppose a client attempts a behavioral experiment such as a new way of interacting with his manager, but he does not get the response he expects. Reframing might help him maintain motivation by viewing the result of his efforts as feedback rather than failure, e.g., "Okay, that didn't work so what can I do differently the next time?"

Cognitive experiments are also used to eliminate mental roadblocks to success. Limiting assumptions, erroneous conclusions, and maladaptive self-talk can stand in the way of progress toward client goals, especially when those goals include a change in attitude or mood. This topic was the subject of Chapters 6 and 7. If you believe that your client's thinking is acting as a barrier to what he or she wants to achieve, then moving into Challenge-for-Thought to explore and adjust her thinking will eventually lead to cognitive experiments in Challenge-for-Action as a means of changing contaminated self-talk and counterproductive beliefs.

Behavioral Experiments

What is the answer to the following riddle? If five green frogs are sitting on a log, and four of them decide to jump off, how many frogs are left on the log? The answer: five. Deciding to do something is not doing it. Doing means behaving differently to achieve some end, but deciding what to do and how to do it is a necessary first step. There are several ways to use the coaching process to generate possibilities for behavioral experiments. In fact, possibilities for behavioral experiments commonly surface in quadrants other than Challenge-for-Action (e.g., when defining demonstrable indicators of success during Challenge-for-Thought). It is merely a matter of noticing when they occur and deciding whether to move directly to Challenge-for-Action or waiting until your work in other quadrants is finished.

1.   Recover Unspecified Actions

In Chapter 4 you were introduced to the technique of recovering deletions to obtain missing information in the Surface Structure language of clients. One of the deletions, unspecified actions, does not spell out the specific behavior associated with those actions. Suppose you ask your client, "What are you going to experiment doing over the next couple of weeks to take a small step toward your goal?" Your client answers with the statement, "I am going to use influence rather than authority to get things done." The word "influence" refers to unspecified actions. To recover those actions, you might ask "What are you going to *do*, specifically, to use influence rather than authority to get things done?" With this inquiry, you challenge the client to state the actions or behaviors with which she is going to experiment. Her answer can be followed up with questions such as, "How are you going to do this?" and "When are you going to start?" Clients are notorious for stating their proposed actions in the form of Surface Structure language with no behavioral specificity.

2.   Use Behavior Derived from a Well-Formed Outcome

In Challenge-for-Thought, well-formed outcomes are created. A well-formed outcome is:

> A positive statement of what is wanted, which includes demonstrable indicators of success, the attainment of which is under the control or direct influence of the individual seeking that outcome.

For the purposes of Challenge-for-Action, the important words in that definition are "demonstrable indicators of success." Demonstrable indicators of success are descriptions of what the client (or others) will see, hear, feel, or experience when his or her desired outcome becomes a reality. These descriptions commonly include actions that can be converted to behavioral experiments. To illustrate, a CEO of a large, non-profit organization received feedback that some of her leadership practices are causing problems for her staff, e.g., she focuses on details that other members of her team should be handling, and she sugar-coats issues—especially personnel problems—rather than confronting them when she thinks it might upset members of her team. As part of constructing a well-formed outcome, she listed the following indicator of success: "The team will notice that I am very direct, even when discussing uncomfortable subjects." "Being very direct" is an unspecified action that can be recovered with "what," "how," and "when" questions during Challenge-for-Action to create a behavioral experiment, e.g., "How are you going to be very direct with the team?", "What are you going to do, specifically, to be very direct with your team?", and "When are you going to start doing this?"

3.   Use Discrepancy to Generate Action Possibilities

During Challenge-for-Thought, the practice of developing discrepancy is used as a means to induce clients to think about their desired future. In the process of describing how they want things to be different, clients will commonly include behavior in that description. Of course, the descriptions will normally be expressed in Surface Structure language, and there will be much work to do to create behavioral experiments from those descriptions, but they do provide a starting point.

Using Discrepancy to Generate Action Possibilities

Coach: You mentioned that your life is pretty chaotic and that you are, to use your words, burning the candle at both ends.

Client: Yeah, I seem to be reacting to everyone and everything instead of being more intentional about what I'm doing.

Coach: If you were more intentional about what you are doing—in the way that you want to be—what would be different going forward from what it is now?

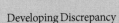

Developing Discrepancy

Client: Well, I think that I would be setting boundaries around what I will or will not do.

In this brief example, "setting boundaries" emerged as a behavioral difference. Now, the coach can recover the unspecified actions embedded in the Surface Structure statement, e.g., "What will you be doing specifically to set boundaries around what you will or will not do?" From there, the coach can nail down the specific behavioral experiments the client will undertake in the near future.

Another use of discrepancy is to ask clients a version of the question "What can you do differently from what you've been doing to move toward . . . [insert the client's desired outcome]?" Asking clients to answer the discrepancy question directs their attention to new actions with which they can experiment. Sometimes this means that they start doing something they have not been doing, and sometimes it means doing less of what they are doing now—or even stopping it altogether. Either way, inducing clients to think about doing something different to affect change is an effective action planning tactic.

4.   *Use Feedback from Previous Behavioral Experiments*

What if the secret to success is failure? The heuristic process is an educated trial and error approach to finding solutions or actions that will work. Progress depends on learning from one's experiences about what works, and especially from what doesn't. Once clients have undertaken a behavioral experiment, their next step depends on what they have learned from what they have tried. Ensuing coaching sessions may start in the Challenge-for-Action quadrant as the coach and client debrief the efficacy of their actions (bridging) and plan for future experiments.

During the debriefing, it is appropriate to ask the following questions:

- Did the client actually do what she said she was going to do?
- If not, what stopped her, and what does she need to do differently to follow through next time?
- If so, how did the actions work?
- Based on what happened, are there other things she might want to do more of, stop doing, or start doing?

If not following through on action experiments becomes a pattern for the client, spend more time in Support-for-Action to test for and, if appropriate, strengthen motivation.

5. Use Success Experiences to Discover What Worked Before

Success experiences are used in Support-for-Action to strengthen confidence. In Challenge-for-Action, they are a source of ideas for behavioral (and cognitive) experiments. Even though a solution-focused approach means looking to the future and finding solutions, it doesn't necessitate ignoring the past when it can be used as a springboard for action in the present. Most clients have previous experiences that, when reflected upon, will provide ideas for dealing with their current situation and achieving desired outcomes. Accessing people's past successes frequently produce insights that stir them to action because they can use what has worked for them before. However, to use the past as a resource, clients must draw upon experiences that mirror their present situation in some way.

> **Using a Success Experience to Generate Action Possibilities**
>
> **Coach**: Has there ever been a time when you've been in a similar situation where you've felt frustrated and been under this kind of pressure, but you were able to handle your emotions and stress in the way that you want to now?
>
> **Client**: (Laughs) Yeah, actually yes. Yeah, it's happened before.
>
> **Coach**: Can you give me a specific example of when you've been able to do that?
>
> **Client**: It would have been when I transitioned into a new role, probably about three years ago. There was a lot of new learning that I had to do.

I needed to absorb a great deal of new information, and then, of course, everyone was coming to me for answers before I was ready. I was stressed out about it and started doubting whether I was providing the right information. So yeah, I can recall having similar feelings.

Coach: And yet that turned out such that you felt successful handling your stress, correct?

Client: Yes, I felt good during that time. I was able to reach a balance.

Coach: What were you doing or thinking that helped you feel good and reach a balance?

Client: Actually, I haven't thought about it in a long time, but I would say to myself, "It's not just about me." That way I'm not just focused on my concerns and feelings; instead, I was able to put myself in the place of the other person. In fact, I remember putting myself in the place of one of the leaders I was trying to support. It shifted the focus away from me. Now that I'm saying this, I realize I'm too caught up in my own little world. So perhaps I can do what I did before, and shift my focus to things other than myself.

Coach: I think that's a great insight.

Client: Yeah, actually I think it will help a lot.

Coach: Is there anything else you did?

Client: It's another thing that I've forgotten while feeling so stressed, and that's to maintain my sense of humor. Sometimes you've got to let things go a little bit and strike a more pleasant and congenial conversation with someone. Does that make sense?

From this point in the conversation, the coach supported his client's ideas and reflected back to her the two things she came up with that might help her handle her emotions and stress currently. By accessing past learnings that could possibly apply to her present situation, the client has simultaneously identified potential action experiments.

When retrieving success stories, remember:

1. A success story can be a time when someone was even *somewhat* successful (e.g., "Can you think of a time when you were able to do this—even in some small way?")
2. Ask for details about the experience, i.e., what the client specifically did or thought that helped.
3. Use stories where the person actively did something to produce the successful outcome, as opposed to success being the result of external factors.
4. Compliment the client to reinforce his or her ideas.
5. Reflect or summarize useful solutions so that they stand out during the conversation.

6.   Help the client connect what he or she did or thought during the success experience to his or her current situation.

6.   *Offer Suggestions*

Many coaches believe it is inappropriate to offer suggestions. However, suggestions are nothing more than a form of information exchange. Coaches are not robots. They have personal and professional experience as well as the advantage of learning from the experiences of their clients. When delivered in a coach-like manner, suggestions can provide your client with valuable ideas and speed up the action formulation process.

What does a coach-like manner mean? First, it means that suggestions are only offered with client permission (e.g., "Would you be interested in a suggestion that might help?"). Second, suggestions are delivered out of the Adult ego state so that there are no Parent imperatives (i.e., "shoulds" and "musts"). In fact, phrasing your suggestion as a "Have you thought about . . . ?" question avoids the trap of advice-giving by placing an idea in the minds of clients where they can develop it on their own if it makes sense to them. For instance, you might ask a client who is bemoaning the fact that he impulsively succumbs to the requests of his peers, but later regrets taking on more commitments, "Have you thought about waiting a day before you respond to a request so that you don't make an impulsive or ill-advised decision?" You are offering a helpful suggestion, but leaving it up to the client to consider what he wants to do with it—which brings up the third guideline: Always emphasize personal choice so that the client feels free to take your suggestion or ignore it (e.g., "You may want to wait a day before responding so that you have time to think about it, but that's really your choice" or ". . . but that's really a decision for you to make at the time").

Go Slow to Go Fast

For the last couple of decades, there has been a movement in science away from the perception that scientific progress is the result of sudden flashes of insight and giant leaps of movement. Instead, it is argued that most discoveries are the result of continuing, persistent, methodical practices and study. This approach to scientific research is termed "Slow Science." In his article, "Fast Science vs. Slow Science, or Slow and Steady Wins the Race," Eugene Garfield (1990) writes, "[I]mportant discoveries generally are made by those who doggedly plug along in a field that is ripe for discovery and who are intellectually prepared to recognize and exploit unexpected results" (p. 380). Similarly, in the field of behavioral change and solution-focused endeavors, it is the client who makes small and consistent progress over time that is most likely to achieve sustainable results. Change is rarely easy and requires a gradual progression of small steps toward the desired result. When helping a client decide on new actions, ask "What is the least that can be done and still make progress?" By asking the client this question, you introduce the strategy of making small changes over time and follow Solution-Focused Principle #3: "Small steps lead to big changes."

Small Steps Can Overcome Inertia

Have you ever tried to change your thinking or behavior only to realize that you have slipped back into your old patterns? Have you ever vowed to start doing something different only to realize that you've never gotten around to it? The problem: inertia, the resistance or disinclination to motion, action, or change. What causes it? There are several possibilities, but competing priorities and feeling overwhelmed are heavy contributors. Since most professionals feel a tremendous amount of job pressure, the time it takes to deal with the day-to-day necessities often leaves little room for the discretionary attention and energy needed to pursue other goals and objectives. This problem is exacerbated when the actions that need to be taken are perceived to be overwhelming. Something needs to happen to get the ball rolling—even slightly. Small steps reduce these barriers to action.

Small Steps Can Lead to Early Success Experiences

When clients try to do too much too fast, they may become disillusioned if they do not experience the success they expect. This is not an uncommon experience given the heuristic nature of change. There will inevitably be some actions that are taken that do not work. It is best to encourage your clients not to complicate matters by trying to do too much too fast. Instead, create early successes through successive approximations.

The use of successive approximations was first articulated by the father of behavioral psychology, B. F. Skinner (1953). Essentially, this method involves a process of developing complex behaviors by sequencing a series of less complex behaviors such that they build upon one another until the final behavioral goal is reached. The same principle can be applied to change efforts. When planning an action sequence that will result in a behavioral change goal, start with a simple behavior that can be easily accomplished and will lead to an early success experience. As an example, for the client who is shy but wants to learn to speak in public, the first step may be to speak up more in team meetings. Follow it with the next logical step, and so on until the final goal is reached. As a person goes through this process, their behavior progresses in successive increments and is continually reinforced; it is the behavioral equivalent of "success breeds success."

Small Steps Can Increase Options

A third rationale for encouraging clients to take small steps is so that they can learn from doing, and in the process, discover options they may not have heretofore considered. Clients choose actions based on their current assessment of their situation and what it will take to get what they want, but they follow a heuristic path. The key to using the heuristic process successfully is to take small steps and use the feedback from one's actions to adjust behavior accordingly. "Once a person makes a small change, then everything tends to look different from this changed perspective" (Berg & Szabo, 2005, p. 19).

This strategy is consistent with action learning whereby a person studies his or her actions and experiences to improve in some way (Marquardt, 2004). Taking small steps gives clients time to reflect upon and learn from their experience, so they generate better ideas, make better decisions, and take more effective actions in the future. Ultimately, it is a quicker path to sustainable change.

Scaling Can Help

As previously stated, scaling has many uses. In Challenge-for-Thought, it is used to help clients create well-formed outcomes by identifying numerical starting points and describing what success would look like when they have achieved a position on the scale a few points higher. In Support-for-Action, scaling is used to evoke Change Talk by asking clients to pick a number on the scale that represents their assessed level of the importance of their goal, their confidence in achieving it, and their readiness to take action. Scaling, as used in Challenge-for-Action, uses numerical increments to identify and reinforce small steps toward goal achievement. This process begins by identifying where clients are starting from on the scale.

Using Scaling in Challenge-for-Action

Coach: It sounds as if you have a good idea of what you will experience when you have a handle on your emotions and stress. Now, I have a question for you, "On a scale of zero to ten, with ten being that you are handling your emotions and stress in the way that you want—even if it's not perfect—and zero being the opposite, where, on that scale, are you now?"

Client: As I think about it, I guess I would have to say that I'm probably at a six on the scale.

Once clients identify where they are on the scale, highlight what is going right and then plan the next small step forward.

Highlighting What Is Going Right

It is quite common that clients will be so preoccupied with what they want to be different in the future that they fail to note that there are already positive things happening in the present. A positive rating, no matter how small, implies that something must already be working for them. By identifying what they are already doing that is working—even a little—you are following a very simple, solution-focused axiom for designing actions: If something is working, do more of it! (de Shazer et al., 2006).

Using Scaling to Highlight What Is Going Right

Coach: It sounds as if you have a good idea of what you will experience when you have a handle on your emotions and stress. Now, I have a question for you, "On a scale of zero to ten, with ten being that you are handling your emotions and stress in the way that you want, even if it's not perfect, and zero being the opposite, where, on that scale, are you now?"

Client: As I think about it, I guess I would have to say that I'm probably at a six on the scale.

Coach: Given that you have rated yourself a six, you must be doing something right that would keep it from being lower. What are you doing right now that's helping you rate yourself at that level?

Client: I think I'm keeping my emotions to myself. I don't think I'm letting my stress show when I'm with the department heads.

Coach: That's good. What are you doing to stay under control when you're with the department heads?

Client: I think one thing that is helpful is that I'm reminding myself that even though things are stressful due to the lack of resources, this will change. I believe that I will have additional people available to me over the next six months. So I guess I think, "This, too, shall pass."

Coach: Great. It sounds like that's important for you to keep doing.

What if clients say zero? That is a very rare answer, but if they do, it is a sign that they are deep in the midst of a troubling situation and are trying to dig themselves out. Show empathy, and ask what they are doing to cope with this situation given that their current rating would suggest that they view themselves as being very far away from what they want. In short, reinforce their coping capability. As soon as possible, plan the next small step forward.

Planning the Next Small Step

Scaling makes it easy to plan the next small step because it is merely asking clients what they would have to *do* to move up the scale one or two points. For example, "What would you have to do to move up from a six to a seven, or maybe even to an eight, on the scale?" These small steps then translate into cognitive or behavioral experiments. While simple, this is not necessarily easy with clients who are used to ambitious action plans. They are impatient, and their need for achievement pushes them to want to succeed at whatever they take on as quickly as possible, even though the heuristic process requires that they go slow to go fast. Too often they are inclined to overreach with their action steps, which can lead to a sense of failure and discouragement. Stick with the plan: small steps and early successes.

Using Scaling to Plan the Next Small Step

Coach: Given that you have rated yourself a six, you must be doing something right that would keep it from being lower. What are you doing that's helping you rate yourself at that level?

Client: I think I'm keeping my emotions to myself. I don't think I'm letting my stress show when I'm with the department heads.

Coach: That's good. What are you doing to stay under control when you're with the department heads?

Client: I think one thing that is helpful is that I'm reminding myself that even though things are stressful due to the lack of resources, this will change. I believe that I will have additional people available to me over the next six months. So I guess I think, "This, too, shall pass."

Coach: Great. It sounds like that's important for you to keep doing. Now given that you're at a six on the scale compared to where you want to be, what might you experiment with doing over the next week or two that might move it up to a seven, or possibly even an eight?

Client: Well, if I were to reach out and maybe be proactive, especially with some of the top leaders that have a lot of challenges, it would enable me to meet with them on my own terms. That would probably relieve my stress because I could carve out the time and work it into my schedule as opposed to being reactive. That's what's happening right now; my phone rings, an e-mail pops up, or I'm asked to attend a meeting, and I'm not prepared. When those things happen, it elevates my stress, so being proactive with a few targeted executives would help.

Coach: I like that idea. It seems like it would help to put you back in control as opposed to just reacting to unexpected events. [Complex reflection]

Client: Yeah. I think that would make a big difference.

Coach: Are there some opportunities coming up in the next few days where you'll be able to do this?

Client: Yes, absolutely.

From this point in the conversation, the coach can pinpoint what those opportunities are and how, specifically, the client is going to act on her idea. The coach will then use follow-up discussions to review the client's progress by using the scaling technique to show indications of progress.

Using Scaling to Show Concrete Indications of Progress

Scaling can also be used to measure the results of actions taken. Checking in with clients to assess how things are going with their action experiments, and then asking for a new estimation of where clients are on the scale relative to where they started, records and reinforces any movement that has occurred. When clients rate themselves as higher on the scale than where they were previously, they are compelled to notice progress. Documenting client progress in this way also provides a natural springboard to Support-for-Action and Change Talk. Eliciting and exploring statements from clients about their demonstrated ability to make progress strengthens confidence.

> ### Using Scaling to Show Progress and Transition to Support-for-Action
>
> **Coach**: Last session you said that you were going to experiment with reaching out in a proactive way with some of the top leaders so that you could meet with them on your own terms. You thought that doing so would relieve some of your stress. How did it go?
>
> **Client**: I did that, and I think it helped. I felt more in control and less stressed out. Less stress also helped me keep my emotions under control.
>
> **Coach**: That's good. Now, let's go back to the scale we talked about last time. I asked you to rate, on a scale of zero to ten, where you were in your ability to handle your stress and keep your emotions under control. You rated yourself at a six. Is that still accurate or has there been a change?
>
> **Client**: Feeling more in control and less reactive has really helped. I think I probably moved up a notch.
>
> **Coach**: So, you're more like a seven now.
>
> **Client**: I think so.
>
> **Coach**: Now, I want to ask you another question. What do you think helped you succeed in doing that? I mean, it must not have been easy. What abilities did you use to move up the scale a notch? [Transition to Support-for-Action: Confidence Talk]

Spending time in Support-for-Action and using elaboration, affirmation, reflection, and summary with the Change Talk that emerges strengthens the client's willingness, ability, and readiness to try new actions in pursuit of her objective. As you can tell, scaling is one of the most flexible coaching tools available to you.

Chapter Summary

The common thread running through all issues that clients bring to coaching is the desire for change, but change does not happen without action. Since action is what clients do *outside* of the coaching conversation, the most that coaches can accomplish within the session is to ready clients for action by ensuring that they know what steps they are going to take, how they are going to go about taking them, and when and where they are going to start—and then support them as they find their way to what they want.

Because of the nature of the heuristic process, the path to change is fraught with uncertainty because there are no textbook answers. Therefore, actions are best thought of as experiments so that the pressure of coming up with the perfect action the first time is reduced. There are three types of action experiments: informational experiments, cognitive experiments, and behavioral experiments. Informational experiments are actions clients can take to gather information that will help them decide what cognitive and behavioral experiments they wish to try. Cognitive experiments are attempts at different ways of thinking and understanding to change how one behaves in or reacts to situations. Behavioral experiments mean trying new behaviors or acting differently to achieve the desired end state. Several methods and techniques were offered for use with these experiments, including the use of scaling. Regardless of whether clients engage in informational, cognitive, or behavioral experiments, the number one guideline is "go slow to go fast." Small steps are the secret of success when implementing a heuristic change process because they facilitate ongoing learning and maximize the probability that clients will make consistent progress over time.

Challenge-for-Action is the final quadrant of the Framework explained in this book; however, that does not mean it is the last to be accessed in a coaching discussion. In fact, it may be the first if bridging is done (i.e., starting the session with a review of what the client has done and how it has worked as a "bridge" to the current session). Challenge-for-Action is meant to provoke movement toward goals through action and can be accessed any time you want to generate action experiments with your clients.

The ICF competencies (ICF Core Competencies—International Coach Federation, n.d.) addressed by the content of this chapter are:

- **Active Listening**
    - Integrates and builds on the client's ideas and suggestions.
- **Powerful Questioning**
    - Asks questions that evoke discovery, insight, commitment, or action (e.g., those that challenge the client's assumptions).
    - Asks open-ended questions that create greater clarity, possibility, or new learning.
- **Creating Awareness**
    - Communicates broader perspectives to clients and inspires commitment to shift their viewpoints and find new possibilities for action.
- **Designing Actions**
    - Brainstorms and assists the client to define actions that will enable the client to demonstrate, practice, and deepen new learning.
    - Helps the client to focus on and systematically explore specific concerns and opportunities that are central to agreed-upon coaching goals.
    - Engages the client to explore alternative ideas and solutions, to evaluate options, and to make related decisions.
    - Promotes active experimentation and self-discovery, where the client applies what has been discussed and learned during sessions immediately afterward in his/her work or life setting.
    - Challenges client's assumptions and perspectives to provoke new ideas and find new possibilities for action.

- Helps the client "Do It Now" during the coaching session, providing immediate support.
- Encourages stretches and challenges but also a comfortable pace of learning.

- **Planning and Goal Setting**
  - Consolidates collected information and establishes a coaching plan and development goals with the client that address concerns and major areas for learning and development.
  - Creates a plan with results that are attainable, measurable, specific, and have target dates.
  - Makes plan adjustments as warranted by the coaching process and by changes in the situation.
  - Helps the client identify and access different resources for learning (e.g., books, other professionals).
  - Identifies and targets early successes that are important to the client.

- **Managing Progress and Accountability**
  - Clearly requests of the client actions that will move the client toward his/her stated goals.
  - Demonstrates follow-through by asking the client about those actions that the client committed to during the previous session(s).
  - Keeps the client on track between sessions by holding attention on the coaching plan and outcomes, agreed-upon courses of action, and topics for future session(s).
  - Focuses on the coaching plan but is also open to adjusting behaviors and actions based on the coaching process and shifts in direction during sessions.
  - Is able to move back and forth between the big picture of where the client is heading, setting a context for what is being discussed and where the client wishes to go.
  - Promotes client's self-discipline and holds the client accountable for what he or she says he or she is going to do, for the results of an intended action, or for a specific plan with related time frames.
  - Positively confronts the client with the fact that he/she did not take agreed-upon actions.

CHAPTER 10

The Coaching Alliance
Putting the Framework in Context

The heuristic nature of the coaching process makes it a messy business. As described in Chapter 2, your role in this process is analogous to that of a guide: someone who helps clients navigate through a confusing jungle of ideas, thoughts, needs, wants, goals, and actions that confront them until they reach their destination. The path taken on this journey is not straight, nor is the journey generally completed in a single conversation. The Foursquare Coaching Framework is a structure that maps the process of the coaching conversation so that you can navigate its changing landscape, but it does not account for the overall relational factors that affect the coaching process, generally. In other words, the FsCF functions within a broader context that consists of the professional relationship between coach and client. This is known as the Coaching Alliance.

The Coaching Alliance

Based on emerging agreement across disciplines, the *Alliance* is a universal concept that has proven to facilitate positive outcomes in a variety of helping contexts—including coaching. The Coaching Alliance has both cognitive elements (goals, roles, and responsibilities) around which consensus must be reached and relational aspects (trust, respect, and caring) that define the complexion and strength of the professional bond between coach and client. The Coaching Alliance facilitates collaboration and partnership between coach and client.

If the FsCF were a house, then the professional bond between coach and client is its foundation. Without a solid foundation, the house will not stand; without a strong working alliance between coach and client the coaching process will suffer—regardless of the conceptual structure or approach used by the coach. The concept of an alliance between coach and coachee was not invented in coaching. Like so many of coaching's concepts, it has been borrowed from elsewhere—in this case, psychotherapy. The term *alliance* is also referred to in the literature as the *therapeutic alliance, working alliance, helping alliance,* and of course in coaching as the *coaching alliance.* The concept of an alliance between practitioner and client began with Freud in the 1940s, but by the 1970s it had expanded from its dynamic roots to include the relational components of all types of helping endeavors:

> [A] working alliance between a person seeking change and a change agent can occur in many places besides the locale of psychotherapy. The concept of the working alliance would seem to be applicable in the relation between student and teacher, between community action group and leader, and, with only slight extension, between child and parent.
>
> (Bordin, 1979, p. 252)

Bordin goes on to state that "the working alliance between the person who seeks change and the one who offers to be a change agent is one of the keys, if not *the* key to the change process" (p. 252). This view has been substantiated in recent years. Martin et al. (2000) concluded that the relationship between alliance and outcome is consistent no matter what variables may influence the development of the alliance. This is an area where, once again, the research and writings in psychology, and more specifically psychotherapy, can inform the practice of coaching.

Horvath and Bedi (2002) write that the alliance refers, in part, to the quality and strength of the collaborative association between the client and practitioner. This collaborative relationship is inclusive of positive affective bonds such as trust, liking, respecting, and caring, all of which are important elements of the coach-client relationship. The words used to depict this relationship describe *how* coaches behave toward their clients throughout the coaching process and the professional bond that is developed while they do what they do. By contrast, terms like "coaching tools" or "techniques" are used to describe *what* is done by the coach to facilitate client-driven goal achievement and outcomes. Norcross and Lambert (2011) draw attention to the fact that "[i]n reality, of course, what one does and how one does it are complementary and inseparable" (p. 5). They use the following analogy to illustrate their point:

> Suppose you want your teenager to clean his or her room. Two methods for achieving this are to establish clear standards and to impose consequences. A reasonable approach, but the effectiveness of these two evidence-based methods will vary on whether the relationship between you and the teenager is characterized by warmth and mutual respect or by anger and mistrust.
>
> (p. 5)

Similarly, the methods used by the coach always take place within the context of a relationship with the client. No matter how masterful you are in navigating the Foursquare Coaching Framework and using evidence-based practices while doing so, without a positive relationship between you and your client, your effectiveness is reduced.

The concept of a Coaching Alliance also extends to the cognitive aspects of the coaching relationship, such as consensus about goals and the desired coaching outcomes for the overall coaching engagement. This involves a mutual understanding as to how the coaching engagement will work, including the tasks and role expectations for both the coach and the client. A particularly important part of the role responsibilities for the coach is that he or she behave in accordance with the ethics and standards expected from a professional in this role. Ethics violations not only breach the cognitive component of the Coaching Alliance but have a spillover effect on the relational component, as well. Ultimately, the concept of the Coaching Alliance suggests a dynamic partnership in which both parties in the coaching relationship are actively committed to their specific and appropriate responsibilities: a partnership that—like any relationship—is not a static state but continually evolves. O'Broin and Palmer sum up the evolutionary nature of the Coaching Alliance nicely in their definition:

> The Coaching Alliance reflects the quality of the coachee's and coach's engagement in collaborative, purposive work within the coaching relationship, and is jointly negotiated, and renegotiated throughout the coaching process over time.
>
> (O'Broin & Palmer, 2010, p. 4)

The Coaching Alliance does not happen by accident, nor is it an inevitable part of the coaching process. Horvath and Bedi (2002) state that developing and maintaining a working alliance between helper and helpee is a conscious and purposeful act. Novice coach practitioners cannot presume that, given enough time, a good alliance will naturally develop. Instead, they must ensure that it does so by doing what is necessary from the outset to produce it. Part of what is necessary is to demonstrate the personal qualities and competencies that nourish the relational aspect of the Coaching Alliance so that the Foursquare Coaching Framework has a strong foundation to support its use.

Two Foundational Traits

Self-Control

Establishing and maintaining the coaching relationship requires a highly sophisticated skill-set that requires a great deal of self-regulation. This includes the self-discipline of controlling one's attentional focus, restraint in managing self-talk and making judgments, the ability to control one's emotional reactions, and the willpower to find positive qualities in the client, regardless of their personal characteristics or situation. It is not surprising, then, that self-regulatory processes are one of the three major subcomponents of the neuroanatomical correlates of the ability to relate to other people so as to establish a positive helping relationship (Elliott et al., 2011). It will be apparent from the discussions below about self-awareness, empathy, positive regard, genuineness, and presence that self-control is a prerequisite for each and, as such, must be a part of any coach's trait profile. In fact, self-control is so essential to our capabilities as human beings that Rachlin (2000) claims "that human happiness is inseparable from self-control" (p. 8). This is an assertion that philosophers and religious leaders have been trumpeting since ancient times.

Psychological-Mindedness

Psychological-Mindedness (PM) is a relatively new term in the coaching literature, even though it has been part of the psychological literature for decades. For example, Appelbaum (1973) referred to PM as, "A person's ability to see relationships between thoughts, feelings, and actions, with the goal of learning the meanings and causes of his experiences and behaviour" (p. 36). Over the years, there have been variations on this definition. Wolitzky and Reuben (1974) defined PM as "a tendency to understand or explain behavior in psychological terms, that is, to view behavior as expressing and communicating information about the needs, wishes, purposes, intentions, conflicts, and defensive strategies, etc. of the person in question, oneself or another" (p. 183). Gough (1975) defined PM as a general interest in psychological phenomena that results in responsiveness to the inner needs, motives, and experiences of others. Dollinger et al. (1983) and his colleagues define PM as simply the ability to "read between the lines of behavior" (p. 183). Beitel et al. (2005) summed it up well when they wrote that "[p]sychological mindedness (PM), in its broadest sense, involves awareness and understanding of psychological processes, such as thoughts, feelings, and behaviors" (p. 740).

The above definitions call attention to PM as a higher-level competency that gives coaches the ability to be aware of their own thoughts and feelings, as well as the thoughts and feelings of others. This capacity to reflect on oneself and others implies an awareness of internal psychological states and signals, the use of which enables coaches to respond more adequately when working in the realm of the personal with their clients. For example, psychologically minded coaches can step back and look objectively at their thoughts, feelings, and behavior within the coaching context so as to consider their impact on the coaching process, reevaluate what they are experiencing or doing, and potentially act on it or change it. Similarly, they are more sensitive to and are able to observe the thoughts, feelings, and behavior of their clients while suspending judgment about what they observe. Psychological-mindedness and self-control are two traits that support the five pillars of the coaching relationship.

The Five Pillars of the Coaching Relationship

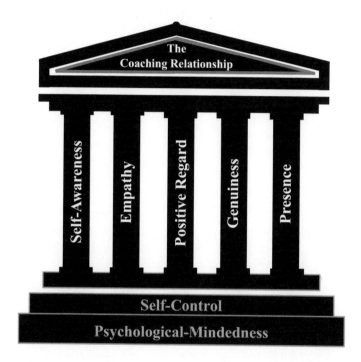

The five pillars of the coaching relationship—self-awareness, empathy, positive regard, genuiness, and presence—are the coach-related competencies required to establish and sustain the relational component of the Coaching Alliance. These five pillars denote the psychological capacities and the behavioral patterns of action that nurture the relational aspects of the Coaching Alliance.

Self-Awareness

"Wherever you go, there you are" is a quote that has been attributed to many sources, including movies (*The Adventures of Buckaroo Banzai Across the 8th Dimension*— 1984) and readings such as Buddha's Reflections on Mindfulness. Regardless of its source, the message is clear: You bring your "self" to everything you do during each moment of the day. It makes sense, then, that the more *self*-awareness you have, the more likely it will be that you bring your best *self* to coaching conversations. According to Lee (as cited in Bluckert, 2005, p. 174), self-awareness, as a function of psycho-logical-mindedness, makes it possible for coaches to:

- Stand back from their own experience and notice the preferences, biases, and blind spots that underpin their behavior;
- Give an account of their personal history, with emotional relatedness to the meaning of key events;
- Reflect on their own behavior, and surface unconscious motivations;
- Examine their feelings, thoughts, and reactions, and distinguish those evoked by others from those deriving from their own psychology;
- Shift their focus of attention across different aspects of their mental and emotional experiences (e.g., actions, cognitions, emotions, systemic context) and entertain multiple explanations for events.

From this list of capacities, it is evident that self-awareness includes the ability to reflect on one's experiences and learn something about oneself which can be used to make one a better coach over time. This is similar to the learning process of the Reflective Practitioner described in Chapter 1. Self-awareness requires the ability to focus one's attention internally, in real time, to ascertain if and how one's needs, motivations, and feeling responses are impacting the coaching process. The impact of self-awareness on the coaching process is illustrated in the following example.

Self-Awareness

Supervising Coach: As homework from our last session I asked you to think about your personal history, how it has shaped who you are, and how it plays itself out in your coaching. Specifically, how it affects your ability to connect with and engage your clients. Have you done that?

Coach-in-Training: Yes, I have. It's interesting because I came up with something that I haven't really thought about before, but now that I do, I realize it's something that I need to be aware of and manage during my coaching.

Supervising Coach: Really? What is that?

Coach-in-Training: To explain, I need to tell you a little about my personal history. I grew up in a household with a very dominant father and a submissive mother. Over the years, the conflict between the two led my mother to turn to prescription drugs and alcohol as an escape. In the process, she began to see herself as very much a victim. She believed she had no control of her life and was unwilling to take steps to help herself. She would complain and do nothing about it. I saw that every day for so many years that I've become overly sensitive to people who present themselves as victims.

Supervising Coach: How does it affect the way you relate to them or coach them?

Coach-in-Training: When I hear someone talking or thinking like that, I sort of shut down. I lose my ability to empathize, and I have an urge to lecture them on the fact that they are playing the role of victim. It is the same thing that I tried to do with my mother—to no avail. I totally lose my connection with the client.

The coach-in-training has taken an important first step in developing her self-awareness by considering how specific attitudes or the behavior of clients trigger her pet peeves, personal standards, or biases in such a way as to cause her to become judgmental and opinionated. This is sometimes called being "hooked" by the client, and once this happens, the tendency is to jump in with premature solutions or to take up a righteous or over-zealous stance. Once coaches become distracted by their subjective responses, they are no longer connected to, or engaged with, their clients. However, when coaches become aware of these dynamics and how consciously or unconsciously they are affected by them, they have taken the first step in overcoming their limitations. Master-level coaches know this because they know themselves.

Countertransference and Coaching

Countertransference is a term that is not usually associated with coaching. It is linked to the fields of psychotherapy and psychoanalysis, where the concept originated. It is, however, something that everyone in the helping profession has experienced—including coaches. Have you ever had feelings in response to a client, and yet there is no apparent reason for those feelings to be there? If so, you probably have experienced countertransference. According to psychoanalytic theory, countertransference occurs because the client has triggered feelings, thoughts, and behaviors (usually unconscious) associated with a person or a situation in the past, and you react to the client based on those past associations. This is exactly what happened with the coach-in-training in the above example when she encountered clients that behaved in ways that she unconsciously associated with those of her mother. Subsequently, this caused her to react to her clients just as she responded to her mother.

As with any helping conversation, coaching involves a partial identification with the client and, thus, makes countertransference a natural occurrence. It becomes a problem, however, when the coach is not aware that the feelings he or she is experiencing are due to this phenomenon. A clue to knowing if you may be experiencing countertransference is when you find yourself experiencing feelings or acting outside of your normal pattern of behavior with a client. For example, you find yourself sympathizing with rather than challenging a client— even though challenging would be your normal approach in that specific situation. The solution to the problem of countertransference is to be alert to your feelings, stop to investigate them, and analyze what's going on, especially if they are out of the ordinary.

In the case of the coach-in-training, the next developmental step is to become an objective observer of her internal processes as she coaches so that she can use the necessary self-management skills during her coaching sessions to remain present and engaged. Master-level practitioners can maintain awareness of their internal states by directing an appropriate amount of their attention toward the self (second-channel communication) while still maintaining their connection with the client. It is a balancing act that comes with time and practice. The kind of self-observation involved in psychological-mindedness is different from the stressful self-monitoring or anxious self-preoccupation that characterizes the novice and even some journeyman-level practitioners. Stressful self-monitoring interferes with their insightfulness because of their fear of making mistakes. In contrast, master-level practitioners have developed the ability to look objectively at their thoughts, feelings, and behaviors by using their "observing self" so as to avoid getting in their own way:

> This is a vital aspect of coach development because this is what psychological-mindedness requires—an ability to notice one's own experiencing and to be able to helicopter above it to observe and reflect on it. This is equally true of the coaching conversation. The coach needs to be able to fully turn up and be present yet also to be able to step back and notice patterns and connections some of which may be to do with the connection between the coach and client.
>
> (Bluckert, 2005, p. 177)

Empathy

A part of psychological-mindedness is self-awareness, but as noted above, it is also an awareness of, and interest in, the thoughts and feelings of others. For this reason, psychological-mindedness is a pre-condition for empathy because one cannot empathize with another without first attending to what that person is thinking and feeling. The Empathy Cycle is discussed in detail in Chapter 3 as a means of connecting with and engaging the client during the coaching session, so a further discussion of the topic is not needed here. Suffice it to say that for decades empathy has been recognized as having an important role in facilitating change in a helping relationship.

Empathy, whether cognitive or affective, is one of the most basic capacities for understanding one another. Along with positive regard and genuineness, it is central to establishing a positive relationship between the practitioner and the client. Stober perceptively summarizes the benefits of empathy this way:

> In addition, by demonstrating empathy the practitioner is performing several important tasks: allowing clients to become more fully aware of their own construction of reality, demonstrating positive regard for the self of the client, and building trust in the relationship. When this understanding is communicated, clients can then gain another's view to their own experience, which often is then felt as a deeply rewarding sense of being known and at the same time can allow clients to know themselves more fully, too. Empathy builds trust that the practitioner seeks to understand and that this relationship is one in which the client's experience holds the ingredients for future growth.
>
> (Stober, 2006, p. 23)

Positive Regard

Brett is a charming client. He is self-confident, assertive, and highly successful. As the CEO of a large pharmaceutical firm, his creative vision and determination to succeed have helped the firm grow and prosper. The first few coaching sessions left you feeling very impressed with Brett and his ability to get things done. Lately, however, you see a different side of him. While he professes to want to develop himself through the coaching experience, he seems to have an unrealistic view of himself and his capabilities. You have concluded that his lack of insight stems from extreme over-confidence. In each subsequent session, you see more and more arrogance in his behavior and attitudes; frankly, it's starting to annoy you. In talking about his goals, he is preoccupied with fantasies of unlimited success, power, and brilliance. None of your attempts to bring him down to earth have succeeded. The worst part is when he describes how he is able to take advantage of others to achieve his own ends and feels no sense of remorse. When he talks about problems that have arisen in his interactions with others, he takes no responsibility for anything that happened. In your opinion, he is not very likable—certainly not to you. Word has gotten to the board of directors about Brett, and they have given him a thorough dress down and expect some changes in his attitude and behavior.

What are you thinking now? Perhaps, it is, "Good; it's about time he gets taken down a few notches" or "Maybe now he'll realize that he is not as good as he thinks he is." While these thoughts may be normal, and even justified, they will not help you to maintain the kind of coaching relationship that bolsters the Coaching Alliance. Carl Rogers maintained that it is virtually impossible to establish a helping relationship if the practitioner cannot accept the person with whom he or she is working. He believed that acceptance meant treating clients as persons of worth and respect and that such acceptance is uppermost if clients are to fulfill their potential. Rogers framed these desirable attitudes within an overarching concept he called *positive regard*. Rogers (1958) framed this concept as a question: "Can I let myself experience positive attitudes toward this other person—attitudes of warmth, caring, liking, interest, respect?" (p. 12).

In most discussions of positive regard, it is referred to as *unconditional* positive regard. However, to behave toward all clients with unconditional positive regard is an unrealistic expectation. Even Rogers himself admits this in his 1957 article, "On the Necessary and Sufficient Conditions of Therapeutic Personality Change":

The phrase "unconditional positive regard" may be an unfortunate one, since it sounds like an absolute, an all-or-nothing dispositional concept. . . . From a clinical and experiential point of view I believe the most accurate statement is that the effective therapist experiences unconditional positive regard for the client during many moments of his contact with him, yet from time to time he experiences only a conditional positive regard—and perhaps at times a negative regard, though this is not likely in effective therapy. It is in this sense that unconditional positive regard exists as a matter of degree in any relationship.

(p. 101)

So while positive regard is not something that the average coach will be able to exhibit 100% of the time, it is something to strive for because it has been proven to be significantly associated with client success—at least from the client's perspective. Farber and Lane (2002) report that decades of research indicate that, similar to other constructs such as empathy or the helping alliance, it is the client's perspective of the practitioner's positive regard that is most often associated with good outcomes. This does not mean that practitioners have to provide a stream of compliments nor a gushing of positive sentiment, but it is important that practitioners ensure that a respectful and positive attitude is communicated to affirm their clients' sense of worth. Farber and Lane go on to offer these additional insights: 1) Practitioners vary in the extent to which they are able to convey positive regard to their clients (some are just plain better at it than others) and 2) clients vary in the extent to which they need to be affirmed by the practitioner's display of positive regard. Remember, each client is an individual, but also keep in mind that at least some positive regard must be communicated because, at a minimum, it sets the stage for other interventions, such as empathy, and positively influences the relational aspect of the Coaching Alliance.

Positive regard cannot be faked. Respecting, caring about, and liking someone are conveyed as part of a significant body of information that is exchanged between two people at a neuroanatomical level. We are hardwired to extrapolate the intentions of others from birth (Decety & Ickes, 2009). Liking a client (such as Brett) may be difficult, but you can convey a sense of respect for him as a person and not let your personal judgments interfere with maintaining positive regard. If positive regard is not present your client will sense it, and the coaching relationship will suffer.

Genuineness

The fourth pillar of the coaching relationship is *genuineness*, sometimes called authenticity or congruence. If clients cannot relate to you or trust you as a person, the coaching relationship will stall. To put it another way, it is not always about what you do, but who you are that matters to your clients. However, coaches must be able to discern the differing needs and expectations of their clients in order to tailor the expression of genuineness to what is appropriate for the specific client at a given time. For example, some clients need and expect greater formality than others and a coach would not be "genuine" if he or she did not realize this. Being yourself during your coaching sessions is essential (after all, who else can you be?), but genuineness must always take place within the context of your role as coach.

What does it mean to be genuine? First, it means openness: appropriately sharing your thoughts and feelings as you experience them. This may include information about you in the form of self-disclosure, or your thoughts and feelings about the client in the form of feedback. Genuine responses are honest, but they are "not disrespectful, overly intellectualized, or insincere (although they may involve irreverence)" (Klein et al., 2002, p. 210). Klein and her colleagues caution that genuine responses require mindful attention and self-reflection and are guided by normative role behavior for the practitioner. Genuineness also means asking the tough questions and not being afraid to challenge the client when your intuitive-self says to do so. Finally, being genuine means owning and taking responsibility for what you say.

Self-disclosure is a distinct way of being genuine and deserves special mention. Hill and Knox (2002) offer some useful insights about the use of self-disclosure in the professional context. First of all, they note that self-disclosure on the part of the practitioner makes the practitioner seem more real and human in the eyes of the client, and occasionally leads to new insights for the client, e.g., "Gee, maybe I'm not the only one that feels that way." At the very least, self-disclosure can improve the working relationship by serving as a model for openness and honesty. For these benefits to accrue, however, practitioners should follow strict guidelines for when and how to utilize self-disclosure.

1. Self-disclosure can be helpful when: a) it validates the client's reality; b) it normalizes what the client is experiencing; c) it models aspects of the coaching relationships (e.g., honesty or trust); d) the coach believes it will strengthen the coaching relationship; or e) it illustrates alternative ways to think or act, thereby increasing the client's choices.
2. Self-disclosure may be particularly effective when it is in response to self-disclosure on the part of the client because it may help the client feel normal and reassured.
3. Coaches need to observe very carefully how their clients respond to their disclosures and use that information to conceptualize how to use disclosure going forward. It is also important to disclose more with some clients than others because of the personality of the client or as a way of building trust.
4. Self-disclosure should *not* be used: a) to meet the coach's own needs instead of facilitating client outcomes; b) to take the focus of attention away from the client; c) when it interferes with the flow of the coaching conversation; d) when it burdens or confuses the client; or e) when it blurs the boundaries between coach and client.
5. Use self-disclosure judiciously. One reason self-disclosure may be useful is because it occurs so infrequently. That being said, coaches are often fearful of engaging in any type of self-disclosure because coaching is supposed to be "all about the client." And yet, what can be more helpful to the client than genuineness, of which self-disclosure is a part?

Presence

The assertion that empathy, positive regard, and genuineness are essential to the practitioner's ability to affect change in his or her clients was held by Carl Rogers for most of his life. Geller and Greenberg (2002) remark that in his later years, however, Rogers began writing about "one more characteristic" that was the most important component of his person-centered approach to individual change. During an interview with Baldwin (2000), Rogers said the following:

> I am inclined to think that in my writing I have stressed too much the three basic conditions (congruence, unconditional positive regard, and empathic understanding). Perhaps it is something around the edges of those conditions that is really the most important element of therapy—when my self is very clearly, obviously present.
>
> (p. 30)

While Rogers did not name it explicitly (as it was only beginning to unfold as a therapeutic concept), he was unmistakably referring to what is now known as *presence*. Presence is most commonly defined as a quality of self or a way of being with clients (Gehart & McCollum, 2008). It is "the state of having one's whole self in the encounter with a client by being completely in the moment on a multiplicity of levels" (Geller & Greenberg, 2002). By being completely present, the coach has an enhanced sensitivity to his or her own reactions to what clients are experiencing as expressed through their narratives and non-verbal cues. Just as a classical guitar resonates to the strumming of its strings, the coach's presence allows for an attuned responsiveness based on a cognitive, kinesthetic, and emotional sensing of the client's expressed and felt experiences. So in effect, by being present, the coach becomes an instrument that resonates to the dynamics of the interpersonal exchange. This receptive state is a precursor for accessing the knowledge, professional skills, and wisdom the coach brings to the relationship. Coaching presence acts as a receptor—and a guide—for using the Foursquare Coaching Framework.

Presence is distinct from the Empathic Attention that is a part of the Empathy Cycle and the active listening techniques used to connect with clients during Support-for-Thought. Gehart and McCollum (2008) point out that these techniques, while important, focus on the *content* of the practitioner's communication with his or her client, as opposed to the practitioner's "being" or "presence" in the room. In their view, presence is "the attitude or stance toward present experience that the [practitioner] brings to the moment-to-moment therapeutic encounter" (p. 178). Coaches sometimes shy away from words like "therapeutic," but in this case, the most general use of the term is appropriate because presence is therapeutic in that it produces good effects and contributes to the well-being and goal attainment of the client. Presence is not a replacement for technique; instead, it is an essential way of being with the client that enhances the overall coaching relationship.

Dual Level of Consciousness

A concept unique to the state of being present is Robbins's (1998) dual level of consciousness. As he describes it, the practitioner is open to the client, while simultaneously remaining separate and clear. The dual level of consciousness is a paradox in the experience of presence because it is the act of being a part of the coaching experience while simultaneously being apart from it. As Geller and Greenberg (2002) explain, "[I]t involves a careful balancing of contact with the [practitioner's] own experience and contact with the client's experience, while maintaining the capacity to be responsive from that place of internal and external connection" (p. 83). A dual level of consciousness supports the use of the FsCF because the coach must be deeply engaged and immersed in the client's experience, yet remain appropriately objective to access and utilize the schema which the FsCF represents. To put it another way, the coach must be open and receptive, yet maintain a consistent focus on the cognitive map of the conversation.

Presence versus Mindfulness

Recently, the topic of mindfulness has become of vogue in both the psycho-therapeutic and coaching literature. While there are certainly overlaps between the two concepts, technically there are important distinctions. *Mindfulness* has its roots in Buddhism and refers to a practice or meditation technique as a way of calming the mind or gaining insight. For example, Brahm (2006) in his book, *Mindfulness, Bliss, and Beyond*, offers a course in mindfulness meditation that enables readers to explore aspects of Buddhist meditation they may know little about as a means of improving their overall quality of life. Additionally, mindfulness is often taught as a technique for clients to use as a way of dealing with "problems of the mind," such as stress, pain, or illness (Kabat-Zinn, 1990). Although mindfulness practice began as a meditative technique, admittedly it has "evolved into a way of being in the world" (Geller & Greenberg, 2002, p. 30). It is taught as a gentle, open, and non-judgmental approach to living. Mindfulness is a way of facilitating an acceptance of things as they are from which right actions and responses flow. It is both an approach to living and a philosophy of life.

Presence, on the other hand, is not a technique or a way of being in the world; instead (as described above) it is a way of being present with the client during a helping conversation. In other words, "it is a relational experience of being fully in the moment that is bodily, sensory and interpersonal, whereas mindful awareness is within the self, a mind-based present-moment awareness" (Geller & Greenberg, 2002, p. 182). There is no doubt that coaching presence can be nurtured by practicing mindfulness. Presence is being fully engaged with the client in the moment during the coaching session. Mindfulness practices are a way of cultivating the present-moment attention needed to be fully present for your client. Furthermore, mindfulness teaches practitioners to withhold judgment and engage the world (and others) with acceptance, both of which are a part of client-focused presence.

In their article, "The Role of Mindfulness in Coaching," Passmore and Marianetti (2007) suggest that coaches use a brief mindfulness exercise to help center themselves before each coaching session. They reference their own personal experiences of rushing from client to client with their minds filled with a myriad of thoughts and distractions allowing very little time to leave behind the thoughts, pressures, and anxieties of the day. They advocate a short mindfulness session involving a series of breathing exercises accompanied by observation of one's bodily sensations in the present moment. This is followed by a review of the notes from their previous meeting with the client.

Try It!

Let me invite you to pause briefly to uncover your personal obstacles to being fully present with focused attention. Read the directions below, follow them, and then answer the subsequent questions.

- Take a moment to pause from reading this book and turn your attention inward. Close your eyes or soften your gaze in front of you.
- Focus briefly on your breath and allow yourself to bring awareness to your bodily experience of breathing.
- Now, quiet your mind and focus your attention *only* on your internal and external sensory experience in the moment.
- Try it for sixty seconds.

What were you first aware of when you paused? Did you notice the busyness of your mind? What were you saying to yourself? Were you making judgments? Were you aware of any discomfort in your body that prevented you from maintaining a state of focused attention? Did you notice any rushed feeling, as in wanting to "get on with it,"—or did you skip the exercise entirely? Care to try it again? If so, notice these things without judgment, keeping your awareness focused on your sensory experience only and letting go of the thoughts or judgments about what you are experiencing. Allow each breath to put you back in the moment.

Before you are dismissive of an exercise such as this, it may interest you to know that research in the field of neuroscience clearly shows that practicing mindfulness—paying attention to the moment with openness and non-judgment—changes the neural structure of the brain so that *presence* is more easily experienced. Scientists are showing that the mind, experience, and the brain routinely change each other.

Chapter Summary

The Coaching Alliance has both cognitive and relational aspects to it. The cognitive component includes a mutual understanding as to how the coaching engagement will work, including the tasks and role expectations of the coach and client. Role expectations for the coach include the expectation and obligation to follow professionally established ethics and standards. The establishment and maintenance of the relational components of the Coaching Alliance require a pyramid of elements that build on and intertwine with each other. These include both traits and competencies.

Self-control and psychological-mindedness are traits that support the five pillars of the coaching relationship: self-awareness, empathy, positive regard, genuineness, and presence. The use of the Foursquare Coaching Framework assumes that both the cognitive and relational components of the Coaching Alliance are present and accounted for. If the Coaching Alliance is strong, then the coach is at liberty to confidently guide the client through the ever-changing landscape of the coaching conversation in pursuit of his or her desired goals and outcomes. The presence of such an alliance means that there is a powerful and healthy professional relationship with the client that adds synergy to the coaching process. Like any relationship, the Coaching Alliance is not static, but is dynamic and evolutionary and, therefore, must be maintained throughout the coaching engagement.

Final Thoughts

The Foursquare Coaching Framework works for three fundamental reasons: 1) It rests upon a strong foundation in the form of the Coaching Alliance; 2) it is a schema that gives you the ability to understand and control the process of the coaching conversation for the benefit of the client; and 3) it utilizes evidence-based practices for its implementation. Furthermore, when the methods and practices prescribed by the framework are used within the context of a strong Coaching Alliance, all of the ICF competencies are demonstrated. Those competencies that are not directly exhibited when following the coaching process dictated by the Framework are embedded within the Coaching Alliance. The cognitive component of the Coaching Alliance employs behaviors and guidelines that demonstrate the ICF competencies *Meeting Ethical Guidelines and Professional Standards* and *Establishing the Coaching Agreement*. The relational facet of the Coaching Alliance encompasses traits, behaviors, and attitudes that satisfy broader aspects of two ICF competencies: *Establishing Trust and Intimacy with the Client* and *Coaching Presence*.

In Chapter 1, you were reminded through Mickey Mouse's errant attempt at sorcery that technique does not a master make. The same is true with coaching; knowing how is not the same as knowing when and what for. Knowing the when and why of everything you do in a coaching conversation means that you are coaching with intention. The Foursquare Coaching Framework makes the coaching process explicit so that you can connect intention with technique. The more you connect the two, the more you will be able to allow this knowledge to inform your intuitive responses when it resonates with the requirements of the moment. This is the demonstration of mastery.

Coaching: The Big Picture

What is the purpose of coaching? It seems to depend on whom you ask. Downey (1999) and Parsloe and Wray (2000) view the purpose of coaching as facilitating learning and development for increasing performance and effectiveness. Rogers (2004) supports this viewpoint in that coaches serve to increase a client's efficiency at work through focused learning. Zeus and Skiffington (2002) offer a variation on this theme. They propose that the purpose of coaching is to foster growth, overcome maladaptive behaviors, and replace them with new ones to create more adaptive and successful actions. Similarly, Greene and Grant (2003) view coaching as a means of creating positive, directed change for transformational purposes. Although there is an assortment of definitions, there is a common theme: change! As Whitworth et al. (2007) perceptively point out in their book *Co-Active Coaching*, people come to coaching for individual reasons, but, in the final analysis, people want change. They no longer want things to stay the same; they want something in their lives to be different. They see coaching as a vehicle for making that change happen.

The themes and issues that people bring to coaching are varied. Many coaches are unclear about the range of topics coaching can address because most articles and books focus on a subset of coaching issues and themes. It is very much like the famous parable of the blind men and an elephant. In this parable by John Godfrey Saxe (1816–1887), six blind men went to learn, through direct experience, the make-up of an elephant. Each man, touching a different part of the elephant, came to a different conclusion. The man who felt the trunk said it was like a snake, the man who felt the tusk said it was like a spear, the man who felt the knee said it was like a tree, etc.; and so it is with coaching. Coaches whose clients come to them for skill development will define it one way. Coaches whose clients come for personal transformation define it another; and still differently, are those coaches whose clients seek help with problems in the workplace. What is more, according to Bluckert, coaches themselves often define the purpose of coaching through the prism of their profession and educational background:

> Definitions of coaching tend to group around learning and development linked to performance improvement or coaching to facilitate personal growth and change. The particular emphasis often reflects the professional background of the coach/author. A significant proportion of academics and those from HR, consultancy, and organisational development tend to stress learning and

development. Those from highly results-focused environments such as sport and business tend to major on the performance theme often seeing coaching as about skills development. Coaching psychologists, counselors and therapists typically define coaching in terms of change, mainly behavioural change.

(Bluckert, 2005, p. 171)

The purpose of coaching, then, can be considered from two perspectives: that of the client and that of the coach. While these views are usually concordant, it would seem to make the most sense to define the purpose of coaching from the standpoint of the client since the coaching agenda is *always* client driven. Therefore, a brief examination of the themes and issues for which clients seek coaching is worthwhile because it demonstrates that, from a client perspective, coaching serves many purposes. That being the case, the answer to the question, "What is the purpose of coaching?" is as simple as "It is what the client wants it to be."

Increasing Competence

Increasing the competence of the coached client lies at the heart of coaching. Virtually any definition of coaching will include a phrase that refers to personal or professional improvement, growth, or development. When clients seek coaching to increase their competence, it is a focused endeavor. That is to say they are looking to boost their competence in a particular way, e.g., their ability to lead change in their organization, to communicate more effectively, to relate better to people. Developing competence is a comprehensive developmental goal that requires deliberate, systematic, sustained, and purposeful effort. Clients develop their competence through coaching by learning specific skills, developing attributes and changing behavior, and acquiring relevant knowledge and understanding.

Learning a Skill

Skills are specific learned abilities used to perform an activity. A skill can be taught to anyone with the aptitude to learn it. Coaching is historically connected to skill development. From the earliest days of humankind, the young were taught (i.e., coached) how to hunt and cook and survive in a hostile world. Coaching and athletics have been linked since antiquity. Just like their counterparts in modern sports today, ancient Greek coaches—former athletes themselves—helped the competitors of their day achieve personal excellence. It is not surprising then that even though coaching has moved well beyond the traditional references to sport, the uninformed person will instinctively connect coaching with athletics, and by inference, skill development generally.

Skills coaching in organizations emerged in force during the mid-twentieth century. Skills coaching is appropriate for all levels; however, the specific skill or ability needed by the client may vary depending on the person's position or level within the organization. Coaching for skills has high clarity because the goals tend to be well defined and concrete (i.e., " I want to enhance my sales skills!"). The coaching process usually entails assisting clients in assessing their needed abilities, discovering learning resources, and—where expert knowledge exists—teaching and modeling the skill. The coach provides a mix of information, advice, guidance, and rehearsal with feedback so that the client develops proficiency in the skill being targeted. The coach helps keep the client focused and on track, and this may require a somewhat aggressive approach. "The coach sometimes functions as 'a drill master,' insuring that coachees practice new skills or behaviors over and over until they are solidly entrenched" (Skiffington & Zeus, 2005, p. 28).

Developing Attributes and Changing Behavior

When people learn a skill, it is because they want to become better at performing an activity. When people develop an attribute or change their behavior, they want to become a better or more productive person. They may wish to improve a personal quality, such as patience, or they may desire to change behavior, such as being more honest and forthright with people. Whatever it is, they see it as a way to become more productive, satisfied, or both. Attributes and behavior are interconnected. An attribute is a quality or characteristic of a person. Attributes are revealed by displaying specific behaviors. Patience, for example, is shown when a person controls their annoyance or temper while in a frustrating situation or dealing with an irritating person, or endures an inconvenience without complaint. These and other similar behaviors define the attribute called patience. If a client wants to develop this quality, it will be accomplished through changes in behavior. Changing behavior to grow an attribute is challenging. It involves adjustments in what a person does and how a person thinks. Gallwey (2002) refers to these adjustments as changes to one's "outer game" and changes to one's "inner game." Changing internal behavior goes hand in hand with changing external behavior when developing personal attributes.

Altering Maladaptive Behaviors (Derailers)

Sometimes people's personality or more accurately the toxic behavior caused by their personality creates problems that can *derail* their career. This phenomenon is especially true if they are in positions of leadership, regardless of how talented and motivated they are. Derailers are weighed, not counted. That is to say, a person may have ten strengths and one derailer, but the derailer will outweigh the ten strengths because it makes success in the role or on the job impossible.

Derailers almost always stem from a lack of emotional intelligence (EI). In his bestselling book, *What Got You Here Won't Get You There*, Marshall Goldsmith explains why emotional intelligence is crucial for leaders:

> At the higher levels of organizational life, all the leading players are technically skilled. They're all smart. They're all up to date on the technical aspects of the job. You don't get to be, say, your company's chief financial officer without knowing how to count, read a balance sheet, and how to handle money prudently.
>
> That's why behavioral issues become so important at the upper rungs of the corporate ladder. All other things being equal, your people skills (or lack

of them) become more pronounced the higher up you go. In fact, even when all other things are not equal, your people skills often make the difference in how high you go.

(2007, pp. 42–43)

Overcoming a derailer requires transformative learning: changes in understanding of one's self, a revision of one's belief system, and a change in one's behavior. According to Mezirow (1997), transformative learning is triggered by a life crisis, or what he terms a "disorienting dilemma"—which is certainly the case when a client's career is in jeopardy. The coaching process is a way for individuals to reflect consciously on their assumptions and beliefs, change their frames of reference, and implement plans that bring about new ways of managing themselves and interacting with others.

Making Decisions

Clients bring difficult decisions to coaching—decisions that require the client to make tough choices. "Do I let the senior person who is stepping down and whom I'm replacing stay on?" "Should I remove someone from my senior leadership team who doesn't support me, but who has influence with colleagues and is popular with direct reports?" "Do I stay in my role as VP, even though my boss doesn't give me the authority commensurate with that role, or take a lateral move to a less prestigious position where I can make a difference?" "Should I take the position that's being offered to me, even though the person to whom I would be reporting is difficult to work with?" "Should I try to rebuild a relationship with a colleague with whom I've had a falling out?" These are the types of decisions that clients face and for which they want help. They are challenging decisions because there is no single correct answer; they require a person to make a judgment call. Faced with decisions such as these, clients often feel stuck and want to talk about them with someone they trust—a thinking partner. A thinking partner is someone who:

- listens to ideas and opinions, without judgment—a sounding board;
- helps another person access and clarify ideas by asking the right questions at the right time;
- creates a conversational environment that supports a free flow of thought; and
- is more interested in understanding the thinking of the other person than in telling the other person what he or she thinks.

Even a cursory examination of the literature on coaching reveals that being a thinking partner is central to the coaching process.

Handling Problem Situations

The problems for which people seek help come from crises, troubles, doubts, difficulties, frustrations, or concerns. These problems are messy, complex, have no clear-cut solutions, and often cause emotional turmoil. They are problems that stem from the trials and tribulations of professional life or occur in the normal course of living. Problem situations "arise in our interactions with ourselves, with others, and with the social settings, organizations and institutions of life" (Egan, 2010, p. 5). So, while coaching is a means of learning, development, growth, and transformation, it is also a method for helping people work through, or cope with, problem situations encountered while living and working in a complicated world. It is often the help that coaches provide in sorting these problem situations that clients value most. Problem situations are different from decisions, even though they often require a person to make decisions in the process of dealing with those situations. Decisions require the client to choose among alternative courses of action, but problem situations require the client to find answers to questions that have a considerable degree of subjectivity, multiple variables, and incomplete information.

Some clients ask for coaching but, in truth, want consulting advice. Coaching assumes that the answers are within the client; consultants are paid to have the answers. Consultants offer clients a different type of expertise. They bring domain specific knowledge and analytical processes to the engagement. When clients ask questions such as "How can I increase revenue?", "How can I reduce business costs?", "How should I set up my nationwide promotion campaign?", or "How can I improve my business strategy", they are looking for specialized answers that they are not capable of providing. They are looking for consulting help: the kind of help that comes from someone who can diagnose the problem or situation and present workable solutions. Consultants are in the business of giving professional or technical advice to people based on their expert knowledge and experience in a particular field. Even though coaching and consulting can work together very well, the purpose and nature of the relationship between a consultant and client are very different from the relationship between a coach and client.

Finding Meaning and Personal Satisfaction

Erik Erikson (1959) proposed a lifespan model of development in which he maintained that all people go through predictable life stages. Each stage presents particular challenges that must be surmounted, and each stage builds on the successful completion of earlier stages. If the challenges of a particular stage are not overcome, they reappear as issues in the future. According to Erikson, in mid-life (i.e. forty to sixty-four years), people are challenged to answer the question, "Can I make my life count?" Given that coaches often work with people in this stage of life, they will frequently be asked to help clients make greater sense and meaning of their work or life.

Coaching someone that is in search of meaning and personal satisfaction is a very gratifying experience. Some would say that it is the highest and best use of coaching. In fact, many definitions of coaching accentuate this purpose. Brock (2014), for example, defines coaching as a process that fosters, among other things, personal growth and conscious choice for the highest good. Whitworth et al. (2007) state that coaching is a process that enhances human learning, effectiveness, and fulfillment. Grant (2003) views coaching as a way to enhance one's total life experience. Although clients seek to be coached for many purposes, finding meaning and personal satisfaction in their lives is one of the highest and best uses of the coaching experience.

The Coach as Change Agent

Admittedly, there may be some overlap between themes, but the issues for which people seek coaching tend to fall into three areas: increasing competence, help with decisions and problem situations, and finding meaning and satisfaction. In the process of working through their individual issues, clients grow, learn, and become more capable and self-reliant. Each client determines the specific purpose for the coaching engagement and sets the agenda for each coaching conversation. Consequently, coaching is considered to be a client-driven activity. Regardless of the client-driven purpose, coaching is the vehicle for whatever change the client is seeking. People look to coaching to help transport them from where they are now to where they want to go. This change process is *coach driven* because it is the coach's expertise in facilitating individual change that the client wants and needs. Essentially, the coach's role is to be a catalyst for change: a change agent. In this, there is broad agreement; however, agreement about how the coach should carry out this role is more elusive.

The point of controversy about the coach's role centers on the use of personal and expert knowledge in coaching. Undoubtedly, clients need information, sometimes at critical moments, to help them with their thinking:

> That information is power is never more true than when you want people to think well. If ideas are based on error, the action that follows won't work. Fact, figures, concepts, directions, interpretations, policy—it doesn't matter; any information composing an accurate picture of reality is crucial to clear thinking on any subject. Withholding information from someone is an act of intellectual imperialism. Not bothering to see accurate information is an act of intellectual recklessness.

> (Kline, 2008, p. 79)

Because coaches have knowledge borne of their professional experience, education, or both, it is not unusual for a coach to have information that will make a difference in the direction, content, or progress of the client's thinking. Suppose that you are an internal coach helping an employee, Beth, think through a decision as to whether to apply for the position of sales director. As you listen, you become aware that the Beth's primary concern about applying for the post is apprehension about working for the VP of Marketing, given his reputation. You, on the other hand, have had frequent interactions with the VP and believe that, while he is an "acquired taste," he certainly isn't as bad as what Beth is imagining. In fact, given what you know about both people you do not see that there will be any problem if she just keeps a few things in mind, which you share with her. Your input gives her an entirely different perspective on the situation. You also affirm, "If you can put up with his quirks, I think you can learn a lot from him while he is here. I think that applying for that position would be a good thing for you and your career aspirations." In telling Beth what you know, you have provided information that may very well influence her decision.

The Ask-Tell Continuum

The notion of a coach as information provider or advice-giver, however, is at odds with what many in the field believe the coaching approach should be: an exclusively non-directive, facilitative activity. Rather than framing the argument as a battle between two approaches, i.e., directive versus facilitative, Cavanagh et al. (2005) offer an alternative perspective. They believe that these two approaches are end points on a continuum and that both have their place within the context of coaching:

> However, these are not categorically different approaches to coaching. Rather, these two approaches lie on a continuum. The issue is not which is right and which is wrong, but rather which best helps the client reach their goals, and which is the most apt at particular points in any specific coaching conversation. In essence, this issue is about striking the right balance between process facilitation and content or information delivery, and this balance varies at different points in the overall coaching engagement and within individual coaching sessions. The skillful and experienced coach knows when to move across the ask-tell dimension and knows when to promote self-discovery and when to give expert-based authoritative or specialised information.

(p. 3)

The methods and practices of coaching unquestionably favor the "ask" direction on the ask-tell continuum. However, it is also true that coaching includes activities that move along the continuum depending on what the client wants and how best to accomplish it. As Brock explains,

> What I do is look at the definition of coaching as a range of activities on a continuum. For example, some say that coaching must be facilitative, and yet there are times when being directive is required. Background experience, culture, and personality of the coach (as well as the client, situation, and context) all affect where the coach falls within the range of activities.

(2014, p. 137)

Coaching as an Engagement versus Coaching as an Activity

One means of establishing clarity about the use of the ask-tell continuum within the context of coaching is to make a distinction between coaching as an *engagement* and coaching as an *activity*. When clients look to coaching to serve their purpose, whether it is learning a skill, developing an attribute, changing behavior, making a decision, handling a problem situation, or finding meaning and personal satisfaction, they enter into a coaching engagement. During the life of that engagement, it is incumbent upon the coach to use whatever approach best helps clients reach their goals. Obviously, the *activity of* coaching (i.e., facilitating self-determined and self-directed problem solving or change through inquiry) will be at the forefront. However, to serve the client's purposes over the course of a coaching engagement, there are three additional activities the coach may employ. These activities fall at the "tell" end of the continuum: teaching, providing feedback, and mentoring.

Teaching

As previously noted, learning new skills is one of the reasons people come to coaching. If so, it is assumed that you, as a coach, have expert knowledge that will help in their skill development. Even if it is not their primary goal, skill development may be needed to achieve other ends. For example, if a client wants to become more assertive and be able to say "no" to unfair requests, teaching assertiveness skills will be a necessary step for meeting the client's objective. Some may argue that it is possible to develop a client's skills with a purely facilitative approach, such as encouraging the client to engage in self-directed learning to grow this capability. This argument has merit, but if the coach can teach, it expedites the client's progress. Knowledge is a critical part of any competency; therefore, when a client's goal is to increase his competency in some way, teaching is a legitimate part of the coaching engagement when the coach has expert knowledge that will help.

Providing Feedback

Feedback is essential to learning, and learning is an important outcome of the coaching process; therefore, coaching and feedback go hand in hand. Giving feedback is a supportive act intended to develop clients' skills or capability in accordance with a goal or desired outcome. For instance, a client, Amadeo, was discussing his frustration with one of his direct reports—a manager of operations. The manager in question was lobbying to hire someone into the department that, in Amadeo's opinion, was not qualified. Not wanting to be authoritative, Amadeo gave the manager several "hints" that the person was not a viable candidate, all of which were ignored because of the manager's strong positive feelings about the person. Amadeo turned to his coach for help in planning for and practicing the conversation he would have with the manager to inform him that the job applicant would not be hired, in spite of the manger's wishes. Amadeo's goal was to feel confident about what he was going to say, how he was going to say it, and how he was going to handle his manager's inevitable push back and objections. Role-playing the conversation with his coach and receiving feedback along the way helped him achieve his goal.

Process observations are a particularly valuable form of feedback for the client. Process observations are remarks about what the coach is noticing about the client during the coaching process. Pointing out, for instance, that the client is embroiled in a narrative about how bad things are, but never talks about what he or she wants to be different sheds light on how the client is getting stuck by becoming entangled in problem talk. Or there might be a pattern of behavior across sessions that seem inconsistent with the client's stated goals. Suppose a client stresses the importance of a goal but never takes actions toward that goal. Sharing the observation that the client's behavior is inconsistent with the expressed importance of the goal brings to the forefront of the coaching conversation a contradiction that can be explored. In fact, noticing client contradictions and bringing them to light is essential in coaching. Whitworth et al. (2007) refer to this as "truth telling" and reminds us that there is no inherent judgment in telling the truth. The coach is merely providing feedback as to what he or she sees. They go on to say that withholding the truth serves no purpose because the coaching relationship is not built on being nice, but on being real.

Feedback is essential for accurate self-perception, and yet leaders (especially senior-level leaders) rarely get the feedback they need. Their superiors no longer have the opportunity, or need, to observe their daily behavior. Subordinates often believe that providing feedback to their superior is risky. They do not want to offend their boss, or may feel that their feedback is unwelcome and, thus, fear the consequences of giving feedback. Therefore, leaders—due to the lack of feedback—are often confused or have misperceptions about their strengths and weaknesses, and, consequently, their developmental needs. To counter this, many coaches include feedback from others as part of the coaching engagement. The purpose here is to help the client develop an accurate picture of their leadership skills, interpersonal style, and so forth. With such information, goals and objectives can be identified, and actions pinpointed to help achieve those goals and objectives. Delivering data-driven feedback and being an impartial source of interpretation for that feedback is an activity regularly undertaken by those who coach leaders and professionals in the workplace.

Mentoring

Mentoring is similar to teaching; one person is transferring information to another. The critical difference is that with mentoring, the information is derived from knowledge and wisdom rooted in one's personal or professional experience. It is not learned in the classroom or from a book. In this sense, mentoring is more personal than teaching because you are sharing a part of yourself—your wisdom born of experience—with another. The more you coach, the more experience you have with how people achieve their goals, overcome obstacles, and effectively deal with different situations. The more wisdom you accumulate from your coaching experiences, the more sage advice you can offer clients, at the right time, and in the right amount. Providing mentoring advice so that a better decision is made, a problem is solved, an obstacle overcome, or a change in thinking occurs may be just what your client needs.

As a coach, it is important to remember that when you do put on your mentoring hat, it is only temporary; you are not a mentor per se. The distinction between mentor and coach is often blurred as illustrated by the definition of the role of mentor as set out by the Institute of Knowledge Transfer:

The mentor spends a great deal of their time listening, asking questions and helping the mentee to develop insights that are beyond their individual perspectives and sometimes outside their comfort zone.

(as cited in SQW Consulting, 2009, p. 4)

This definition clearly describes coaching. However, make no mistake there is a difference in role requirements between a mentor and a coach. Mentoring is a relationship that ordinarily exists within the confines of an organization, whereby more experienced professionals or managers—usually in the same specialty—provide advice to less experienced colleagues. It is an open-ended relationship, frequently formal in that mentors are matched with mentees and exclusively associated with the mentee's career development or performance improvement. Unlike coaching, the relationship is hierarchical in the sense that the mentor is considered to be the expert and of higher rank.

Teaching, providing feedback, and mentoring are activities that are all part of the ask-tell continuum. While they do not represent the *activity* of coaching per se, they can be used within the framework of a coaching engagement. Each, in its own way, serves a purpose that benefits the client. That said, coaching is an activity unique unto itself and is a catalyst for the changes that clients seek from the coaching experience.

So, What Is Coaching?

The French poet, novelist, and critic Remy de Gourmont (1858–1915) stated that a definition is a sack of flour compressed into a thimble. Perhaps that is why there are different definitions of coaching in books, essays, and discussions; there is not enough room in one definition to cover all facets of coaching. So, rather than adding another "thimble" to the pile, perhaps it is better to summarize the common elements that characterize this "sack of flour" called coaching. Coaching is:

- **A Methodology**: Coaching utilizes a person-centered, non-directive, inquiry-based methodology for assisting clients in transformative learning and constructing solutions as a path to goal attainment. Via incisive questioning, the coach guides the client in critical reflection, self-discovery, self-directed learning, and problem solving. This methodology imitates the Socratic Method in that it is a form of inquiry and discussion between the coach and the client, based on asking and answering questions to stimulate critical thinking and to illuminate ideas. It is not assumed that the coach has, or needs, expert knowledge about the subject matter for which the client is being coached.
- **A Relationship**: Coaching is a collaborative and egalitarian relationship between the coach and the coachee. Unlike an authoritative relationship, e.g., teacher-student, the coach and the client are considered to be equal, but having different roles. The client brings the agenda and has domain-specific expertise, while the coach brings know-how in the process of coaching and relates to the client in the spirit of partnership. It is a powerful alliance—a

professional partnership—in which the client holds the ultimate responsibility for, and ownership of, the desired outcomes.

- **A Purpose**: Coaching deals with a wide-range of *normal* issues. Its purpose is not to promote emotional healing or relief from psychological pain, such as that which accompanies clinically significant mental health problems. Rather, its purpose is transformative learning to enhance the client's life experience and goal attainment in both the personal and professional setting. The coach is someone trained in, and devoted to, guiding others into increased confidence and commitment so as to optimize their potential, performance, and happiness.

- **A Philosophy**: Coaching is a philosophy of empowerment. It is a philosophy built on the premise that clients bring a foundation of life experiences and knowledge from which they can draw upon to solve their problems, make decisions, and reach their goals and objectives. With help from their coach, clients use their resourcefulness, skills, and confidence in finding solutions to problems and pathways to goals. It is believed that answers come from within the client. Therefore, clients are encouraged and expected to take charge of their lives and be responsible for the choices they make.

- **A Process**: Coaching is a process of supporting and challenging clients so that they are encouraged to learn, discover, understand, and solve problems independently of the coach. The process is heuristic and favors experiential learning whereby the client engages in critical reflection, evaluates possible answers or solutions, and then experiments to gauge the efficacy of those solutions. Some experiments might be purely exploratory, with actions taken only to see what follows. Others might be performed to initiate change, and still others to test hypotheses. It is a process in which a coach and client work together utilizing the mediums of inquiry, deliberation, and dialog.

In the parable about the blind men and the elephant, each part of an elephant does not, by itself, provide a complete picture of the elephant; and so it is with coaching. Each element, by itself, does not define coaching nor distinguish it from other forms of helping conversations. However, all of the elements, in concert, provide a realistic picture of this activity called coaching.

References

Adams, J. S. (1965). Inequity in social exchange. *Advanced Experience in Social Psychology*, 62, 335–343.

Ahmadi, M. R., Gilakjani, A. P., & Ahmadi, S. M. (2011). The relationship between attention and consciousness. *Journal of Language Teaching and Research*, 2 (6), 1366–1373.

Appelbaum, S. A. (1973). Psychological-mindedness: Word, concept and essence. *The International Journal of Psycho-analysis*, 54 (1), 35–46.

Arden, J. B. (2010). *Rewire your brain: Think your way to a better life.* Hoboken, NJ: John Wiley & Sons.

Argyris, C., & Schön, D. A. (1974). *Theory in practice: Increasing professional effectiveness.* San Francisco: Jossey-Bass.

Arkowitz, H., & Miller, W. R. (2008). Learning, applying, and extending motivational interviewing. In H. Arkowitz, H. Westra, W. R. Miller, & S. Rollnick (Eds.). *Motivational interviewing in the treatment of psychological problems* (pp. 1–25). New York, NY: The Guilford Press.

Baldwin, M. (2000). Interview with Carl Rogers on the use of the self in therapy. In M. Baldwin (Ed.). *The use of self in therapy* (2nd ed., pp. 29–38). New York, NY: Haworth Press.

Bandler, R., & Grinder, J. (1975). *The structure of magic.* Palo Alto, CA: Science and Behavior Books.

Bandura, A. (1982). Self-efficacy mechanism in human agency. *American Psychologist*, 37 (2), 122–147.

Bandura, A. (1994). Self-efficacy. In V. S. Ramachaudran (Ed.). *Encyclopedia of human behavior* (Vol. 4, pp. 71–81). New York: Academic Press.

Bandura, A. (1997). *Self-efficacy: The exercise of control.* New York, NY: Freeman.

Baron-Cohen, S. (2012). *Zero degrees of empathy: A new theory of human cruelty.* New York, NY: Penguin Group.

Baron-Cohen, S., & Wheelwright, S. (2004). The empathy quotient: An investigation of adults with Asperger syndrome or high functioning autism, and normal sex difference. *Journal of Autism and Developmental Disorders*, 34 (2), 163–175.

Barrett-Lennard, G. T. (1981). The empathy cycle: Refinement of a nuclear concept. *Journal of Counseling Psychology*, 28 (2), 91–100.

Bateson, G. (2000). *Steps to an ecology of mind: Collected essays in anthropology, psychiatry, evolution, and epistemology*. Chicago, IL: The University of Chicago Press.

Beck, A. T. (1964). Thinking and depression: II. Theory and therapy. *Archives of General Psychiatry*, 10, 561–571.

Beck, A. T. (1976). *Cognitive therapy and the emotional disorders*. New York, NY: International Universities Press.

Beck, J. S. (1995). *Cognitive therapy: Basics and beyond*. New York, NY: The Guilford Press.

Beck, J. S. (2005). *Cognitive therapy for challenging problems: What to do when the basics don't work*. New York, NY: The Guilford Press.

Beitel, M., Ferrer, E., & Cecero, J. J. (2005). Psychological mindedness and awareness of self and others. *Journal of Clinical Psychology*, 61 (6), 739–750.

Bem, D. J. (1972). Self-perception theory. In L. Berkowitz (Ed.). *Advances in experimental and social psychology* (Vol. 6, pp. 1–62). New York, NY: Academic Press.

Benjamin, A. (1981). *The helping interview* (3rd ed.). Boston, MA: Houghton Mifflin Company.

Berg, I. K., & Szabo, P. (2005). *Brief coaching for lasting solutions*. New York: W.W. Norton & Company.

Berne, E. (1964). *Games people play*. New York: Grove Press.

Berne, E. (1972). *What do you say after you say hello? The psychology of human destiny*. New York: Grove Press.

Blakey, J., & Day, I. (2012). *Challenging coaching: Going beyond traditional coaching to face the FACTS*. London: Nicholas Brealey.

Bluckert, P. (2005). The foundations of a psychological approach to executive coaching. *Industrial and Commercial Training*, 37 (4), 171–178.

Bordin, E. S. (1979). The generalizability of the psychoanalytic concept of the working alliance. *Psychotherapy: Theory, Research and Practice*, 16 (3), 252–260.

Brahm, A. (2006). *Mindfulness, bliss, and beyond: A meditator's handbook*. Somerville, MA: Wisdom Publications.

Brammer, L. (1973). *The helping relationship: Process and skills*. Englewood Cliffs, NJ: Prentice Hall.

Brock, V. G. (2014). *Sourcebook of coaching history* (2nd ed.). Los Angeles, CA: CreateSpace Independent Publishing Platform.

Brockbank, A., & McGill, I. (2013). *Coaching with empathy*. Maidenhead, UK: McGraw-Hill.

Burns, D. D. (1980). *Feeling good: The new mood therapy*. New York, NY: Avon Books.

Burns, D. D. (1999). *The feeling good handbook*. New York, NY: Plume.

Cameron-Bandler, L. (1985). *Solutions*. San Rafael, CA: FuturePace, Inc.

Carkhuff, R. R. (2009). *The art of helping* (9th ed.). Amherst, MA: Possibilities Publishing.

Cavanagh, M., Grant, A. M., & Kemp, T. (Eds.). (2005). *Evidence-based coaching volume 1: Theory, research and practice from the behavioural sciences*. Bowen Hills Qld, Australia: Australian Academic Press.

Chi, M. T. H. (2006). Laboratory methods for assessing experts' and novices' knowledge. In K. A. Ericsson, N. Charness, R. R. Hoffman, & P. J. Feltovich (Eds.). *The Cambridge handbook of expertise and expert performance* (pp. 167–184). New York, NY: Cambridge University Press.

Core Competencies. (n.d.). Retrieved from http://www.coachfederation.org/credential/landing.cfm?ItemNumber=2206&navItemNumber=576

Costa, A. L., & Garmston, R. J. (1994). *Cognitive coaching: A foundation for renaissance schools*. Norwood, MA: Christopher-Gordon Publishers, Inc.

Cranton, P. A. (1992). *Working with adult learners*. Toronto: Wall & Emerson.

Daloz, L. A. (1999). *Mentor*. San Francisco: Jossey-Bass.

Daloz, L. A. (2012). *Mentor: Guiding the journey of adult learners*. San Francisco: Jossey-Bass.

Davis, M. H. (1983). Measuring individual differences in empathy: Evidence for a multi-dimensional approach. *Journal of Personality and Social Psychology, 44*, 113–126.

DeBacker, T. K., & Nelson, R. M. (1999). Variations on expectancy-value model of motivation in science. *Contemporary Educational Psychology, 24*, 71–94.

Decety, J., & Ickes, W. (Eds.). (2009). *Social neuroscience of empathy*. Cambridge, MA: MIT Press.

De Jong, P., & Berg, I. K. (2008). *Interviewing for solutions* (3rd ed.). Belmont, CA: Thomson Brooks/Cole.

Dekeyser, M., Elliott, R., & Leijssen, M. (2009). Empathy in psychotherapy: Dialogue and embodied understanding. In J. Decety & W. Ickes (Eds.). *Social neuroscience of empathy* (pp. 3–15). Cambridge, MA: MIT Press.

de Shazer, S. (1985). *Keys to solution in brief therapy*. New York, NY: W.W. Norton & Company.

de Shazer, S., Berg, I. K., Lipchik, E., Nunally, E., Moinar, A., Gingerich, W. C., & Weiner-Davies, M. (1986). Brief therapy: Focused solution development. *Family Process, 25*, 207–221.

de Shazer, S., & Dolan, Y. M. (2007). *More than miracles: The state of the art of solution-focused brief therapy*. Binghamton, NY: Haworth Press.

de Shazer, S., Dolan, Y. M., Korman, H., Trepper, T. S., McCollum, E. E., & Berg, I. K. (2006). *More than miracles: The state of the art of solution focused therapy*. Binghamton, NY: Haworth Press.

Dewey, J. (1938). *Experience and education*. New York: MacMillan.

Dollinger, S. J., Reader, M. J., Marnett, J. P., & Tylenda, B. (1983). Psychological-mindedness, psychological-construing, and the judgment of deception. *The Journal of General Psychology, 108*, 183–191.

Downey, M. (1999). *Effective coaching*. London: Orion.

Dreikurs, R., Grunwald, B. B., & Pepper, F. C. (1982). *Maintaining sanity in the classroom*. New York, NY: Bantam.

Eccles, J. (1983). Expectancies, values, and academic behaviors. In J. T. Spence (Ed.). *Achievement and achievement motives* (pp. 75–146). San Francisco: W. H. Freeman and Company.

Egan, G. (2010). *The skilled helper: A problem-management and opportunity-development approach to helping* (9th ed.). Belmont, CA: Brooks/Cole Cengage Learning.

Elliott, R., Bohart, A. C., Watson, J. C., & Greenberg, L. S. (2011). Empathy. In J. C. Norcross (Ed.). *Psychotherapy relationships that work: Evidence-based responsiveness* (2nd ed., pp. 132–152). New York, NY: Oxford University Press.

Ellis, A. (1962). *Reason and emotion in psychotherapy*. New York, NY: Lyle Stuart.

Erikson, E. H. (1959). Identity and the life cycle. *Psychological Issues, 1*, 1–171.

Farber, B. A., & Lane, J. S. (2002). Positive regard. In J. C. Norcross (Ed.). *Psychotherapy relationships that work: Therapist contributions and responsiveness to patient needs* (pp. 390–395). New York, NY: Oxford University Press.

Fauth, J., & Williams, E. N. (2005). The in-session self-awareness of therapist-trainees: Hindering or helpful? *Journal of Counseling Psychology*, 52 (3), 443–447.

Finlay, L. (2008). *Reflecting on reflective practice*. Practice-based professional learning centre. Milton Keynes, UK: The open university. Retrieved from http://www.open.ac.uk/opencetl/resources/pbpl-resources/finlay-l-2008-reflecting-reflective-practice-pbpl-paper-52

Fishbein, M., & Ajzen, I. (1975). *Belief, attitude, intention, and behavior: An introduction to theory and research*. Reading, MA: Addison-Wesley.

Foulds, L. R. (1983). The heuristic problem-solving approach. *Journal of the Operational Research Society*, 34 (10), 927–934.

Gallwey, T. W. (2002). *The inner game of work*. New York: TEXERE.

Garfield, E. (1990). Fast science vs. slow science, or slow and steady wins the race. *The Scientist*, 4 (18), 14.

Gehart, D., & McCollum, E. (2008). Teaching therapeutic presence: A mindfulness-based approach. In S. Hicks & T. Bien (Eds.). *Mindfulness and the healing relationship* (pp. 176–194). New York, NY: Guilford.

Geller, S., & Greenberg, L. (2002). Therapeutic presence: Therapists' experience of presence in the psychotherapy encounter in psychotherapy. *Person Centered and Experiential Psychotherapies*, 1 (1–2), 71–76.

Glasser, W. (1984). *Control theory: A new explanation of how we control our lives*. New York: Harper & Row.

Goldsmith, M. (2007). *What got you here won't get you there*. New York: Hyperion.

Gough, H. (1975). *California psychological inventory*. Palo Alto, CA: Consulting Psychologists Press.

Grant, A. M. (2003). The impact of life coaching on goal-attainment, metacognition and mental health. *Social Behavior and Personality*, 31, 253–264.

Grant, A. M., & Stober, D. R. (2006). Introduction. In D. Stober & A. M. Grant (Eds.). *Evidence-based coaching handbook* (pp. 1–14). Hoboken, NJ: John Wiley & Sons.

Gray, D. E. (2006). Executive coaching: Towards a dynamic alliance of psychotherapy and transformative learning processes. *Management Learning*, 37 (4), 475–497.

Greenberger, D., & Padesky, C. (1995). *Mind over mood: Change how you feel by changing the way you think*. New York, NY: The Guilford Press.

Greene, J., & Grant, A. (2003). *Solution-focused coaching*. Harlow: Pearson Education.

Harris, T. A. (1969). *I'm OK-you're OK: A practical guide to transactional analysis*. New York, NY: Harper & Row.

Hart, V., Blattner, J., & Leipsic, S. (2001). Coaching versus therapy: A perspective. *Consulting Psychology Journal: Practice & Research*, 53 (4), 229–237.

Hatfield, E., Cacioppo, J. L., & Rapson, R. L. (1993). Emotional contagion. *Current Directions in Psychological Sciences*, 2, 96–99.

Hettema, J., Steele, J., & Miller, W. R. (2005). Motivational interviewing. *Annual Review of Clinical Psychology*, 1, 91–111.

Hicks, R. F. (2014). *Coaching as a leadership style: The art and science of coaching conversations for healthcare professionals*. New York: Routledge.

Hill, C. E., & Knox, S. (2002). Self-disclosure. In J. C. Norcross (Ed.). *Psychotherapy relationships that work: Therapist contributions and responsiveness to patient needs* (pp. 255–265). New York, NY: Oxford University Press.

Hoag, D. (2012). *NLP meta programs*. Retrieved from http://www.nlpls.com/articles/metaPrograms.php

Holland, J. L. (1959). A theory of vocational choice. *Journal of Counseling Psychology*, 6 (1), 35–45.

Hollenbeck, J. R., & Klein, J. R. (1987). Goal commitment and the goal-setting process: Problems, prospects, and proposals for future research. *Journal of Applied Psychology*, 72 (2), 212–220.

Horney, K. (1950). *Neurosis and human growth: The struggle toward self-realization*. New York, NY: W.W. Norton & Company.

Horvath, A. O., & Bedi, R. P. (2002). The alliance. In J. C. Norcross (Ed.). *Psychotherapy relationships that work: Therapist contributions and responsiveness to patient needs* (pp. 37–69). New York, NY: Oxford University Press.

Humes, J. C. (1997). *Nixon's ten commandments of leadership and negotiation: His guiding principles of statecraft*. New York, NY: Simon & Schuster Inc.

Ives, Y., & Cox, E. (2012). *Goal-focused coaching: Theory and practice*. New York, NY: Routledge.

Iveson, C., George, E., & Ratner, H. (2012). *Brief coaching: A solution focused approach*. New York: Routledge.

Jackson, P. I., & Decety, J. (2004). Motor cognition: A new paradigm to study self-other interactions. *Current Opinion in Neurobiology*, 14, 259–263.

Jarvis, P. (1987). *Adult learning in the social context*. London: Croom Helm.

Jarvis, P., Holford, J., & Griffin, C. (1998). *The theory and practice of learning*. London: Kogan Page.

Kabat-Zinn, J. (1990). *Full catastrophe living. How to cope with stress, pain and illness using mindfulness meditation*. London: Piatkus.

Kemp, T. J. (2005). Psychology's unique contribution to solution-focused coaching: Exploring clients' past to inform their present and design their future. In M. Cavanagh, A. M. Grant, & T. Kemp (Eds.). *Evidence-based coaching volume 1: Theory, research and practice from the behavioural sciences* (pp. 37–47). Bowen Hills Qld, Australia: Australian Academic Press.

Kendzierski, D. (1980). Self-schemata and scripts: The recall of self-referent and scriptal information. *Personality and Social Psychology Bulletin*, 6 (1), 23–29.

Klein, M. H., Kolden, G. G., Michels, J. L., & Chisholm-Stockard, S. (2002). Congruence. In J. C. Norcross (Ed.). *Psychotherapy relationships that work: Therapist contributions and responsiveness to patient needs* (pp. 195–215). New York, NY: Oxford University Press.

Kline, N. (2008). *Time to think: Listening to ignite the human mind*. London: Ward Lock, Cassell illustrated, A member of Octopus Publishing Group Ltd.

Koch, C., & Tsuchiya, N. (2007). Attention and consciousness: Two distinct brain processes. *Trends in Cognitive Sciences*, 11 (1), 16–22.

Korzybski, A. (1994). *Science and sanity: An introduction to non-Aristotelian systems and general semantics* (5th ed.). Brooklyn: New York Institute of General Semantics.

Kotter, J. P. (2008). *A sense of urgency*. Boston, MA: Harvard Business School Press.

Lazarus, R., & Folkman, S. (1984). *Stress, appraisal, and coping*. New York: Springer Publishing Company.

Leahy, R. L. (2003). *Cognitive therapy techniques: A practitioner's guide*. New York, NY: The Guilford Press.

Lefcourt, H. M. (1982). *Locus of control: Current trends in theory and research*. Hillsdale, NJ: Lawrence Erlbaum Associates Publishing.

Lewin, K. (1952). *Field theory in social science: Selected theoretical papers by Kurt Lewin*. London: Tavistock.

Locke, E. A. (1996). Motivation through conscious goal setting. *Applied & Preventive Psychology*, 5, 117–124.

Locke, E. A., & Latham, G. P. (1990). *A theory of goal setting and task performance*. Upper Saddle River, NJ: Prentice Hall.

Locke, E. A., & Latham, G. P. (2006). New directions in goal-setting theory. *Current Directions in Psychological Science*, 15 (5), 265–268.

Marquardt, M. J. (2004). *Optimizing the power of action learning*. Palo Alto, CA: Davies-Black.

Martin, D. J., Garske, M. P., & David, M. D. (2000). Relation of the therapeutic alliance with outcome and other variables: A meta-analytic review. *Journal of Consulting and Clinical Psychology*, 68, 438–450.

Masuda, A., Kane, T. D., Shoptaugh, C. F., & Minor, K. (2010). The role of a vivid and challenging personal vision in goal hierarchies. *The Journal of Psychology*, 144 (3), 221–242.

Maultsby, M. C. (1986). *Coping better . . . anytime, anywhere: The handbook of rational self-counseling*. Alexandria, VA: RBT Center.

Meichenbaum, D. (1977). *Cognitive-behavior modification: An integrative approach*. New York, NY: Plenum Press.

Merriam-Webster. (n.d.). "Ambivalence." Retrieved December 29, 2015, from www .merriam-webster.com/dictionary

Mezirow, J. (1994). Understanding transformation theory. *Adult Education Quarterly*, 44 (4), 222–223.

Mezirow, J. (1997). Transformative learning: Theory to practice. *New Directions for Adult and Continuing Education*, 74, 5–12.

Miller, W. R. (1983). Motivational interviewing with problem drinkers. *Behavioural Psychotherapy*, 11, 147–172.

Miller, W. R., & Rollnick, S. (2002). *Motivational interviewing: Preparing people for change* (2nd ed.). New York: Guilford Press.

Moyers, T. B. (2004). History and happenstance: How motivational interviewing got its start. *Journal of Cognitive Psychotherapy: An International Quarterly*, 18 (4), 291–298.

Mozdzierz, G. J., Peluso, P. R., & Lisiecki, J. (2014). *Advanced principles of counseling and psychotherapy: Learning, integrating, and consolidating the nonlinear thinking of master practitioners*. New York: Routledge.

Napper, R., & Newton, T. (2014). Transactional analysis and coaching. In E. Cox, T. Bachkirova, & D. Clutterbuck (Eds.). *The complete handbook of coaching* (2nd ed., pp. 91–103). London, UK: Sage Publications.

Neenan, M., & Palmer, P. (2012). *Cognitive behavioural coaching in practice: An evidence based approach*. New York: Routledge.

Norcross, J. C., & Lambert, M. J. (2011). Psychotherapy relationships that work II. *Psychotherapy*, 48 (1), 4–8.

O'Broin, A., & Palmer, S. (2010). The coaching alliance as a universal concept spanning conceptual approaches. *Coaching Psychology International*, 3 (1), 3–6.

O'Connell, B. (2003). Introduction to the solution-focused approach. In B. O'Connell & S. Palmer (Eds.). *Handbook of Solution-Focused Therapy* (pp. 1–11). London: Sage.

Osterman, K. F. (1990). Reflective practice: A new agenda for education. *Education and Urban Society*, 22 (2), 133–152.

Parker, L. E., & Detterman, D. K. (1988). The balance between clinical and research interests among boulder model graduate students. *Professional Psychology-Research & Practice*, 19 (3), 342–344.

Parsloe, E., & Wray, M. (2000). *Coaching and mentoring*. London: Kogan Page.

Passmore, J., & Marianetti, O. (2007). The role of mindfulness in coaching. *The Coaching Psychologist*, 3 (3), 130–136.

Pemberton, C. (2006). *Coaching to solutions: A manager's toolkit for performance delivery*. Oxford, UK: Elsevier.

Perls, F., Hefferline, R. F., & Goodman, P. (1951). *Gestalt therapy: Excitement and growth in the human personality*. New York: Dell.

Persons, J. B. (1989). *Cognitive therapy in practice: A case formulation approach*. New York, NY: W.W. Norton & Company.

Pope, V. T., & Kline, W. B. (1999). The personal characteristics of effective counselors: What 10 experts think. *Psychological Reports*, 84, 1339–1344.

Porter, L., Bigley, G., & Steers, R. M. (2002). *Motivation and work behavior* (7th ed.). New York: McGraw-Hill.

Prochaska, J. Q., & DiClemente, C. C. (1983). Stages and processes of self-change of smoking: Toward an integrative model of change. *Journal of Consulting and Clinical Psychology*, 51, 390–395.

Prochaska, J. O., Norcross, J. C., & DiClemente, C. C. (2005). Stages of change: Prescriptive guidelines. In G. P. Koocher, J. C. Norcross, & S. S. Hill III (Eds.). *Psychologists' desk reference* (2nd ed., pp. 226–231). New York: Oxford University Press.

Pucci, A. R. (2006). *The client's guide to cognitive-behavioral therapy: How to live a healthy, happy life . . . no matter what!* New York, NY: iUniverse.

Pucci, A. R. (2008). *Feel the way you want to feel . . . no matter what!* New York, NY: iUniverse.

Rachlin, H. (2000). *Science of self-control*. Cambridge, MA: Harvard University Press.

Rankin, K. P., Gorno-Tempini, M. L., Allison, S. C., Stanley, C. M., Glenn, S., Weiner, M. W., & Miller, B. L. (2006). Structural anatomy of empathy in neurodegenerative disease. *Brain*, 129, 2945–2956.

Robbins, A. (1998). Introduction to therapeutic presence. In A. Robbins (Ed.). *Therapeutic presence: Bridging expression and form* (pp. 20–21). Bristol, PA: Jessica Kingsley Publishers Ltd.

Rogers, C. R. (1951). *Client-centered therapy: Its current practice, implications, and theory*. Boston: Houghton Mifflin.

Rogers, C. R. (1957). The necessary and sufficient conditions of therapeutic personality change. *Journal of Consulting Psychology*, 21, 95–103.

Rogers, C. R. (1958). The characteristics of a helping relationship. *Personnel and Guidance Journal*, 37, 6–16.

Rogers, C. R. (1961). *On becoming a person*. Boston: Houghton Mifflin Company.

Rogers, C. R. (1980). *A way of being*. Boston: Houghton Mifflin Company.

Rogers, J. (2004). *Coaching skills*. Buckingham: Open University Press.

Rolfe, G. (2002). Reflective practice: Where now? *Nurse Education in Practice*, 2 (1), 21–29.

Rollnick, S., Miller, W. R., & Butler, C. (2008). *Motivational interviewing in health care: Helping patients change behavior*. New York: The Guilford Press.

Rosengren, D. B. (2009). *Building motivational interviewing skill: A practitioner workbook*. New York, NY: The Guilford Press.

Rotter, J. B. (1954). *Social learning and clinical psychology*. Englewood Cliffs, NJ: Prentice Hall.

Saleebey, D. (Ed.). (2007). *The strengths perspective in social work practice* (4th ed.). Boston: Allyn & Bacon.

Schmeichel, J., & Baumeister, R. F. (2014). Effortful attention control. In B. Bruya (Ed.). *Effortless attention: A new perspective in the cognitive science of attention and action* (pp. 29–49). Cambridge, MA: MIT Press.

Schön, D. A. (1983). *The reflective practitioner: How professionals think in action.* New York: Basic Books.

Schön, D. A. (1987). *Educating the reflective practitioner.* San Francisco: Jossey-Bass.

Shapiro, D. (2002). Renewing the scientist-practitioner model. *Psychologist*, 15 (5), 232–234.

Sheldon, B. (2011). *Cognitive-behavioral therapy* (2nd ed.). New York, NY: Routledge.

Siegel, D. J. (2012). *Pocket guide to interpersonal neurobiology.* New York: W.W. Norton & Company.

Skiffington, S., & Zeus, P. (2005). *Behavioral coaching: How to build sustainable personal and organizational strength.* Sydney: McGraw-Hill.

Skinner, B. F. (1953). *Science and human behavior.* Oxford, UK: Macmillan.

Spinelli, E. (2014). Existential coaching. In E. Cox, T. Bachkirova, & D. Clutterbuck (Eds.). *The complete handbook of coaching* (2nd ed., pp. 91–103). London, UK: Sage Publications.

SQW Consulting. (2009). *A review of mentoring literature and best practice.* NESTA, p. 4.

Stewart, I., & Joines, V. (1987). *TA today: A new introduction to transactional analysis.* Chapel Hill, NC: Lifespace Publishing.

Stober, D. (2006). Coaching from the humanistic perspective. In D. Stober & A. M. Grant (Eds.). *Evidence based coaching handbook* (pp. 17–50). Hoboken, NJ: John Wiley & Sons.

Stoltenberg, C. D. (1993). Supervising consultants in training: An application of a model of supervision. *Journal of Counseling and Development*, 72, 131–138.

Stoltenberg, C. D. (1997). The integrated developmental model of supervision: Supervision across levels. *Psychotherapy in Private Practice*, 16 (2), 59–69.

Trevino, J. G. (1996). Worldview and change in cross-cultural counseling. *Counseling Psychologist*, 24, 198–215.

Watson, J. C., & Greenberg, L. S. (2009). Empathic resonance: A neuroscience perspective. In J. Decety & W. Ickes (Eds.). *Social neuroscience of empathy* (pp. 125–137). Cambridge, MA: MIT Press.

Whitworth, L., Kimsey-House, K., Kimsey-House, H., & Sandahl, P. (2007). *Co-active coaching: New skills for coaching people toward success in work and life.* Palo Alto, CA: Davies-Black.

Wigfield, A. (2000). Expectancy-value theory of achievement motivation. *Contemporary Educational Psychology*, 25, 68–81.

Wilson, K. G., & DuFrene, T. (2008). *Mindfulness for two.* Oakland, CA: New Harbinger.

Wolitzky, D. L., & Reuben, R. (1974). Psychological-mindedness. *Journal of Clinical Psychology*, 30 (1), 26–30.

Zeus, P., & Skiffington, S. M. (2002). *The complete guide to coaching at work.* New York: McGraw-Hill.

Index